Taking Root

This series of publications on Africa, Latin America, Southeast Asia, and Global and Comparative Studies is designed to present significant research, translation, and opinion to area specialists and to a wide community of persons interested in world affairs. The editor seeks manuscripts of quality on any subject and can generally make a decision regarding publication within three months of receipt of the original work. Production methods usually permit a work to appear within one year of acceptance. The editor works closely with authors to produce a high-quality book. The series appears in a paperback format and is distributed worldwide. For more information, contact the executive editor at Ohio University Press, Scott Quadrangle, University Terrace, Athens, Ohio 45701.

Executive editor: Gillian Berchowitz
AREA CONSULTANTS
Africa: Diane Ciekawy
Latin America: Thomas Walker
Southeast Asia: William H. Frederick

The Ohio University Research in International Studies series is published for the Center for International Studies by Ohio University Press. The views expressed in individual monographs are those of the authors and should not be considered to represent the policies or beliefs of the Center for International Studies, Ohio University Press, or Ohio University.

Taking Root

Narratives of Jewish Women in Latin America

Edited by Marjorie Agosín

For Rassi Lebo,
With great admiration
For your work and
Committment to social
Justice —

Marjorie Agosín

2002

Ohio University Center for International Studies
Research in International Studies
Latin America Series No. 38
Athens

The books in the Ohio University Research in International Studies series
are printed on acid-free paper ∞

11 10 09 08 07 06 05 04 03 02   5 4 3 2 1

Mary Berg translated the introduction and the following chapters from the
Spanish: 12 (Nedda G. de Anhalt), 13 (Graciela Chichotky), 14 (Sonia
Guralnik), 15 (Rosita Kalina de Piszk), 16 (Angelina Muñiz de Huberman),
17 (Teresa Porzecanski), 18 (Mercedes Roffé), 20 (Ana María Shua),
21 (Ivonne Strauss de Milz with Marjorie Agosín), and 22 (Nora Strejilevich).
Chapters not mentioned here were written in English.

Library of Congress Cataloging-in-Publication Data

Taking root: narratives of Jewish women in Latin America / [edited by] Marjorie
Agosín.
        p. cm. -- (Research in international studies. Latin America series ; no. 38)
ISBN 0-89680-226-4 (pbk. : alk. paper)
1. Jewish women--Latin America--Biography. 2. Jews, Latin American--United
States--Biography. 3. Latin America--Emigration and immigration. 4. Immigrants--
Latin America. I. Agosín, Marjorie. II. Series.

F1419.J4 T36 2002
305.48'892408'0922--dc21
[B]
                                                        2002016986

Contents

CONTENTS

CONTENTS

Acknowledgments

AMONG THE JOYS of editing *Taking Root,* I am grateful for the commitment and authenticity of each of the writers included, as well as for their belief in and passion for sharing their stories as Jewish women in the Americas. Each of the authors included so graciously agreed to write an essay specially for this collection, and I thank them for their effort and their grace. I am also grateful for the chance to know them better and to share in their world of memories of displacement and permanence.

Each one of them is not only a contributor but a friend.

I ALSO WISH TO THANK the Littauer Foundation. Their generous support of this project made it possible for me to travel to Latin America to interview the writers.

I ALSO WISH TO THANK Mary Berg for her elegant translations and her commitment to excellence in rendering one language into the other.

MY SPECIAL THANKS to the staff at Ohio University Press, especially to Gillian Berchowitz, whose generosity and belief in this project have been a source of strength and inspiration. I must also thank Sharon Rose for her warmth, her delicacy as an editor, and her dedication to this project.

ALL CREATIVE WORK is shaped by our communities, and I thank my friends and family all over the world, who have helped me gather my own roots, and my husband, who is my tree.

Introduction

Marjorie Agosín

SOME OF MY EARLIEST childhood memories are of stories and of women who told them, always gathered at teatime. They seemed to form a magic circle where words invoked other lives and other times. Foreignness, the strangeness of having come from another place and being in a new place, seemed to pervade the conversations in our house. Señora Victoria Mizrahi spoke in Spanish with a French accent, although sometimes Ladino intonations could be heard in her voice, especially when she sang. Señora Lucia told us about her summers in Alexandria, and my great-grandmother Helena described her strolls through the Prater or the forests of Vienna.

All of these women were immigrants and uncertain travelers tossed upon the shores of Latin America by the vicissitudes of history. They were women who had come to that "other America" as they used to say, the poor America, far from gold and opportunities. In this new continent they forged new identities, they learned skills and languages. Yet they always conserved a tone of profound sadness, a nostalgia inevitably inherent in those who have departed abruptly from their countries, their neighborhoods, and their beloved gardens. It is worth mentioning, too, that these women, who formed an integral part of our everyday lives, were Jewish. Being Jewish united them not so much because they shared a religion, but rather because being Jewish had forced them to leave their countries due to the pogroms in distant Russia, the Holocaust in Europe, or the war between Egyptians and Israelis. Being Jewish was really equivalent to being from somewhere else, and that often meant "ready to go" and ready to move on, to repeat the journey of the ancestors, as well as to embrace a new life. I often picture my grand-mothers with suitcases and seeds to plant flowers in a new soil.

From an early age, I associated Judaism with a historical and no-madic condition. It seemed to me that my family's suitcases were al-ways at hand, and I remember my grandmother saying that with a handful of salt and candles, we could get through the sorrows of living in a foreign land. As time went by, I understood that being Jewish in the twentieth century was implicitly associated with coming from an-other place, with being an outsider or a permanent foreigner, always ready to move on, burdened with new languages and old memories.

I remember being especially confused and startled when the Six-Day War broke out in Israel in 1967. People would ask my father, "What are you going to do now, without a homeland?" and I wondered what homeland they were referring to since I had come to Chile when I was three years old. I began to understand my great-grandmother Sonia, who escaped from Odessa because her house had been burned down. She always had a packed suitcase ready for the moment when things got dangerous for the Jews, and, all too often, life was indeed dangerous for the Jews.

The oral histories told by first-generation immigrants live on perma-nently in my memory, but I cannot write them down because I was a child when I heard them, and most of my informants have died. I also sensed that my life was surrounded by traces of a world profoundly lost; a vanished world that seemed to be made up of the shapes of "ghosts" and the living, a world of unfinished stories and interrupted conversa-tions. This is why I became a writer, to finish these stories and to cele-brate memory. I have been lucky to write about the private and public lives of my parents in *A Cross and a Star* and *Always From Somewhere Else,* both historical memoirs. These two books inspired me to continue exploring the lives and tribulations of contemporary Jewish women of Latin America. Then I decided to gather essays for this collection, which focuses on an essential question: What has it meant to be a Jewish woman in Latin America? I asked this question of a group of women

whose interests and professions range from rabbis to journalists to
cooks, because I am convinced that the Jewish identity of these women
is an open treasure chest of memories which connects us to our past.
If memory only exists in oral form, how can it be made permanent?
How can it be inscribed in the book of life? This is what I attempted to
do when I gathered the voices of diverse women spanning various generations. How did they inscribe their Judaism in the book of daily life?
How did they translate their memories, which are both personal and
historical? Although Jewish settlements in the New World go back to
the arrival of the Spanish, very little has been written about the Jewish
presence in Latin America. Most of the existing accounts are from the
nineteen seventies and they are historical and sociological visions of the
Jewish presence in Latin America. Though there have been a few brief
articles on and anthologies of Jewish literature written by women—my
own *House of Memory: Jewish Women Writers of Latin America* (Feminist Press, 1999) and *Miriam's Daughters: Jewish Women Poets of
Latin America* (Sherman Asher Publishers, 2000) among them—little
is known about what it means to be Jewish in Latin America, and even
less about what it means to be a Jewish woman there. I am interested in
exploring what it means to be a Jewish woman in Latin America at the
end of the twentieth century, which may mean being a woman rabbi or
a woman who begins to write at the age of sixty. One of the women included here, Joan Friedman, is a translator who, as she read other Jewish women's writings, remembered her own childhood and birth in
Shanghai and thus decided to spend her life translating the work of
other Jewish women. A similar curiosity allowed me to think about and
create this book of diverse and ordinary voices, of hybrid and border-
land experiences, but mostly of a mixture of two universes: the Jewish
and the Christian. *Mestizaje,* or the mixing of races, has been the most
outstanding characteristic of the Americas, but even so, the Jewish
presence has gone almost unnoticed by historians, and the history of
the Jewish presence in Latin America remains largely unwritten, filled
with secrets, forgotten memories, and stories yet to be told. America

the continent is old, older than the European conquest. It had and continues to have the dimensions of an alien presence, watched over and separate, often all but invisible except for the times when it is brought to light as the special target of some persecution.

This collection was spawned by a very general set of questions about genealogies and travels sent out to a wide range of women. I wanted to ask them about their families' migration routes and the objects they brought with them from other lands. Above all, though, I wanted the respondents to edify their own historical and personal memories, their sense of private, as well as public, self. In my questionnaire, I hoped to suggest that we all have itineraries and landscapes of our travels, that we are all outsiders as well as insiders within the memories of our own imaginations. I was curious about how being Jewish had affected their lives as women, professionals, and citizens. I sent my survey out to the contributors, but I asked them to let their narratives flow. I told them they should tell the stories of their lives and the memories that are important to them. Thus, the reader will find here a very personal and intimate vision of what it is like to be a Jewish woman in Latin America.

THE CONTRIBUTORS WHO APPEAR in this collection were chosen for a variety of reasons. Many of them are writers of international distinction; others have occupied pivotal professional lives in their respective countries. I believed that each of these women had an important story to tell, ancient and new wisdoms that would shed light on a diasporic existence that is not exclusive to Jewish experience. Many contributors followed my questionnaire; others were audacious and created their own visions and narratives of their journeys. In each, the story of authenticity and endurance prevails. Each writer has also addressed her own story with a spirit of individualism as well as a sense of belonging to a great collective thread of historical experience both unique and universal.

If the oceanic crossings, forced exiles, and fear of always being from somewhere else have characterized most Jewish immigrants in the twentieth century, other factors have also loomed large: a yearning for permanence, the desire to survive, and the hope of belonging to the new land that offers a safe haven. Several of the essays are by women who, blown by the winds or historical change, have undertaken a second migration. These women, who have already lived with their grandparents' and parents' memories of journeys, begin to live their own exiles, remembering their countries while they adapt to new countries, in most cases the United States. This last group might be described as postmodern and very centered on the experiences that relate to modernity. Many of those who emigrate from Latin America gradually articulate a kind of post-memory of their grandparents and parents fused with their own memories and the collective memory of the Jewish people. The writers who emigrate to North America experience a double loss: their language and the identity associated with it. Perhaps, as Ester Shapiro speculates, rebellion might have something to do with living in two cultures.

As Darrell Lockhart points out in his introduction to Rita Gardiol, et al.'s anthology of Jewish Argentine literature, *The Silver Candelabra and Other Stories* (Pittsburgh: Latin American Literary Review Press, 1997), these voices and discourses demonstrate, through the culture of Jewish women immigrants, that Latin America has not had a homogeneous history or culture. It is important to point out that these writers also expose a side of history long minimized or omitted by patriarchal official historians in Latin America. In some cases, being Jewish has helped to evade patriarchal silencing, particularly for those who participate in secular Judaism.

THIS COLLECTION IS ABOUT exploring, about finding a horizon from which to speak and address others. This anthology does not theorize about the conditions of an exile or the sociological aspects of Jewish women and immigration, but focuses on how these women with varied experiences and professions have been able to construct a *self* that has many selves; how, through the experience of displacement, these women have been able to construct a self.

The topic of the Jewish people's emigration and the topic of the diasporic condition are inseparable. Since childhood, I've wondered about my genealogical tree with all its missing branches, lopped off by the randomness of history. I've wondered about those stately ladies seated in old photo albums suspended in time and in an uncertain memory. Where did they go? Where could they hide? If the contemporary history of Jews has been a history of forced displacement, this book wants to focus on life stories, to collect narratives that have allowed a rootless people to acquire a sense of permanence in literature.

When I invited Edna Aizenberg to participate in this project, she said that she could certainly tell me about her thousand and one migrations through Argentina, Venezuela, Israel, and New York. When I received her essay, I noticed she had begun with a quote from Borges and his marvelous poem dedicated to Israel, in which he says that all of us, all inhabitants of this planet, are children of Israel. The universalization of the Jewish experience is a central focus of these essays, as is the obsession with identity, a twentieth-century phenomenon of the multicultural Americas. Aizenberg discusses how "Latin Americans have been as obsessed with the big Who are we? as have Jews, the original inventors of identity angst. Who are we? Are we Spanish? Are we Indian? Mestizo? Mulatto? The cosmic race? Did we descend from the boats? The bridge over the frozen Arctic? Is Buenos Aires the Paris of the South, or is Macondo what we're all about? . . . Like Jews, Latin Americans are blessed and burdened by a knotty and discordant heritage."

Aizenberg's essay opens the collection and suggests a hybrid and complex identity, both blessed and cursed by history. Fundamental to this is the fact that Latin American and Jewish identities, despite multiple origins, are fused together by the experience of living in Latin America and feeling part European, part indigenous, and part mulatto. The experience of being Jewish is connected to being part of the ethnic multiplicity of Latin America. For that reason, we include in this collection women like Verónica de Darer, who is part German and part Caribbean, and Angelina Muñiz de Huberman, who is of Sephardi heritage, French by birth, and a Mexican citizen.

Ruth Behar, who came to New York with her family, addresses an important issue recurrent in this collection of essays: the tensions between Sephardi and Ashkenazi Jews, and how these tensions affect immigrant women. In her essay, "A Sephardi Air," she discusses how a union between an Eastern European Jew and a Sephardi Jew was regarded as a mixed marriage, a dangerous liaison. Behar's essay describes how, in the Diaspora, Sephardi communities of Spanish descent have often felt themselves to be "others," even among Jews. This may be one reason why Sephardi communities in Latin America seemed to adapt more quickly to Hispanic cultures than did Ashkenazi communities.

The history of Jewish immigrations to the Caribbean has received less attention than has immigration to South America. Many of the explanations of the presence of Jewish settlements on Caribbean islands are purely speculative. The Jewish communities with the longest histories are those of Curaçao and Aruba, where the oldest synagogues in the Caribbean still stand. But North American transplants compose the main part of the Jewish community in Aruba. It is also of interest to point out that the majority of Caribbean Jews are of Ashkenazi descent rather than Sephardi.

In contrast to other small communities such as the ones in Uruguay or Chile, very little has been written about the Jewish community of Lima, Peru. This has always been a mystery to me as well as to others who are interested in Jewish history. I wonder whether Peru's powerful indigenous tradition and its bias against Western scholars have kept the Peruvian Jewish world wrapped in a veil of mystery. The only exception is Isaac Goldenberg, who has given an international readership complex possibilities of a hybrid existence coexisting between the Jewish and the mestizo worlds. It is a great privilege to have in *Taking Root* an essay by Fortuna Calvo-Roth. Through her words we discover the story of Lima's Jewish community as well as the tense divisions between the Sephardi and the Ashkenazi world. Fortuna points out that "Sephardi Jews may have been the first to land in the New World and be burned at the stake of the Inquisition, but the German Jewish community has the oldest continuous congregation in Peru." Her essay makes us think about and explore the complex balance of power between the Sephardi and the Ashkenazi worlds, and the fact that the world of the Sephardi Jews was never totally accepted by Jews of European ancestry. One wonders whether this is the reason we know so little about the world of the Peruvian Jews.

Calvo-Roth's essay allows us to feel the ways in which her family's Sephardi heritage, with its origins in Turkey, found resonance in the Spanish-speaking world, a home away from home. She also reminds us of the longing of the Sephardi communities. Calvo-Roth points out that many Ashkenazi Jews arrived in Latin America on the eve of World War II, but the Sephardi Jews had left behind a disintegrating Ottoman Empire where their ancestors had lived for at least five centuries. In this poignant essay, she shows us how the world of *burekas* coexists with matzo balls and gefilte fish. It is within this hybrid tension and complex history that the celebration of identity transcends times and geographies.

Although many of the writers in this collection first spoke Yiddish, Hebrew, or German, they all write in Spanish. Two Venezuelans, Joan Friedman, who was born in Shanghai, and Verónica de Darer, born in Caracas, help us to understand this hybrid and complex zone. The case of Darer is revealing and touches upon what has been a ferocious silence for many people, but she also discusses the marked Germanic identity of many of the Jews who migrated to America, where they fused their old ways with their new lives in their host countries.

Darer addresses the legacy of emigrant parents and the vocation of daughters who become activists. Her article is also very perceptive and truthful in its articulation of how the German past is so tidily linked with her Venezuelan heritage and how the Venezuelan concept of being a "nation" becomes part of the European model. Darer's text clearly shows her great capacity to be part of Venezuelan culture, to not enter into certain prejudices that the Jewish community has toward non-Jews, and to both establish profound dialogue with those who are different and embrace the most complex diversities. In Darer's words:

> I constantly predicated to my friends in the Jewish community about the implications of the racist overtone of the words they used to describe Venezuelans. They never have understood my point of view, and I never perceived any change in attitude or use of language. The distancing, or, better said, the self-distancing, of Venezuelan Jews from Venezuelan society has never been part of dialectical discussions in either Venezuelan or Jewish social circles. . . . Slowly I understood that for members of the Jewish community in Venezuela, it was impossible to be Jewish and at the same time part of a Christian society.

With absolute clarity, Darer sets forth one of the paradoxes that have distinguished Latin American Jewish identity in both Latin America and North America: Is it possible to be a Venezuelan Jew or an Argentine Jew and participate in both parts of this identity and not live a polarized life? One may also ask whether it is really possible to be Hispanic or North American without engaging in stereotypes pertaining to hair color or accent. How can one unify all the diverse concepts that go into the formation of Latin American or North American Jewish identity? I think that it is precisely this generation, the one just arriving now in North America, that will be able to fulfill this vision of the world, this reason for being, for existing and participating in varied and multiple identities. Darer describes the utopia that is gradually becoming a reality. "My diverse worlds, the Jewish, the Venezuelan, and the German, have interlaced to influence my work as a professor, researcher, and writer. The Jewish dialectic viewpoint, together with a deep respect for education, is the spiritual guide of my pedagogical work. The warm and generous hospitality and welcome given to Jewish immigrants by the Venezuelan people left in me the imprints of compassion and an acceptance of every student as a unique human being."

This is the same pluralistic, reconciliatory spirit that permeates Joan Friedman's testimonial about her parents, who came from Western Europe, and her own birth in Shanghai. Friedman's text, like Darer's, shows how Venezuelan society openly incorporates the implications of what it means to be Jewish. Unlike Darer, Friedman's parents were Jewish immigrants of limited means who from the very beginning worked hard to improve their circumstances and took learning Spanish very seriously. "As children will, I quickly learned the language, and even excelled at it. Never wanting special dispensation or to be treated differently, I even studied catechism, which was one of the subjects averaged into the final grade. . . . Our family never felt any personal anti-Semitism. Quite the contrary: we were not only accepted, but warmly welcomed by the community."

The story of Ethel Kosminsky, full of personal as well as historical vision, allows us to understand the complicated routes of emigration Eastern European Jews have taken. Through her story, a reader comes to comprehend the extent and difficulties of their travels and ultimately the remoteness and alienation they found in the place they settled. The story of Ethel Kosminsky and her parents reads like a saga of fortitude and courage. As she takes us back in time to the road her parents took from Imperial Russia in 1914, to the colony of Entre Rios founded by Baron Hirsch, to their lives in northeastern Brazil in the colony of Recife, Ethel is able to create vivid portraits of the lives of her parents and relatives, as well as her own, in a dialectic that negotiates with an ancient past as well as an uncertain future.

Ester Levis Levine's view of Jewish migration is different from those of the other writers because she writes about leaving Cuba, the yearned-for country to which Levine has not yet been able to return. She speaks of that absent country, imbued with memories of flight and the dreams of childhood. Referring to Cuba, she says: "The glimpses only live in my memory. Unlike others who left their native countries, I have not been able to return to Cuba and search for my roots. I have only a few photographs to remind me of my youth." Levine's text, steeped in a profound sadness, reminds us that memory can be ever so painful, as it was for those post-Holocaust Jewish refugees whose photographs became their only link between the past and the present. For Levine, who came to the United States early in life, those photographs are the only bridge to her childhood.

Levine also discusses the problems of identity and accent, topics which recur throughout this book. Her girlhood friends tell her that she has an accent in Spanish, even though she is the daughter of first-generation Cuban parents. Then, when she moves to the United States, people constantly ask her "You're Jewish? I thought you were Cuban. You can't be Cuban and Jewish! As a matter of fact, aren't you a bit too white to be Cuban? And your English doesn't have a Cuban accent." Levine talks about the sense of dichotomy so often seen in all of these essays: the almost impossible task of crossing boundaries, of participating in two worlds and two identities while not feeling fully part of either one.

Several essays engage in the ambiguous and often difficult discussion of how many identities are combined. Like Joan Friedman and Verónica de Darer, Natania Remba Nurko, who has immigrated to the United States, is preoccupied by this process. What did it mean to Nurko to be a Mexican Jewish woman *gringa?* She begins her essay by discussing this topic: "In the United States, people tend to label ethnic groups. When I filled out my application for admission to UCLA, there was a blank that called for 'Ethnic origin.' What am I? I wondered. I tried to pick one by excluding the others. The options included Caucasian, African American, Hindu, Asian, Latino, and Other. I thought: 'I'm not Caucasian. I'm not Anglo-American. I don't have any African, Hindu, or Asian ancestors. Maybe I fit under Latino.' Finally I picked Other and specified 'Jewish Mexican.'"

But even this characterization is problematic. An art restorer, Nurko dedicates much of her writing to exploring the hybrid identity

of a Jewish woman in Mexico surrounded by prejudices and established traditions. She goes even further in her scrutiny of what it is like
to be a Mexican Latina in the United States. Nurko's text reads like a
dramatic narrative—*ranchera* music is mixed with klezmer tunes
throughout her childhood and adolescence. Then she tells us about
her arrival in the United States, where we realize that an obsession
with identity is part of being Jewish. She comments on how difficult it
is to be accepted in the United States as a Latina Jewish woman.

Few countries have suffered political violence on the same scale as
Colombia. That might be the reason why the Jewish community in
there has remained silent and alienated from other Jewish communities in Latin America. We know very little about it. The essay by
Cecilia Rosenblum sheds some light on the interaction between non-
Jews and Jews in Colombian society. Her writing shows us how this
community has kept itself separate from other religious communities.
This isolation has produced a positive result within Colombian society.
As Rosenblum tells us, Judaism and being a practicing Jew were seen
as a sign and a possibility of privilege. Nevertheless, as Rosenblum
shows us in her essay, as the years go by, this self-enforced isolation is
one of the factors that motivated her migration to the United States. In
Rosenblum's case , arrival in the United States caused radical personality and identity changes. "My identity had suddenly changed. I was
now seen as a Latin American. I had another persona. I was now interesting not for being Jewish, but for being 'Hispanic.' Was I really
Hispanic? What made me Hispanic? Was it the language I grew up
with? But I grew up with two other languages! Where did I really belong in this American world?"

Ester R. Shapiro, the next contributor to *Taking Root,* is a contemporary of Ruth Behar. Ester arrived in Miami at the age of six in the
early sixties, when many Cubans came to the United States. She belonged to a close-knit Jewish Cuban family, and her gradual accultura-
tion to the United States took place within the protective world of
Polish grandparents and aunts. Her family ties were retained even

when the family was exiled from Cuba due to historical events. Reading Shapiro's essay, we begin to understand how the complexity of the vanished world of the Yiddish language and the shtetel seems related to the lost world of her Cuban roots, her language and her identity. Her essay reveals her deep sadness at the loss of language and historical place and her difficulty in defining her Jewish Cuban identity in the United States. In her essay, Shapiro addresses this sense of being "lost in translation" and discusses the way loss of language and a sense of impermanence continue to be felt by even second- and third-generation immigrants.

Through the mediated text of her granddaughter Jessica P. Alpert, we are able to travel with Wilma Bloch Reich across continents and time. From the Netherlands to Guatemala to El Salvador, Reich recreates, with delicacy and nostalgia, a life in El Salvador—the beauty of its countryside, the smell of fresh coffee, and the ever-present sense of living at the edge, in a society that in subtle ways has always questioned ethnicity and religion. What is significant to remember is that in small Central American and Caribbean countries like El Salvador and the Dominican Republic, Jewish life was even more difficult due to the very small Jewish communities in which these settlers dwelled. It is also remarkable how they loved the landscape of life and the Spanish language and how they learned to thrive in their new environment. This story is made more poignant by its proof of fortitude: the way it shows how the acceptance of a Jewish destiny was allowed to survive on a distant island. A similar feeling can be found through the voice of Ivonne Strauss de Milz.

THE EXPERIENCE OF CUBAN immigrants to the United States is radically different from that of women who migrated to other Spanish-speaking countries, such as the Cuban journalist and writer Nedda G. de Anhalt. Anhalt was born in Cuba, but she emigrated to Mexico in 1968. It is obvious that the Spanish language is the link among all of these women. Language occupies their imaginations and unites the memories of their past to their present. In Anhalt's case, just as for Ruth Behar and Ester Shapiro, we see a passion for preserving Judaism, but also Cuban culture, and, to a certain degree, a desire to vindicate her own roots, lost in so many diasporas. Anhalt's text asks a question central to all of the essays in this collection: what does it signify to be a Jewish woman in Latin America? Anhalt is a clear example of the hybrid nature of Latin American Jews, of a people moving across cultures, continents, and oceans, always articulating new selves and identities. She, in turn, answers one of my questions with this thought-provoking statement: "What does it mean to be a Jewish woman in Latin America? The question is asked from an abstract point of view. The concept of Latin America, an apparently magnificent idea, is utopian. We are twenty-two very different countries, strangers to each other. No one could be more different from an Argentinean than a Bolivian, for example. If you add to this gap their Jewishness, you have to find out whether it is Sephardi or Ashkenazi." This quote touches upon the very essence of this collection of essays, which celebrates memory, but a constant memory, one which flows and remembers that the ancestors brought to the New World their memories as a way to create a new life where the past would be linked to the present.

Graciela Chichotky is an Argentine who now resides in Santiago, Chile, and is married to a rabbi. She explores Jewish life in both Buenos Aires and Santiago, but believes that the strength of Jewish culture will always be found in its own uniqueness, not necessarily in its hybrid nature.

Sonia Guralnik arrived in Chile in the middle of summer from the distant Russian winter with her fur coat. For a while she lived the traditional life of a woman of her time; then, after taking several university courses and working as a pastry chef, she decided to take up her pen and write. She stopped teaching her traditional cooking classes and decided to write the story of her migration. Guralnik began with a collection of stories entitled *Relatos en sepia* and a marvelous semi-autobiographical novel called *Para siempre en mi memoria* (Buenos

Aires: Planeta, 2000). Chile, unlike Argentina and Mexico, does not have a large Jewish community—altogether, there are only some twenty thousand Jews—and Guralnik's efforts to describe the multiple experiences of Jewish settlers in a nation that does not think of itself as a country of immigrants is of special significance.

One of Guralnik's most memorable passages points out the gaps between oral and written speech and the relationship between language and identity. "By the time I started school in Chile, I knew how to speak some Spanish, but I didn't know how to write. . . . I had no idea how to write the alphabet in Spanish. It might as well have been Chinese. And then I was baffled by the relationship of sounds to letters: I didn't understand the *s* or the *c*, the *ch*, the silent *h*. They were all puzzles to work out. Several years later, I could speak and write Spanish, but my dreams were always in Russian."

Many of these women's life stories simultaneously invent and deny themselves. They run in parallel on a symbolic level and on a real and spiritual level. For these immigrants, the journey is also a path toward understanding, a new possibility of being and of continuing to be what they were before.

Rosita Kalina de Piszk from Costa Rica alludes in her text to the presence of anti-Semitism in daily life, to the constant desire to be accepted, to feeling left out, to the preponderant role that memory has played in her life, her poems, and her stories. Her constant preoccupation with bringing into the open Jewish writers in various languages helps to bring them to life in Spanish, as is the case of Isaac Bashevis Singer, Bernard Malamud, and Elie Wiesel. Just as Aizenberg discusses endless possibilities, de Piszk says: "As a Costa Rican of Jewish origin, I lived intensely through the years of the 1948 revolution in Costa Rica, and I have always been interested in the politics of my country and of Latin America. I cannot imagine how being Jewish would make me turn away from something as essential as the land where I was born and lived my whole life, just as I cannot imagine how I could stop being Jewish or separate myself from the meaning for a Jew of the state of Israel." De Piszk is of an older generation, and she speaks of the experience of integrating into another world and belonging to it. Angelina Muñiz de Huberman, the next contributor, is a well-known writer, poet, and essayist who lives in Mexico. Huberman's story and her first words relate directly to the inspiration and motivation behind this book. She begins by saying, "Mine is . . . a tale about a life story. . . . The key to what happened was a war. But this is not unusual. Many lives are changed by war."

There is no doubt that chance and the vicissitudes of history have played a key role in the migrations and life histories of each one of these women, but Huberman's occupies a special place in memory. She was born in the remote and very small town of Hyéres, in Provence, a place chosen by her parents when they escaped from the Spanish Civil War. Later, Huberman went to Mexico where she became, like so many others of Spanish descent, one more refugee who arrived on board the ship *Oropesa*. Her story then becomes radically different from the norm. Huberman's grandmother tells her secretly about their Jewish origins, which go back to the era of the Inquisition. From that moment on, Huberman's identity multiplies: she is Jewish, of Spanish parents, born in France, living in Mexico. Finding out about her Jewish ancestors gives her a passionate force which propels her along a literary path to become one of the most acclaimed Latin American writers with the publication of her novels, *Tierra adentro* (1998) and *Huerto cerrado* (1982) (both books, Fondo de Cultura Mexico). These books are about extraordinary converts such as Saint Teresa of Avila and the merchant Benjamín de Tudela, who traveled around the Mediterranean with his illustrated calendars. Like many of the contributors to this collection, Huberman also took on the role of rescuer and preserver of others' memories in her collections of Judeo-Spanish poetry.

Teresa Porzecansky's essay could be read as a mythical fable, a story of love and of triumph. Very little is known about the Jewish community in Uruguay, only that, like Chile's, it is one of the smallest in Latin America. Despite this, it founded one of the first Jewish cemeteries in

Latin America. Porzecansky is an anthropologist, writer, and poet. A large part of her anthropological and academic labor has been documenting the memories of Jewish immigrants to Uruguay. She alludes to the secular experience of being Jewish and the possibility of including the history of Jewish immigrants in a more universal vision of the significance of migration, an awareness of difference, and an embracing of diversity. Porzecansky speaks of memory, and this image remains with great constancy throughout her pages. She says, "If all my writing is a journey, memory is the essence of travel. Memory is a mobile entity. It transforms itself, it rewrites itself unbidden, it resists my control."

Next we hear the voice of the poet Mercedes Roffé, whose family came from Morocco and who now lives in New York. Her reflections are revealing. Unlike her colleagues, she does not identify with being a Jewish writer or with her fellow writers who have defined their work as part of a Judeo-Latin American tradition. Roffé does share—with both her ancestors and her contemporaries—an obsession with memory in the best rabbinical tradition. She comments at one point that it is difficult to separate Sephardi and Spanish poetry and culture from each other. It is hard to separate the texts of Saint Teresa and Saint John of the Cross from those of Ibn Gabirol, which also allude to a kind of continuity and migration occurring from the time of the Inquisition to the arrival of Columbus in the New World. Thus, the Spanish language presents the possibility of union between these two continents and cultures.

Ana María Shua's essay follows that of Roffé. Shua is a very important cultural figure in Argentina. She represents a generation, or rather a type of Jewish woman, for whom the Jewish component, political and cultural, is important but who also has a profound connection with being Argentine in the immediate present.

Shua explains that to be a Jewish writer in Latin America means to reclaim the past and forge a covenant with the future. Both she and Roffé have tried through their fiction to keep the past alive and to conjure a present by becoming transmitters and listeners. Shua speaks of herself as "woman, Argentine, Jew, and writer, in that order or any other." Thus, like all the contributors, she recreates a universe shattered but unified by the vital force of memory and by the impact that these stories have had on younger generations. The experience of oral history is transmitted and relived through writing. In the last paragraph, Shua discusses a theme that is central to many of the works presented here: "And so, here I am, Latin American, a woman, a Jew, a writer—in that order or any other—writing with all I am, with all I have been, with my gender, with my Argentineness, with my Judaism, with my history, my memories, my readings, my personality, staking it all, playing for keeps, putting all of myself into every line."

The next chapter concentrates on the Dominican Republic, the town of Sosua, with an interview with Ivonne Strauss de Milz, the descendant of a founding family, whose parents and grandparents came from Shanghai in the forties. As I have said, most of the essays in this volume were adapted from authors' responses to a questionnaire. The Sosua text is based on a personal interview with the author. The town of Sosua may be the symbol of greatest hope in the Caribbean as well as a unique chapter in the history of Jewish migration to Latin America from 1800 to the post-Holocaust years. It is well known that during the period between the two World Wars, it was difficult for Jews to migrate and there were strict quotas (with the exception, perhaps, of Baron von Hirsch's colony, Entre Rios, in Argentina to which the first Jews from Russia came). The Jewish colony of Sosua occupies a unique place in history. Trujillo, a Dominican dictator who in the years prior to the Holocaust gave visas to Jews, approved thousands of visas for Jews fleeing from the Nazis. Some eight hundred Jewish immigrants arrived, mostly between 1940 and 1942. The Jews who were able to escape did so primarily from countries that were relatively neutral, such as Switzerland, Luxembourg, and China.

Nora Strejilevich, who has lived in Argentina, Israel, Canada, and now the United States, speaks of a people unjustly persecuted and expelled from everywhere, a people who have developed an extraordinary capacity to survive and transcend death. She manages to link the prejudices against Jews to the present and shows the many dilemmas and contradictions of this collection. Being a Jewish Latin American woman, the daughter of Jewish parents who are survivors of the Holocaust, postulates the possibility of creating a new memory, a post-memory where the story of a vanished lineage merges with the story of the possibilities of a new life, complete with all of society's prejudices.

Strejilevich's words help us create a new millennium filled with the possibility of peace and joy: "Woman, Jew, Latin American—three labels that don't seem favorable for climbing the social ladder. I identify fully with these, my great attributes, and I feel even more part of a *mestiza* community which proclaims sincerity, citizenship, mixtures of cultures, languages, and colors. The unidimensional is nearly extinct, although many still yearn to preserve an illusory purity of blood, of mind, and of sex."

THROUGH EXILE, LOSS, DEATH, and uncertain travels, these daughters and granddaughters of immigrants have celebrated their families' journeys and have traveled inward as well, exploring, meditating, doubting, and considering their Jewish lives in Latin America.

Taking Root

Chapter 1

Latin American Jewishness
A Game with Shifting Identities

Edna Aizenberg

ONE OF MY FAVORITE poems by Borges is called "A Israel" (To Israel). In it, the blind sage explores his possible Jewish ancestry, and asks if Israel might be flowing in the lost labyrinths of his blood, wandering like a majestic and ancient river. Well, it doesn't really matter, Borges responds in the end. Whether or not Israel's in his veins, it's still an inescapable part of him through the Sacred Book that mirrors everything, that makes us all Children of Israel.

What a brief, yet so borgesianly superb, commentary on Jewish identity! In a few short lines, Borges compresses the kaleidoscope of Judaism—the Torah and the commentaries; Judaism's magnificence and antiquity; its venerable offshoots; the exiles and the exoduses; and Jewish biology, both praised and damned. Biology may be part of the mix, Borges says, but it's just one small part, perhaps the smallest, of Jewish identity. Despite the rantings of racists and fundamentalists, identity is a conglomerate, a combinatoria created and recreated, formed by culture, choice, place, and time.

I'm not surprised that Borges, an Argentinean, wrote these words, because Latin Americans have been as obsessed with the big Who are we? as have Jews, the original inventors of identity angst. Who are we? Are we Spanish? Are we Indian? Mestizo? Mulatto? The cosmic race? Did we descend from the boats? The bridge over the frozen Arctic? Is Buenos Aires the Paris of the South, or is Macondo what we're all about? Are we premodern, peripheral modern, postmodern, postcolonial, hybrid resistors of capitalist globalization? Is it OK for us to say *surfear* when we surf the web? Like Jews, Latin Americans are blessed and burdened by a knotty and discordant heritage. No wonder psychoanalysis, dreamed up by a conflicted Viennese of the Mosaic persuasion, finds its most devoted adherents in Argentina, where almost everybody lies on the after all Jewish couch.

This rough-and-tumble identity, with its heterogeneous bits and pieces, best suggests my Jewish Latin Americanness, or, if you prefer in this game of shifting ethnicities, my Latin American Jewishness. My identity is a work in progress: lost labyrinths of genes weave in and out of it, as do immigrant itineraries, remarkable people, reading and writing. Even as I write *these* words, fragments might be floating in and out, since self-conscious meditation always shapes by omitting, highlighting, occasionally falsifying the facts. It's a risk I'll take, because writing, my own and others', has been so essential to my Jewish Latin Americanness.

Too Jewish, or What's Latin American About It?

1982: I'm ready to send off my first book, *The Aleph Weaver,* on the Bible, Kabbalah, and Judaism in Borges, to a university press. It's highly recommended, highly praised, pathbreaking, innovative, etc., the usual blurbs. After the requisite wait, I receive an answer: yes, yes, all of the above, *and yet.* The study won't interest the general reader. It "will appeal only to certain ethnic communities"; less politely, it's "too Jewish."

In the early eighties, in the great US of A, the field of Latin American studies was unready to accept a book that not only spoke openly about Borges's Jewish connections, but also dared to reveal what was in

Borges's texts: a Jewish model for Latin Americanness. Latin Americans are in a "Jewish" position vis-à-vis Western culture, Borges wrote in his renowned essay "The Argentine Writer and Tradition" (1990): they act within it, yet are not totally of it. They retain much of the outsider in an alien landscape. Jews have turned this double bind into a strength, innovating with unabashed irreverence. Why don't Latin Americans stop preaching either ultranationalist indigenism or deracinated cosmopolitanism, and do the same? Terrific words, ones that established the direction for much of Latin America's hailed twentieth-century literature, but they were "too Jewish" for publishers in the United States or, for that matter, in Latin America. *The Aleph Weaver* was finally published by a small, independent press, and *El tejedor del Aleph,* its Spanish version, by a sympathetic Spaniard who had gotten over the hump that Hispanic geniuses could be in one way or another of the Hebrew persuasion, *ex illus.*

I've purposely begun with a bookish fragment of my identity, not with *la travesía*—the archetypal crossing over the ocean in the archetypal underbelly of an immigrant ship. For what defines Latin American Jewish intellectuals are creative acts, questioning reimaginings on the page. What did the crossing, the settlement on the pampa, the cemetery in Coro, the peddling in the amazon *mean?* And how can they be inserted in national imaginaries that weave stories of Spanish conquistadors, noble and savage indigenes, heroic generals, bearded guerillas? Does Borges have something to say about the intersections of Judaism and Latin Americanism? Alberto Gerchunoff? Marcos Aguinis? Alicia Steimberg? Margo Glantz? Marjorie Agosin? Isaac Chocrón? Elías David Curiel? My writing comes from the need to probe these reimaginings and the tensions that drive them in a time-honored Jewish way, through commentary. But commentary always reveals the self.

Llegada de Inmigrantes/Here Come the Immigrants

It was a fragrant spring morning, fields of daisies dotted the joyously green countryside. . . . A group of new immigrants was

3

> due to arrive on the ten o'clock train to settle near San Gregorio. . . . As the train drew near, a murmur of excitement ran through the waiting crowd . . . the immigrants began to pour out of the cars. They looked sick and miserable, but hope shone in their eyes.

—ALBERTO GERCHUNOFF, "Llegada de inmigrantes"

For Aunt Shaive, the arrival in Buenos Aires was as hopeful as it was for Gerchunoff's Jewish greenhorns. I don't know if it was a fragrant spring morning, or if the daisies were already around, but she was tired of roaming from country to country. My grandaunt Shaive on my mother's side was the one who established our Latin American beachhead while the rest of us still roved—Russia, Poland, Germany, France, Palestine, the U.S., the Argentine. Gerchunoff (Gerch to his friends) was one of the first immigrants to turn his brethren into literary characters in the story collection *Los gauchos judíos* (The Jewish gauchos, 1910). He remembers how they used to sing: To Palestine and the Argentine / We'll go, to sow, / We'll go, brothers and friends, / To live and be free . . . Well, some of us went to one promised land, some to the other, some to both, and it didn't always go so famously, the sun didn't always shine gloriously. When Tia Shaive received us in Buenos Aires, she and her husband were living in a dingy building in El Once, the city's Lower East Side, sharing their quarters with the bolts of cloth they cut to make a living—fabric in the front, family in the back. Shaive, who had once lived in Paris, and had once stopped my Uncle Eddie in another train station from going off to the Spanish Civil War to fight fascism. Eddie—Adolph before Hitler came to power—had beaten up a Nazi, and the German Christian neighbors told him he'd better take off.

So how to compare my Aunt Shaive with Gerch's miserable but expectant future Jewish gauchos, kin to the kibbutzniks of Eretz Yisrael? I've probed Gerchunoff's influential reimagining of Jewish life in the farming pampa colonies established by the Baron de Hirsch again and again, in articles and in a new translation of *Los gauchos judíos*. The Russian immigrant turned Argentine writer, I show, was well aware that fragrant mornings and joyously green countrysides were only one side of the tale, the Garden of Eden version. Despite the fact that he's been cast as no more than a pollyannish *luftmensch*, Gerch would have identified with Shaive, perhaps he even passed her on some street in El Once, where he used to walk, to breathe Jewish air, *aire de judería*, as he put it.

The bard of the Jewish colonies is less well known as the author of "El día de las grandes ganancias" (The day I made big money), a sort of gritty city epilogue to the rural georgics, like the pampa fictions based on his own experiences. Here, the quintessential Jewish peddler, the ambulatory seller of muslin and ribbons, exhausts his hopes and heels on the streets of Buenos Aires without earning a single peso. This is Aunt Shaive's world. If in *Los gauchos judíos* Gerchunoff endeavored to invent utopia—as did so many Jews of his age—to morph Jews into Mestizo Argentinean broncobusters, knowing that it didn't quite click, in "The Day I Made Big Money" he doesn't even make the attempt. The urban realism displays the hardships of *hacer la América*, making it in America, unvarnished, and Gerchunoff demands a space for the frustrations of his folk, too, in Argentina's official story.

Médicos Milagrosos/Miraculous Doctors

> Dr. Yarch's name was uttered with reverential respect. People talked about his miraculous cures and his magic gift of gab. What was the source of his miracle working? No one could explain it, yet no one doubted it. Yarch's fame spread from the humble and misty little Jewish farming villages to the large provincial cities. He was consulted from far and near about the most difficult cases.
>
> —ALBERTO GERCHUNOFF, "El médico milagroso" (1942)

What's a Jewish *mayse* without a doctor? Gerchunoff has his, and I have mine. His is Noah Yarcho; mine is Abraham Finkelstein, whom we called Finky. Yarcho, to tell it encyclopedia style, was one of the first to practice medicine in the Jewish colonies. In 1894, he faced an exanthematic typhoid epidemic which exhausted the newly arrived settlers. He later wrote the first medical study on this disease to be published in Argentina. Yarcho practiced his profession with fervent idealism, striving to give spiritual as well as physical help to the Jewish and native inhabitants of the vast region.

From these barebone facts, Gerchunoff fashions a fable about Yarcho the Miracle Worker, proving that Rachil, the Jewish pampa hamlet of his stories, not García Márquez's Macondo, may have been Latin America's first magical realist town. His Yarcho cures outlaw gauchos, delivers impossible babies, weans drunks, calms hysterics, arranges weddings, reads clouds, envisions golden cities. Many years later, Jews and gauchos still speak of the prodigious physician with awe.

My Dr. Abraham Finkelstein worked miracles of his own, although they may not be as large or famous as Yarcho's. He was my father's friend—both were lifelong Zionists. Finky, whose specialty was joint diseases, and my father, who had graduated from the London School of Economics, where the other students would ask him if Jerusalem was in Palestine or Palestine was in Jerusalem (this was in the thirties), envisioned a state-of-the-art clinic in Israel where Argentinean and Israeli doctors would work side by side, and they actually got the project off the ground. They steered the scheme through the Israeli bureaucracy, which at the time was as friendly to capitalists as it is now to socialists; Finky began to divide his time between Buenos Aires and Jerusalem. In Buenos Aires, he founded a medical research institute that he named "Albert Einstein," with equipment you couldn't then get in Argentina. He was patiently open to new methodologies, no matter how outrageous, like my father's homemade arthritis-buster—two transistor batteries taped to his pinky, which he swore relieved the swelling and pain.

I could wax poetic about Drs. Yarcho and Finkelstein's contributions to Argentina, in the *gauchos judíos* way, or in the way of those huge illustrated volumes that are published periodically with photos of illustrious Jewish philosophers, educators, business people, medical pioneers, tango singers—designed to convince the majority that the minority really did make a difference to the adoptive *patria.* They truly deserve a study of their own, as apologia literature. I would explore why, after a hundred or more years in Latin America, Jews still need to apologize: please, please, remember we are good *argentinos, chilenos, mexicanos, venezolanos,* good Jewish gauchos like Yarcho. Why is Latin American identity still so narrowly construed?

I won't do it here, because for me Dr. Finkelstein's greatest miracle was his matchmaking: he found me a husband. It turned out that Finky's nephew was studying in New York at the same time I was. We arranged a date, went out to see *My Fair Lady,* and grew accustomed to one another's faces. Isidoro, renamed Josh by his Yankee buddies, came from Buenos Aires's Villa Crespo, known for obvious reasons as Villa Kreplach. He and I will one day write our joint memoirs about being Jews on three continents: about Hebrew and Yiddish *morim,* who drummed Judaism into us, and, childish pranks notwithstanding, mostly succeeded; about prissy public school teachers who didn't like little Jew-kids with foreign accents and left us out of field trips; about being proud to be among the stiff-necked folk (even if it sometimes hurt) without needing Hitler to jolt us; about lighting Shabbat candles in coconut shells by the Venezuelan Caribbean waters of Tacarigua de la Laguna after almost drowning with our boys in our one-car barge; about going vegetarian near the Bolivian border among the llamas of the Humahuaca because the llama doesn't clove its hoof; about grandfathers who didn't bring over samovars but wrote their memoirs so that we would know what it's all about.

Ley Etnica/Ethnic Law

Remote generations resound in my being. / My life was kneaded with ashes of the dead, gestated over centuries; / And if in its transmigrations my life force was set free, instinct becoming thought, my heart remained enslaved, anchored to its roots.

—Elías David Curiel, "Ley étnica" (1906)

7

Not many people know about Elías David Curiel, but he tussled with the complexities of Jewish Latin Americanness before Gerchunoff or Borges or, more humbly, Aizenberg did. His is another "steamy" Caribbean novel (or screenplay) awaiting its muse: Cut to Coro, the old colonial city on the torrid northern coast of Venezuela, within eyeshot of Curaçao, circa 1830. Elías David's forebear, Joseph Curiel—Papá Yosi—bearded, stern-faced, the very image of the Dutch-Curaçaoan Sephardi grandee, lands on *tierra firme.* Around him his wife, Deborah, of the Curaçao Lòpez Maduros, the endless dunes, *los mèdanos de Coro,* a few goats, a few townsfolk, stevedores waiting to unload the couple's belongings off the schooner to their new home. Simón Bolivar, liberator of Venezuela from the accursed Spanish, was repaying his debt. They had supported his army and hidden his hounded relatives ("Remember, Yosi, how Mordechai Ricardo took in Bolivar's sister, those poor girls?") Now, Bolivar had kept his promise and abolished the Inquisition; Dutch citizens, Catholic or not, could live openly in Venezuela. No more *marranos* lighting candles in the cellar.

Scene II: Zoom into Papá Yosi's whitewashed house. Brick-floored patio bursting with birdcages and bougainvillea, long columned corridors, hammocks swinging in the high-ceilinged rooms, begrilled windows, sunlight alternating with shadows. The sound of crying: Hanah, their eight-year-old little girl, their jewel, their crown, has died. Thank God, David Hoheb, David Valencia, Samuel Maduro, Abraham Senior, some of the others have come to comfort them. Where to bury the child? Back in Curaçao? "No, the heat and the law demand that we do it quickly, right here, in Coro." "But we have no *haham,* no *beit hayim,* no cemetery. And who knows if we'll stay here. Business isn't bad, *baruh ha-Shem,* but those flyers last year, 'Jews, get out or die,' the gunshots, the riot. . . ." "I'm burying my daughter. There's plenty of land, and we need a cemetery. I'll speak to the authorities." Papá Yosi notes down in his Book of Life, with tears in his eyes, "Hanah, born June 10, 1823. Died, January 14, 1832."

(So far so good. But where's Elías David and the steam? Where am

I?) Coro, 1918: Elías David Curiel, *poète maudit*, staggers into Botica Americana, his brother José David's apothecary. He recites, breath heavy with rum: "On a night of drunken orgy I gave away to a bacchante, / my golden pen case, my diamond ring, / the silver cup my godmother gave me the day of my bloody pact with the Covenant of God. . . ." Elías David was a man after our own contemporary hearts—insomniac, inebriated, substance abused (ether was his drug of choice), fond of damsels from the Coro slums. He struggled with the asphyxiating tedium of his provincial life, and with his genealogy as well, conceiving hallucinatory, nocturnal poems in which dead ancestors, speaking to him in foreign lilts, intone obsessively, "Marco Polo is a Jew, Torquemada is a Jew, Mordechai is a Jew, and Darius is a Jew too." Curiel, who took his own life, vents the anguish of a soul caught between a surfeit of Jewish past and a deficit of Jewish present: remote generations won't let him rest, and current generations have little to offer him. By the turn of the century, Judaism had been diluted into ethnic memory for the shrinking Coro community, isolated, leaderless, engulfed by the Catholic environment, increasingly enticed by the promises of modernity. Science, Progress, Universalism would erase the residues of bloody and enslaving particularistic ties.

Doesn't Elías David, scribbling through sleepless nights in his godforsaken corner, embody the dilemmas of every Jew since the onset of modernity, I thought, as I reread his poetry and Papá Yosi's history? My question isn't academic, since Elías David and his family have become a part of me, and I part of them. Why, I'm even included in the book about *la communidad judía de Coro,* right there in the photo between Dr. José Curiel Abenatar and José Curiel Rodríguez. (The Buendías didn't invent name repetition.) In fact, I'll say with only slight García Marquézian exaggeration that the world would probably never have heard of Coro if it weren't for Josh and for me.

Coro, 1970: The Jewish cemetery on Calle Zamora. Dr. José Curiel Rodríquez, Venezuela's Minister of Public Works, solemnly addresses the crowd: "Señoras y señores, ladies and gentlemen: In the name of the president of the republic, it gives me great pleasure to be here to take part in this simple but deeply symbolic ceremony. Many desires and efforts have converged here today. The desire to restore a monument of great value not only to Venezuela but also to Latin America as a whole, the desire of a people to reestablish links with one of its most important symbols on Venezuelan soil, and the desire of the executive to acknowledge a group that has obviously been of major importance to our national development."

I stand in the heat and listen to Minister Curiel, and think back on the day Josh and I first visited the Coro *beit hayim* after we came to live in Caracas. I think back on the cracked graves, the crumbling chapel, and the weeds, weeds creeping like menacing creditors on Hanah's, Papá Yosi's, and Elías David's stores. The precious stones on the Jews of Coro gone to pot, no one left to care for them. If there were sermons in stones, this one wasn't entirely edifying.

But here we were, spearheaders of the restoration, standing among the sepulchres with their oh so un-Jewish angels, the newly bricked chapel, the garden planted with pine and cypress seedlings brought from Israel. It was exhilarating, but bittersweet. Thanks to us, Venezuelan Jews now had their Jewish gauchos. Minister Curiel, one of Papá Yosi's many Catholic descendants, had said as much. Coro on the dunes was Venezuela's answer to Rachil on the pampas. Jews were no johnny-come-latelies in Latin America; they were good *venezolanos, bolivianos, argentinos,* a minority that really did make a difference to the adoptive *patria,* that fully identified with it. Wasn't Minister Curiel himself a good evidence? Weren't we?

Summa Identitas/Back to Borges

Tired of being confined to gauchos, pampas, and Buenos Aires slums, the standard stuff of "national" culture, Borges looked to the Jews. Complex, discordant, unbound by a single tradition or place, yet paradoxically anchored, they seemed to have what it took to be citizens of the contemporary world. Why didn't Latin Americans, with so much in common, follow them? Oh brave new borgesian world! Discord might be intellectually stimulating, literarily enriching, but it's difficult, even dangerous. Latin Americans have enough knottiness without Jews. Why don't the Hebrews just give up? Some were tempted, some succumbed, but Borges had it right—single-paned identities don't work. My kaleidoscopic borgesian, gerchunoffian, curielian Jewishness, my Latin Americanness, my Latin American Jewishness keeps turning and turning, transmuting, fragmenting, blending its colors, lights, shapes. It is who I am.

Chapter 2

A Sephardi Air

Ruth Behar

I GREW UP WITHIN my mother's Ashkenazi family, hearing Yiddish, eating gefilte fish, and adoring passionately my Russian-born grandfather, who had pale green eyes and spoke so softly you could barely hear him. And yet, always, I was reminded by my mother's family that I resembled my father's Sephardi family. It was not only my dark curly hair, Frida Kahlo eyebrows, and large brown eyes that made me more like *el lado turco* (the Turkish side). I was told that my temperament—which consisted of a terribly strong will, a fierce rage that came from a source I could not begin to fathom, and an inability to forgive those who'd wronged me—was a Sephardi temperament. I learned early to believe that Ashkenazim were logical, rational, reasonable, and modern, and that Sephardim were moody, irrational, hard-headed, passionate, and fixed in their ways. What is more, I learned that no amount of time spent with my Ashkenazi family would ever quite rid me of the Sephardi body and soul I'd inherited from the *turcos*.

If I angered my mother, she would yell, as if uttering a curse, "Eres igualita a tu padre!" (You're just like your father!). But when we were happy, she'd sometimes run her thin fingers through the curls in my hair (her own hair was Indian straight) or watch me gazing into the mirror and say, "Tienes un aire sefardí, una cosa sefardí muy bonita" (You have a Sephardi air about you, something Sephardi that's very beautiful). She recognized, in those moments of affection shaded with detachment, that she'd given birth to a female creature quite unlike herself, a young woman in whom she could see little of her own image.

The union in Cuba, in 1956, of my mother, the child of immigrants from Poland and Russia, and my father, the son of immigrants from Turkey, was viewed, by both sides, as an intermarriage. The Ashkenazi and Sephardi communities that took root in Cuba in the twenties remained apart. They prayed in separate synagogues and lived in separate neighborhoods in Havana, and they settled in different regions of Cuba. My maternal grandmother, hearing of my mother's plans to marry Albertico Behar, a *turco,* despaired, "But how will we talk to his parents? They don't speak Yiddish." Spanish, for my Eastern European maternal grandparents, was the language of the *goyim,* but for my paternal grandparents it was precisely the language of their Jewishness, a thread that wound its way back to Ladino, the fifteenth-century Spanish that Sephardim have sheltered inside Hebrew letters. Little did my grandmother imagine that a few years later, with the coming of the Cuban Revolution, my mother's entire family would depart for the United States, where both Yiddish and Ladino would be lost to new generations and the only language of comfort, love, and longing that would remain to us would be Spanish.

My mother's family was very close and tightly knit, both in Cuba and in the early years in the United States. In our first years in this country, we lived in the same apartment building in Queens, New York, as my maternal grandparents and my mother's sister and her family. I had much less contact with my Sephardi family, who resettled in Brooklyn after leaving Cuba. My father, ashamed of his family's poverty in Cuba, drew away from his parents and the Cuban Sephardi community. In Cuba, he had studied accounting in night school while working days to support his parents and younger siblings. He was ambitious, and there were more opportunities, both in Havana and later in New York City, to rise into the middle class through Ashkenazi business contacts. Yet he would always be the *turco* in that upwardly mobile world, just as he was in my mother's family.

Although my father was too charming ever to have been an outcast, I sensed that he was often treated as "other" in the Ashkenazi settings in which he tried to make something of himself. I wanted to sympathize with him, for I too had been marked as *turca,* and therefore as different within my Ashkenazi family. I understood intellectually how we were alike, but my heart could not warm to my father. He was, in my adolescent years and after, an unyielding authoritarian father, who saw me not as his ally, but as a wild feminist daughter who posed a threat to his power. My Sephardi identity came to me from him—and it came with sorrow and without forgiveness.

The stories I heard about my Sephardi family were told by my Ashkenazi family and therefore were always filtered through a lens that was exoticizing, even racist. The story most often told by my Ashkenazi family to show just how strange were those Jewish *turcos* was the tale of my brother's name. When my brother was born in 1959, the year of the Cuban Revolution, my mother, honoring her father's wish, decided to name him Morris to honor the memory of a brother of her father's who had been killed by the Nazis.

My father's parents arrived at the hospital and were enraged to hear that she'd already named the boy. "Este niño es nuestro, nos pertenece a nosotros!" (This child is ours, he belongs to us), they exclaimed.

Furious, my mother in turn told her in-laws that the child had come from her body and she was honoring a wish of her father's. And my father's parents, convinced of their rights and deeply hurt, said to her, "But we let you name your first child to honor your side of the family, and now this second child belongs to us. And we want you to name him Isaac." My mother was doubly shocked. How could a child "belong" to its grandparents rather than to its own mother? And how could a child be named after a living relative?

"Isaac? Name him Isaac? You're alive! We can't name him Isaac."

And my paternal grandfather replied, "Yes, I'm alive, and I want you to name the boy after me."

My mother, holding to the Ashkenazi dictum that names are given to honor the dead rather than to give joy to the living, refused to change her mind. Finally, she compromised and said she would name her son Morris Isaac. This, however, was not satisfying to my father's parents, who announced they would not attend the *bris* unless the boy was renamed Isaac Morris. As the day drew near and the tensions mounted between my mother and father, my maternal grandparents thought to ask their neighbor, Rabbi Gambach, a Sephardi rabbi from Turkey, to talk some "sense" into my father's parents. My paternal grandparents greatly respected Gambach, and he managed to convince them that even if Isaac were my brother's middle name, El Abuelo Isaac would be honored just the same. So they went to the *bris* and a semblance of family peace and unity was restored.

Why is it, then, that I, in telling this story, want to claim the anger and loss of my Sephardi grandparents? I would probably have been even more furious than was my mother, had my in-laws tried to force me to give my son a name I didn't like and hadn't chosen. But I see now that my grandparents were cowed into accepting an arrangement that put their traditions and their memory in a secondary place within the family, just as at Passover we always went to their house for the second rather than the first seder. We have never once called my brother "Isaac." We never once gave my paternal grandfather that joy in life, and now in death we still deny it to him. Isaac is gone from us, as surely and as bitterly as the lover who sings his goodbye in the old Sephardi ballad and does not return again.

Chapter 3

What! No Yiddish?
Growing up Sephardi in Peru

Fortuna Calvo-Roth

To Evelyne—who helped me remember.
To Julie—who made growing up fun.

SINCE MY EARLY TRAINING in journalism, I have spent more time working on lead paragraphs than on the rest of the story. As a result, I have ended up wishing I could fill a whole chapter such as this one with beginnings.

So far, it is clear that I belong in these pages by virtue of my Sephardi Jewish upbringing in Peru. Recently I heard that the Sephardi congregants in Lima were going to move from their first and only synagogue site, built in the nineteen thirties, around the time I was born, to quarters in the synagogue and community house of the Orthodox Ashkenazi community. My late father, a seemingly old-fashioned but actually forward-looking man, would not have been too surprised. "Everything changes, my dear, everything passes," I can almost hear him saying. His eyes always twinkled when he laughed, a very quick laugh. "Somos hojas al viento, hijita. . . ." We were like leaves in the wind, he would sigh.

My father, Isaac Calvo, was honored in 1983 on the fiftieth anniversary of the construction of our synagogue. My sister Evelyne, who has an academic background in history, researched the archives of the Sociedad de Beneficencia Israelita Sefardí and prepared a text for the commemorative video. When the congregation was established in 1921 (its first president, a Mr. Sasson, was a British subject of Syrian-Lebanese ancestry), services were held at a number of places, among them the Masonic Hall. Our father was a Mason in his youth, and kept the characteristic three-dotted signature until his dying day.

At the time of the fiftieth anniversary, Papá, then in his nineties, was the congregation's sole surviving founder and its first treasurer. Papá would tell his three daughters—Evelyne and Julie are four and two years older than I—how he would go to his coreligionists, one by one, for a modest monthly quota to build the "cal" (kahal) or the local *sefaradí*, as it was known by everyone. Born in Turkey, he arrived in Lima in 1915, set up a business, and for many years traveled constantly throughout the country to sell his wares, often on muleback across the mountains. Less than a decade later, he was one of Lima's prosperous immigrants.

Sephardi Jews may have been the first to land in the New World and be burned at the stake of the Inquisition, but the German Jewish community has the oldest continuous congregation in Peru, first called Sociedad de Beneficencia 1870 and later, almost as cryptically, Sociedad de Beneficencia y Culto 1870. Its founders were French- and German-speaking businessmen who arrived with families and domestic workers, and today their congregation practices rituals associated with Reform Judaism. The Jewish cemetery was built at this time (the 1870s). Among its founders was New York-born Henry Meiggs, who donated the land. He was a well-known businessman, railroad builder, and adviser to the president of Peru. A mountain in the Andes is named after him.

Our parents and our friends' parents lie in that beautifully maintained cemetery, which I visit every time I go to Lima. The tombstones include names like Cohen and Levy, Sarfaty, Behar, Lemor, Franco, Mayo, Varón, Alalú, Aragonés, Sevilla, Alhalel, Bueno,

Cordoví, and also Goldenberg, Roitman, Prag, Nathan, Sterental, Edelman, Weinstein, Zender, Perelman, and Gabel; and birthplaces like Izmir (Smyrna), Constantinople, Novo Zelitza, Odessa, Bucharest, Warsaw, Frankfurt, Hamburg, Berlin, Salonica, Cairo, Alexandria, Aleppo, Beirut, Jerusalem, and Chanakkale and Edirne. Our Jewish community shrinks while the cemetery's population thrives. There were more than five thousand of us in the nineteen sixties. Today, we are about half that many.

Our mother's grave says Rose Penso de Calvo was born in Turkey and died in Lima. Technically, she died at St. Luke's hospital in Houston, Texas, but she was only there for a few days. Her grave also carries an inscription from WIZO—the Women's International Zionist Organization—to its founding co-president. In 1941, a Canadian by the name of Rachel Smiley established WIZO in Peru. The three communities, Sephardi, Ashkenazi, and German, were so divided that each one had to have its own president. Fortunately, as time went by they agreed on a single president. Unfortunately, what unified the communities was the Holocaust.

World War II affected us profoundly. In general, we knew much more than the youth of the United States did about concentration camps and gas chambers. We all had relatives in Europe and the Middle East. David Levy, a first cousin, spent five years as a French prisoner of war of the Germans. I could already read by the time the U.S. entered the war on December 7, 1941, but the naval activities of the SS *Ohio* and the SS *Iowa* confused and worried me: they were pronounced *oyo* and *yova* in Spanish, which sounded suspiciously Japanese.

Mamá participated modestly in the war effort. She couldn't knit or sew for the Allied soldiers, but almost every afternoon she assisted other women who were experts at these tasks, sometimes at the Ashkenazi synagogue, other times at the British Embassy. In addition, she helped refugees from Europe gain a foothold in their new surroundings and regain their self-respect. Thus, we took piano lessons not because we were especially talented, except for Evelyne, but because

Mamá needed to find employment for our two teachers, Frau Jacob and Frau Kirstein. She also recommended them to her friends. We were fortunate to have *la señora* Malca come to the house on a regular basis to alter hemlines, sew buttons, and fix practically anything. And a very distinguished white-haired gentleman in a white three-piece suit with a gold vest-pocket watch came every week to sell chocolates from an elegant leather briefcase. We were much more thrilled to see him than to see the piano teachers.

Until the early postwar years, a mixed marriage in our milieu meant a union between members of ethnically different Jewish congregations. And, among Sephardim at least, marriage between first cousins was encouraged to preserve social, cultural, and economic unity. More to the point, Evelyne married David. Julie married Cuban-born Salvador Salinas, whose family was friendly with Mama's family in Havana. As for me, many arguments with my father ended with this threat: "Just you wait! I'll marry an Ashkenazi." And I did, but by then he no longer believed that "our own" meant Sephardi Jews exclusively.

Ashkenazi Jews initially agreed there was little in common between us: their vernacular was Yiddish, ours Ladino or Judeo-Español, a fifteenth century Spanish to which words from many languages have been added; they ate gefilte fish, chopped liver, and kreplach (dumplings) while we ate *filas* and *burekas* (turnovers), *abudarajo* (dried roe), salted tuna, and a variety of vegetable-cheese-and-egg pies. Many Ashkenazim arrived in the nineteen thirties from Rumania, Poland, Hungary, and Russia on the eve of World War II. Sephardim left a disintegrating Ottoman Empire, home to ancestors for four centuries, in the early 1900s.

Before immigrating to Peru in 1915, our father lived in New York for two years. An enterprising person, he started working at a flashlight factory on the Lower East Side the day after his arrival. Shortly afterward, he became an usher and candy concessionaire at a movie theater in Brooklyn. We loved to hear about those days as much as we loved to hear his Yiddish-accented English. To our "Where's Penn Station,

Papi?" he would answer with a smile, "Toity-toid Street, goils." "And what did you sell?" "Hoishy bar, Cracker Jack, a penny a piece!"

He marveled at the efficient humanity of New York Jewry. He told us that when his ship anchored at the harbor's docks, a man waiting at the gangplank asked him: "Are you Sephardic?" "Yes." "Do you want a job?" "Yes." "Do you want a place to live?" "Yes." He remembered fondly the boarding house at 75 Chrystie Street.

With three days to go before his first paycheck, he had only one nickel left. A handful of peanuts in his pocket, he went to the café where his *paisanos,* people like him, ate and spent their leisure time. He was eating a peanut here, a peanut there as he watched a game of cards, until his friends noticed. He shared the rest of his peanuts with them. Still hungry, he finally swallowed his pride and asked a friend of his older brother's for a loan "until Friday" because, as he explained, his shift did not give him time to go to the bank to change his gold coins. The man opened his wallet. Father took only one dollar, thanked him, and raced back to the café. Years later, he could still taste the food: fish, spinach, rice, a roll, a cup of coffee. Grandly waving the dollar in his hand, he asked: "How much?" The owner answered: "What! Don't you know our regulars get credit until payday?"

Alas, well adjusted though he was to life in New York, tales he heard from an Izmirli on business in New York of untold riches in Peru were too tempting. And there was the added incentive of not having to learn a new tongue. Farther south on the continent, people spoke his language. Almost. He picked up Spanish quickly, but always spoke with a distinctive Sephardi accent: "el Dió" instead of "Dios," "aséntate" instead of "siéntate," "azete" for "aceite," and so on . . ., and used many colorful expressions to describe character traits, such as "desmodrado" (from "desmoderado," meaning without moderation). To him, moderation was of utmost importance. "Everything in moderation," he would advise me, "even virtue." In other words, don't be a goody-goody.

Isaac Calvo became a migrant anew, this time carrying one thousand dollars ("In gold!" he would remind us) in the event things didn't work out in Peru—in which case he would return to New York—plus one thousand (gold) dollars' worth of merchandise, which he shipped separately.

He had left Edirne—Iderné to him, in the region of Andrinople or Adrianopolis—for New York when neighboring Bulgaria laid siege to his hometown during the Balkan war. His father, Salomón Kalvo, spelled with a *K* to preserve the Spanish pronunciation, was a grain broker who was ruined by that war. Papá always said the family was originally from Toledo. In his novel *1492*, Mexican author Homero Aridjis mentions that on April 29, 1492, the Catholic Kings expropriated the possessions of fourteen families, among them the Calvos, in San Martín de Valdeiglesias and elsewhere. My Uncle Rafael told us it was easy to know where in Spain every Sephardi Jew in Turkey came from because they named their synagogues after their erstwhile towns.

As for their mother, Estrella Eskenazi, Papá would tell us how she woke up before dawn to bake bread for the family. German Jews migrated to the Ottoman Empire in the thirteenth century, and she may have been one of their descendants. Although we have no proof of this, the number of redheaded Calvo cousins I met on a recent trip to Istanbul was remarkable. Estrella died young, after bearing four sons and a daughter who all lived to ripe old ages. Aunt Rachel died at 104. The youngest son, Rafael—Rufat to us—who was studying to be a rabbi when he was drafted during the World War I, eventually joined Papá in Peru and lived with him most of the rest of his long life. They were business partners for forty years, went together everywhere, and talked in the same agitated tones. Everyone called them the Calvo twins, even those who only knew them by sight, and many business and social acquaintances thought they were actually twins.

Longevity runs on both sides of the family. Our mother Rosa—her father preferred to call her Rossina—died at seventy-one, but her mother, Hoursi Mouchabac, lived into her nineties. She spent most of her life in Chanakkale, Turkey, in the Dardanelles region, but when her son died she moved with her older daughter, first to France and then to Lima, where she spent the last four years of her life with us. When I met her, the only language she could remember was Ladino, which she called "judezmo" (Jewish), just as Ashkenazim often call Yiddish "Jewish."

A few hours after her arrival in Lima, as she watched in total amazement the strange new world before her eyes, she overheard two women dressed in colorful Indian garments as they passed under the balcony of her bedroom. She couldn't believe her ears! "Vení, vení!" she urged. "Come and look! These are the strangest-looking Jews I've ever seen!" We explained that the women were not Jewish. She looked even more astonished: "Then why are they speaking Jewish?" To her dying day, she was unable to comprehend this great mystery.

Her youngest daughter, our mother, was also born in Chanakkale. She began her education at the Alliance Israélite Universelle, part of a network of French-based schools established to preserve Jewish heritage throughout the Middle East. At home, she had an Italian tutor, *professore* Santa Agata. Later, she learned English at the North American Boarding College in Istanbul. Her parents cherished a good education: her mother was illiterate, which was not uncommon for women of that place and time, while her father, Joseph Penso, a banker and grain dealer, was on the school board. (His family lived in the Austro-Hungarian Empire, which at one time included the Veneto. There are records of Pensos in Venice; of a consul by the name of Joseph Penso in Dubrovnik, also part of that empire; and of another Joseph Penso, an eighteenth-century author in Amsterdam.)

This was a time of war: in the Balkans and later throughout Europe as World War I erupted, and, in the midst of it all, the Russian Revolution, which shattered Joseph's business. In 1917, the Bolshevik government refused to honor debts—our grandfather's among them—incurred by the Czarist regime. Although his fortune was decimated, there was enough money to send Rossina to Vienna to live with her older sister (fifteen years her senior) and brother-in-law and their children. She learned German and took business courses. Four years later, another move, this time to Paris. She now spoke eight languages and found work as an interpreter at the Galleries Lafayette, a well-known department store.

Rose Penso and Isaac Calvo met at the end of September 1924, in Paris. They were married one week later. No, it was not love at first sight. Both were looking for a spouse with similar backgrounds and values: honesty, hard work, modesty. Mama was looking for something else: financial security, which Papá, by now a Peruvian businessman visiting France on a business and wife-hunting trip, could provide.

They lived in Miraflores, the cheerful, upper-middle class suburb of Lima where Evelyne was born. A couple of years later the family moved closer to other members of the Sephardi community, and Julie was born in the new neighborhood. Both of my sisters were delivered by Mrs. Olga Powolotsky, a Russian-born midwife. Conceived in Lima, I was born in Paris when our mother decided to visit her relatives.

Mamá left Paris with her three children a few months after my birth, and we all settled in another house, closer yet to our synagogue, where we lived for the next eight years. Here, Evelyne had her own room, and she filled it with books. As we grew up, now in a lovely new Art Deco house in the suburb of San Isidro, she started to lock her books up in her huge walk-in closet so we wouldn't ruin or lose them. Julie loved romantic novels and magazines from Argentina like *Estampa* and *Para Ti*. I owe my love of reading to my sisters and to Mama, who read Schiller, Shakespeare, and Molière aloud to me before I learned to read. At the age of ten, I was as engrossed by Hans Christian Andersen and the Brothers Grimm as by Alexandre Dumas, Stefan Zweig, Alphonse Daudet, the poetry of Amado Nervo and Gustavo Adolfo Bécquer, or the novels of Rafael Pérez y Pérez. Evelyne preferred Louisa May Alcott, Rafael Sabatini, Emilio Salgari, Jules Verne, Mark Twain, and later Dumas and Edgar Allan Poe.

Evelyne remembers that after every school day, the radio (a huge eighteen-tube Midwest) "belonged" to whoever reached it first. She listened to Mozart, Schubert, Beethoven, and Liszt while Julie and I longed for the songs of Leo Marini, Fernando Torres, Libertad Lamarque, and the late Carlos Gardel. I can still savor the sensual satisfaction of learning the lyrics to every new bolero or tango. We were already familiar with Frank Sinatra and Bing Crosby, Harry James and Louis Armstrong from Hollywood movies and from the U.S. disc jockeys who settled in Lima after the war and brought us the hit parade.

The radio belonged to the grown-ups in the evening, but we were just as interested as they in the dramatized current events of "Esto Sucedió Ayer" (This happened yesterday), which featured musical preludes and postludes from the *William Tell* overture and the "Barcarolle" from Offenbach's *The Tales of Hoffmann* and news of the war. A few minutes before nine, Papá would switch to short-wave radio, where we heard Big Ben's solemn gongs followed, in impeccable Spanish, by "At 2100 hours, Greenwich Meridian Time, this is the BBC of London." I was moved every time I heard that voice. London was being bombed, and yet these people devoted precious time to keep us informed. A noble calling, indeed, which influenced me in choosing journalism as a career.

When I arrived in Columbia, Missouri, to study journalism, my Jewish credentials were met with skepticism: no Yiddish, no gefilte fish, no matzo balls, no *kugel.* . . . Did Jews really live in Peru? It didn't sound kosher. I wasn't even sure whether my family was Orthodox or Conservative, although I was sure we were not Reform. Growing up in a Conservative household and practicing Orthodox rituals at the synagogue did not cause problems for us.

We lived our Sephardi heritage before we knew we were Jewish. We did not keep kosher but would not eat pork or shellfish. Our father's influence was so strong that, as very young children, we felt nauseous when we saw or smelled pork meat. Papá went to synagogue Friday nights, Saturday mornings, and whenever a *minyan* was required. He did not smoke and Mama did not sew during the early hours of Shabbat, although they drove and Papá's business was open on Saturday mornings. Every member of the family gathered for dinner on Friday nights. No exceptions were allowed. I broke this rule during my first week at the School of Journalism of the Catholic University: our curriculum was fixed, and I had class on Friday nights. Papá barely spoke to me for a while. And he did not celebrate when, at the end of the school year, I won the award in Catholic ethics.

Fiercely conscious though we were of our Jewishness, fear of anti-Semitism may have been a factor in our avoidance of the word *Jewish*. During my early childhood, we spent most of our time among fellow Jews in the neighborhood of Santa Beatriz where our synagogue had been built. Most of us lived within a five-block radius. Our families took us almost every evening for a couple of hours to two lovely nearby parks, Sucre and La Reserva, where the grown-ups chatted while the youngsters played tag or hide-and-seek. A few Ashkenazim also lived in our neighborhood and, though they did not attend our religious services, they were active participants in our social events.

Teenagers of different backgrounds came to the synagogue on weekend afternoons to dance to popular music played on a "pick-up" (record changer) and, together with younger children, to put on "veladas," as we called our evening functions. Some played musical instruments while others declaimed in Spanish and Hebrew. On several occasions a member of the Lima Philarmonic, German-born Bronislau Mitman, played the violin. We heard poetry from fourteen-year-old Emilio Cogan and also from the famous Argentine sisters Berta and Paulina Singerman. And we always sang "Hatikvah" and the Peruvian national anthem.

Saturday afternoons and Sunday mornings we attended Hebrew school, where Morá Alcabés taught us about Abraham, Isaac, Jacob, Joseph and his brothers, and Moses and the Ten Commandments. Our parents also went to the synagogue to hear celebrities like U.S. writer Waldo Frank, an ardent socialist, or Communist Chilean senator Berman, not because of their ideology but because they were

Jewish luminaries. And it was the gathering place of young and old, Sephardi and Ashkenazi, on joyous occasions like the end of the war and the establishment of the state of Israel.

The main room of the two-story building (complete with balcony for the women) housed the sanctuary. That same room doubled as community house, theater, and ballroom. Weddings, bar mitzvahs, and other ceremonial events, such as the presentation of awards at the end of the Hebrew school year, were held on a large stage as the spectators sat in rows or around banquet tables, as the occasion demanded.

The High Holidays were exactly that. Attending school was taboo. Regardless of our economic situation (and it became dire for a few years during our childhood when Papá lost his business), we always wore something new. We went to synagogue and came home to celebrate with relatives at a table festively set with the English china and French sterling our parents bought after their wedding. We also observed other holidays, especially Passover, more by having Seders, eating matzah and avoiding *hametz* than by attending services, although the men were always there. Presents were not an important part of any holiday, even Purim or Hanukah. For the young, the synagogue served as a community, rather than a religious, center.

A few weeks into kindergarten, a classmate asked me: "Are you Catholic or Protestant?" Four-and-a-half at the time, I may have heard the words but didn't know their meaning. "I'll ask my mother," I replied. Mom pondered the question, then said she would let me know soon. Maybe my sisters told me before she did, but besides finding out we were Jewish I learned that Jews . . . no, wait a second, Pontius Pilate, it was definitely Pontius Pilate . . . but then, he left it up to the Jews to choose who would get killed, right? And it was Christ who was crucified.

As if by rote, I learned the response we gave to peers who occasionally hurled "You Jews!" at us with scorn and contempt: "And proud of it!" I think I kept saying it until my college years.

The reason a five-year-old asked me whether I was Catholic or Protestant was that our school was run by U.S. Methodist missionaries. Lima High School was founded in 1906 to give women access to the workplace as bilingual secretaries and bookkeepers. They also gave us a solid English-language education and a steady diet of hymns like "Onward Christian Soldiers," "We Three Kings of Orient Are," "Away in a Manger," which we often sang heartily at chapel; that is, unless a church envoy from the United States led a revival-type meeting or a dentist came to teach us the value of good hygiene. Theoretically we could have gotten an exemption from any religious activity, but our parents thought it was important to be an integral part of the class. Besides, "we mustn't call attention to ourselves." Keeping a low profile was best.

Jewish parents did not need to explain why their children, about 15 or sometimes 20 percent of the class, attended a Methodist school. Public, except for magnet, schools were only for the very poor. A few lay schools were sponsored by French, Swiss, Italian, German, British, and U.S. private groups or, at times, governments but, until the postwar period, many were established by religious orders from abroad, some Anglican or Evangelical, the majority Catholic: Santa Ursula (Germany), Villa María and Santa María (U.S.), Belén and San José de Cluny (France). Lima High School had a wonderful reputation, our parents felt there was less anti-Semitism among Protestants than among Catholics, tuition was modest, and our mother insisted on a modern education, for which English was a must.

I did not experience much direct discrimination at Lima High School until the year I graduated. By 1950, the Jewish day school had been established and the new wave of missionaries was more militant. The school's mission was to gain converts, the principal explained to our mother, but not a single Jewish student had converted! "Until now," she added, "we accepted members of your community out of a sense of moral obligation, but now you have your own school and your people should go there."

This new policy applied to future applicants but affected me in several ways. Our teachers knew I wanted to be a journalist, and during my senior year I was awarded literary prizes both in English and in Spanish, yet instead of writing for the yearbook I was asked, together with my two Jewish buddies, to sell advertising. Then, although I had been assured I would deliver one of the graduation speeches—English or Spanish—I was informed at the last minute that my voice did not project. Finally, when I applied for a scholarship, the principal wrote this letter: "Fortuna Calvo has asked me for a letter of recommendation. She says she wants to be a journalist." Overall, however, I have fond memories of my teachers and have remained friendly with many classmates.

During our teenage years, right before and after the establishment of Israel, we formed part of Hanoar Hatzioni, a Zionist organization. There were two other youth groups, also ideologically oriented: the revisionist Betar and the left-wing JJV (Juventud Judía Vanguardista, or Jewish Youth Vanguard). Besides being trained to make *aliyah,* we liked to dance and organize sports and social activities. A few young people did migrate to Israel—some for good, others for a few years.

The three Calvo sisters left home: Evelyne went to Paris, married a few months later, had a child and returned with her family to Lima, where she had twins. Julie went on vacation to Havana, met Salvador, married a few months later, and returned with her husband to Lima, where she had two girls and a boy. I went to college, returned to Lima, and left again. A few weeks after my arrival in New York, a handsome young man with very blond hair and deep blue eyes smiled as we were introduced. "Would that he were a tiny, tiny bit taller," I sighed inwardly, with the certainty that I would spend the rest of my life with him. Felix Roth and I were married forty-three years ago and our two children are Carla and Stephen. But that is a subject for a new beginning.

Chapter 4

My Past Is Present
The Complex Identity of a German-Jewish-Venezuelan-American

Verónica de Darer

MY NAME IS VERÓNICA Zander Udewald Darer. I am a Venezuelan Jew, a German Jew, and an American Jew. I am a citizen of many worlds, a patriot of none. Zander, my father's name, Udewald, my mother's name, and Darer, my married name, are all Jewish, even if they are from diverse national origins. My names, reflections of my amalgamated identity, are the threads that unite my Jewish culture, constructed and reconstructed by incessant emigrations.

Herbert Zander Mayer, my father, was born in Germany. My mother, Ruth Udewald Kaufman, was born in the same town as my father. Even though the two families had some contact, my parents never met as children. Both of my German Jewish parents fled their country around 1937–38 to avoid the persecution of Jews during the Third Reich.

The story of my father's exodus from Germany was different from my mother's. Since my father could not attend university in Germany due to Nazi prohibitions against the Jews, his family sent him to study in Barcelona, Spain, at a college specializing in textile engineering. Unluckily, it was exactly then that the Spanish Civil War broke out. My father escaped by traveling from the city of Barcelona to the port of

Burgos. Thanks to an armistice between Germany and Spain, German citizens living in Spain were allowed to return to their country. My father returned to Germany as a German citizen, on a ship sailing under the German flag, disguised as a member of the Nazi party. Upon his arrival in Germany, his father immediately sent him off once again, this time to Colombia to live with some distant cousins. During the trip, my father met a successful Venezuelan businessman of German origin who convinced him to stay in Venezuela, then a country of magnificent economic opportunities. That is how my father came to disembark at the port of La Guaira, and how the Zander family settled in Caracas, Venezuela, in 1937.

Soon after, in 1938, my paternal grandfather, Moritz Zander, arrived in Venezuela with his second wife, a Catholic woman to whom he had been married for five years. Divorced from his first wife, my paternal grandmother Teresa, my grandfather was not willing to help her leave Germany. Their divorce had been bitter, and he abhorred the idea of importing his former marital problems to his new home. Possibly without knowing it, he condemned her to death in Germany. She died in one of the many Nazi concentration camps. We do not know which one.

In contrast to my father, my mother suffered directly from Nazi policies of persecution against the Jews. Before becoming a refugee in the United States, she was forced to wear the Star of David prominently displayed on her clothing. She was excluded from all school and social activities in her city. She was abused physically and psychologically by her schoolmates. My grandmother, Hannah Kaufman, was a divorced woman in her mid-forties. She knew that the only option she had to save herself and her daughter was to find a sponsor in the United States. Taking advantage of her beauty, she sent her photograph to agencies in New York that found European Jewish women to marry Jewish American gentlemen. Mr. Weinberg, a gentleman significantly older than my grandmother, fell in love with her photograph and brought both mother and daughter to New York, where he and my grandmother were married.

My grandmother's ex-husband, my maternal grandfather still living in Germany, begged his ex-wife to help him escape from Nazi danger. Even though Mr. Weinberg had the economic means to immediately sponsor my grandfather, my grandmother was hesitant and waited too long. My maternal grandfather also died in a concentration camp. My mother never forgave either her mother or her stepfather for her father's death. This momentous event affected the relationship between my mother and grandmother for the rest of their lives.

My parents, two people hurt by hostile divorces, which were so uncommon during this era of traditional families, both living with the shadow of possible paternal or maternal culpability in the tragic destiny of a partner, both hurt by the loss of one of their parents to the Holocaust, fell in love at first sight. It was my father's sister, my Aunt Edith, who introduced my mother to my father when he was in New York on a business trip. After knowing each other for only two weeks, they got married. My mother moved to Venezuela, where my father had established himself as a successful manufacturer's representative. She was happy to distance herself from her mother, whom she still blamed for her father's death. Both my parents lived in Venezuela until they died, my father in 1992 and my mother in 1996.

Neither my father's nor my mother's family had the opportunity to bring to their new home the beloved belongings of their ancestors (except an oil lamp and two silver candlesticks). The lamp and the candlesticks are reminders of an era when my grandmother's family participated in religious traditions. The oil lamp, a copper piece of significant size, could burn for days, so there was no need to turn on lights during Shabbat. Today it proudly hangs in a place of honor at the house of my oldest sister in Venezuela. Till the day of her death, the silver candlesticks rested on my grandmother's night table in New York. After her death, I brought them from New York to Venezuela for my mother. My mother gave them as an engagement gift to the first grandchild who got married. From my father's family, the only object related to his Jewish roots that was brought to Venezuela was a silver kiddush cup to bless the wine. I have this cup, the only physical evidence reminding me of the Jewish life of my German ancestors.

Notwithstanding the personal experience my father had during the Holocaust, he always considered himself a German first, then a Venezuelan, and last a Jew. Once the war was over, he traveled at least once a year from Venezuela to Germany. He established commercial links with Germany, and for years represented German manufacturers in Venezuela. At the end of his life he decided once again to adopt his German nationality and passport.

My father was a profoundly intellectual man. He was a polyglot. He spoke seven languages fluently—German, Spanish, English, French, Italian, Catalan, and Russian—all without a trace of an accent. He was a man of culture, even though he had not been able to complete his university degree. Knowledgeable in the fields of music, numismatics, philosophy, and history, he studied and read assiduously until his death. He was a man with great honors, winner of the government Medal of Merit and distinguished with the highest accolade conferred by the Masons, the order of the thirty-third degree. My father instilled in the minds of his daughters that among the Jews, German Jews were the best educated and most intelligent, the greatest thinkers and creators. The writings of German authors such as Schiller and Goethe and the operas of Wagner and Strauss, always present in our home, were the cultural frame that surrounded our existence. The great vacuum in the multifaceted education of my father was his lack of knowledge regarding secular and religious Jewish traditions, which had been concealed and limited by years of his family's integration to German society before the rise of Nazism.

The German identity and culture of my father together with his scorn for the Jewish religion were critical influences on my life. My first language was German. My first nanny was German. My first school experience was in a German kindergarten. Many say that the first language determines the point of view, the lens that filters the perspective with which a person sees the world (Whorf, 1956). I agree. Even though my German language skills have shrunk to mere basics, the rigidity, the linear chronology, and the sense of exactness of the German language have influenced my way of thinking and writing, which may lack poetry, but always seeks clarity, neatness, and efficiency of words.

Even though my mother was fluent in German, English, and Spanish, she had barely finished high school. My grandmother forced her to work in a factory as a punishment for rebelling against her stepfather. In contrast to that of my father, her encyclopedic knowledge was limited to what she read in best-selling novels, but her Jewish roots were strong and profound. She worked for Jewish organizations such as ORT, WIZO, and B'nai B'rith. Nevertheless, after many confrontations with my father, she bent to his wishes and followed his Germanic social patterns. She had almost no contact with the non-German Jewish community.

In Venezuela, not only my father, but also the majority of German Jews, considered themselves superior to the Jews from Eastern Europe and certainly superior to the Sephardi Jews from North Africa and the Middle East. Consequently, they avoided intimate contact with the Jewish community. Their alienation from the community in general was not out of fear of belonging to a cultural/religious group persecuted and ill regarded by Venezuelan society—from the earliest arrivals, Jewish immigrants were admired and respected members of the rich cultural mosaic that was Venezuela. The Jewish immigrants of the nineteen thirties founded the community as it exists today. The majority of these first Jewish immigrants from Eastern Europe and North Africa became business people, manufacturers, and merchants. There are stories of miraculous economic successes, of men who landed, on that same day found work as street vendors, and later became important and influential business magnates.

For the Jewish community in Venezuela, education was fundamental. Starting with the first immigration, Venezuelan Jews were determined to educate future generations and spared no effort to ensure that their offspring could enjoy all the opportunities of their new homeland. Their Hebrew schools are recognized as some of the best schools in the country. Second- and third-generation Venezuelan Jews, both those of European descent (Ashkenazim) as well as those of African and Middle Eastern descent (Sephardim), have become doctors, lawyers, economists, bankers, important politicians, and powerful industrialists in Venezuela. Due to the economic and educational success of the Jewish community in general, the Jews have held a privileged position in Venezuelan society. Thus, Jews have been a cultural-religious minority that has enjoyed great cultural and religious freedom of expression in Venezuela.

Nevertheless, the first generation of Venezuelan German Jews decided to distance themselves from the Jewish community and not to enroll their children in their renown Hebrew schools. Instead, the children of German Jews attended lay schools where they were an accepted, but marginalized, minority. As the daughter of German Jews, I also went to a secular school.

My years at a mostly Catholic all-girls school showed me what it is to be and feel "different" due to culture, religion, and physical appearance. There were only eight Jewish students in my class. On the surface, all the students, Jews and non-Jews, interacted routinely and were part of all educational and social activities. We were separated only when the Christian students attended catechism lessons, a normal part of even public schools' curricula. The Jews would then sit on benches right outside the class, doing homework. When religion class was over, the Christian students would pass right in front of us. I recall two occasions when they called us "killers of Christ" as they left class. It was then that we knew that we were Jewish, and that our religion set us apart from the other students. Ironically, ours was a religion we did not understand well, a religion that was ours only in name and not in practice. We, the German Jewish classmates, knew we were considered foreign.

Because of our parents' expectations, the German Jewish students distinguished ourselves academically. The pedagogical honors always went to at least one of us. On occasions when I won academic, musical, or artistic prizes, my father never actually congratulated me. It was as if artistic and academic talent were, in his opinion, intrinsic to the German Jewish race. It was my duty to shine as an intellectual, to demonstrate my supposed superiority as a daughter of German Jews. Our academic success only compounded the religious differences, further disconnecting us from our classmates.

Our looks were also a subject of conversation, both in and out of school. Many German Jews had very curly hair or prominent noses. Personally, being a blue-eyed blonde of European appearance, I attracted attention in the multicolor population of mestizos and mulattos. When we walked down the street, the Venezuelans would call us "musiú" or "musiúa," mispronunciations of the French "monsieur" used to refer to foreigners in Venezuela. I have always felt that for the Venezuelans I was not a "true" Venezuelan. The truth is that many other immigrants, not only the Jews, were considered outsiders in their own country, in great part due to their physical appearance.

However, it was the contrast between the Venezuelan cultural, moral, and philosophical values and the Germanic cultural, moral, and philosophical values that hindered my full integration to Venezuelan society. Germanic values that were instilled methodically, every day, in both theory and practice. Values that were constantly being modeled by my father and the German Jewish community. My father was one of the few who paid their taxes on time. He insisted on the absolute punctuality of a Swiss watch in both work and social environments, on keeping all promises, on knowing a person and who his ancestors were before exchanging even a greeting. My father's actions reflected German values such as the importance of time, punctuality, work, and efficiency, the existence of definite and irrevocable laws, adherence to a linear and absolute sense of right and wrong, and a preference for few long-term intimate friendships. These values are in conflict with Venezuelan values such as flexibility in concepts of time and the law, an ephemeral sense of right and wrong, and the importance of close friendships and open communication.

I recall one of many incidents that clearly illustrates the contrast of values of my two worlds, the Venezuelan and the German Jewish. To obtain a driver's license in Venezuela, one must wait in endless lines. To avoid this inconvenience, people utilize social and political contacts, or, if they have the means, they pay a small sum of money to an intermediary who specializes in facilitating the process. My father insisted that he and members of his family had to obtain the documents "legally," without contacts and without intermediaries. After six months and several visits to the registrar of motor vehicles, where each time they asked for another official paper, another stamp, or another certificate, I finally paid an intermediary and was able to obtain my driver's license.

Religious education was not an integral part of my childhood. My parents did not routinely attend services at a temple. During the most sacred days of Yom Kippur and Rosh Hashanah, my mother, my sisters, and I went to Reform services that took place in the B'nai B'rith building, which was converted to a temple during religious holidays. The only time I remember taking Hebrew language or Jewish religion lessons was when, as the youngest of the family, I had to learn the four questions to recite at the Passover table. Passover is the only holiday we celebrated with other German Jewish families. Nowadays, Passover is still the only religious holiday that is joyously celebrated with familiar traditions at my house. The four questions are the only prayer that I can repeat perfectly by memory.

During high school, curiosity about our Jewish roots brought many of the German Jews of my generation, including my sisters and I, to visit the main Ashkenazi synagogue, the Unión Israelita (Israelite union). The services held at this synagogue are traditional Jewish Orthodox in nature. The women sit in the balcony on the second floor, separated from the men. While the men pray, the women do not participate actively in the service. Instead, they chatter about the latest gossip and social events, or they critique and comment about the dress and physical appearance of other women present. The absolute separation of genders was unacceptable to me. After going on various occasions to religious services at the Unión Israelita, I decided that even though I would always be Jewish by tradition, I would not become Jewish Orthodox nor follow Jewish religious laws and rituals. A religion that ignores women in their services was not a religion that I could accept or practice.

Nevertheless, as a result of the visits to the Unión Israelita, many of the young German Jews started to have more contact with the wider Venezuelan Jewish community. At the beach club we frequented with other German Jewish families, we became friendly with young Jews we had seen at the Unión Israelita. They were more involved in the Jewish schools and with Jewish religious tradition. Our parents could not impede our growing sense of Jewish identity. We all married Jews of national origins other than German. At this beach club I, too, met my husband, Enrique Darer, an Ashkenazi of Russian background.

With my husband, I entered wholeheartedly the world of Venezuelan Judaism. Every Friday night, my husband's family would get together for Sabbath dinner at the home of my in-laws. Even though they did not follow the religious rites of lighting Sabbath candles or blessing the bread and the wine, Jewish tradition permeated the food, the conversation, and the music: Hebrew songs sung by my nieces, my nephews, and eventually my daughters. For the first time, I tasted gefilte fish, *malai,* kreplach, and *kasha* accompanied by the latest rumors of the community interlaced with sayings in Yiddish, which I could understand because of its similarity to German. The sum of smells, tastes, and sounds of these dinners is the most vivid and palpable memory that remains of my affiliation to Venezuelan Judaism.

After our two daughters completed kindergarten at a secular institute, my husband insisted on registering them in the Hebrew community school. My daughters' attendance at this school threw me into the universe of traditional Jewish education. My daughters invited me to participate in their Jewish world, in and out of the school environment. They would come home reciting and singing in Hebrew. They would ask me to create decorations and prepare special food to celebrate Jewish holidays they had learned about in school. Even though I pleased them, I regret that I was never able to identify entirely with such traditions. The influence of German logic had not left a place in my head for acceptance or enjoyment of religious myths and legends.

Until I was married, I had felt on the border of my two cultural groups, the Venezuelan and the Jewish. For many years, I was too "Jewish-*musiúa*" to be able to fully integrate into Venezuelan society. At the same time, I was too secular and German to belong to the traditional Jewish group of the community. It was with my husband, a graduate of the Jewish community schools and an active participant in the religious and secular culture of the community, that I started to slowly become part of the Jewish community at large. I became an accepted member, even though I know I was always considered a little eccentric because of my beliefs stemming from my German Venezuelan experience.

One of the great differences between Jews educated in the community schools and me was my perspective about non-Jews in Venezuelan society. Before becoming friendly with members of the Jewish community, I had never heard certain words that I consider contemptuous: Yeque (German Jew); *goy* or *goyim* (non-Jew); *shikse* (non-Jewish girl), usually used in Venezuela to refer to maids; *sheiguets* (non-Jewish boy), usually used in Venezuela to refer to men that do manual labor; and *shvartze* (person of color). I could not fathom how Jews, a people with a history of uncountable persecutions and sufferings caused by the ignorance, prejudice, and racism of others, could in turn measure non-Jews in the same inhuman manner. Venezuelan Jews not only differentiated between themselves—Ashkenazim-Sephardim, Germans-Poles, Russians-Rumanians—but also marginalized and set themselves apart from the population that had sheltered and accepted them into its midst and offered them all the rights and responsibilities of full citizens.

I constantly predicated to my friends in the Jewish community about the implications of the racist overtone of the words they used to describe Venezuelans. They never have understood my point of view, and I never perceived any change in attitude or use of language. The distancing, or, better said, the self-distancing, of Venezuelan Jews from Venezuelan society has never been part of dialectical discussions in either Venezuelan or Jewish social circles. The differentiation of the Jews from the general population was subtle and superficial, therefore difficult to perceive and distinguish.

Slowly I understood that for members of the Jewish community in Venezuela, it was impossible to be Jewish and at the same time part of a Christian society. Among this first generation of Jews, arriving directly from the persecutions and concentration camps of war-torn Europe, reigned the fear of assimilation, of the possible loss of Jewish identity. This terror was like a fog that covered the eyes of Venezuelan Jews and impeded their closeness to any non-Jewish group. The Jewish educations they accordingly gave their children resulted in the establishment of strong ties with Israel, and not with the young people's own country, Venezuela. Many of the economic and social efforts of the community favored Israel and did not significantly contribute to the development of Venezuela. My sparse experience and contact with the Zionist world of the Jewish schools impeded my fully understanding this limitless connection Venezuelan Jews feel for Israel or the absence of ties they perceive with the Venezuelan people, the people with whom they share their lives on a daily basis.

For my daughters, educated primarily in a Venezuelan Jewish environment, there was no difference between being Jewish and being Venezuelan. I recall the time that my husband gave a presentation about Venezuela to my youngest daughter's third-grade class in Norwich, Vermont, where we moved in the eighties. One of the students asked my husband if all Venezuelans were Jews, like us. My daughter, without hesitation or doubt, answered an irrevocable *yes*. Having been educated and raised in a Jewish context, surrounded almost exclusively by Jewish family and friends, learning the language, the religion, and the history of the Jews, it was logical for her to think of her Venezuelan and her Jewish world as one and the same. The self-imposed segregation of the Jewish community protected my daughters from possible racist incidents. However, it hindered them from feeling and experiencing the challenge of dealing with the contradictions of belonging to two very different but compatible worlds. It has been in the United States that my daughters have had to face the problems of being part of many diverse groups—Jewish, Hispanic, and North American—and of being stereotyped as Hispanics and as Jews.

Even without the ample Jewish education my husband and daughters have had, I have learned that I, too, am first a Jew. My Jewish self, so un-Jewish in many ways, is the one that has been with me, that has never abandoned me, that is always present in the Jewish names of my dead ancestors in concentration camps. In spite of the amazement and criticisms of our parents, German Jews of my generation, with the help of our husbands and wives, raised and educated our own children in a secular Jewish manner. My daughters have a great sense of their own Jewishness. One of them attends religious services almost every Friday, no matter where she is living. The other has decided that when she marries, she will marry a Jewish man to continue the Jewish tradition, her tradition. The fact is that in all the places we have lived, Caracas, Venezuela; Hanover, New Hampshire; Gainesville and Naples, Florida; and Boston, Massachusetts, most of our intimate friends have been of Jewish descent. The Venezuelan friends with whom I still maintain contact are mostly my German Jewish classmates from primary school and my Jewish friends from the community.

When we moved from Venezuela to Hanover, New Hampshire, a small college town, it was the Jewish community that first welcomed us. The universality of familiar values and traditions that we found in another Jewish community, so far from and alien to our existence in Venezuela, showed me that Judaism has no geographical, linguistic, or national frontiers. Being Jewish is a passport to all the corners of the world where Jews live. It is to be an immediate member of all the Jewish societies of the world.

Maybe having lived as a minority, differentiated but not rejected, forced me to confront that my cultural and moral home is a Jewish one. It is the only place where I will always be accepted unconditionally, despite my controversial, controverted, and contradictory opinions about Judaism. There has not been a time when I have felt that a fellow Jew judges my being, my soul. At times, my Jewish friends jokingly will call me "Yeque potz," German Jew. Never have I taken it as an insult. It is not the same when a non-Jewish Venezuelan or North American makes a comment about Jews or Judaism. Then I immediately feel the need to raise a barrier to protect myself against the possibility of insensitive or prejudicial opinions that accompany the stereotypical images that still exist about the Jews.

THE TRUTH IS THAT the subtle discrimination rooted in the Jewish community and in Venezuelan society as a whole, the environment of the constant grouping of people according to their religion, their nationality, their physical appearance, or their educational level, left an impression in me. From a very young age I recall saying many times that I wanted to study law to be able to help the blacks of South Africa fight against the system of apartheid. Surely the sense of tearing, of isolation, of marginalization caused by multiple loyalties was what impelled me to become a multilingual/multicultural educator. I feel the need to instill in each student a respect for diverse opinions and points of view. At the same time, I point out the need to balance this respect for others with the right of each student to have and maintain his or her own cultural lens. This notion, which is at the center of my professional and pedagogical interests, is the place where all my diverse worlds are at peace.

After various experiences in other professional fields, teaching is the profession in which my German Jewish and Venezuelan Jewish roots found a line of communication and mutual usefulness. When we moved to New Hampshire from Venezuela in 1983, to keep busy and integrate myself into the community I taught Spanish as a volunteer in the Hanover Middle and High Schools. Spanish was not a part of the educational program in the town's public schools. Students could study German, French, or Latin, but not Spanish. As Spanish is such an important language in the United States, I could not understand why it was not on the list of languages offered by the schools. Angered, I promised myself that I would introduce Spanish to the Hanover public schools. By the time a Spanish program was approved, I had obtained my Masters Degree in teaching second languages. I was very proud to accept the challenge of creating and coordinating the high school Spanish department.

That is how I started to teach. In the classroom, while I offer my students the opportunity to explore other ways of understanding and speaking about the events in their own lives and the world at large, my multicultural past started to take on meaning. Through teaching I learned, together with my students, how languages have words with similar nuances, but never identical meanings. I understood the communicative power of words that have no translation, words impossible to capture exactly in another language. I learned about the lexicon, the expressions, and the idioms interpreted so differently by each person, according to their experience. I began to appreciate the power and the passion of the rhythm and melody of each one of the languages and cultures composing my own personal symphony. Being a teacher of languages has allowed me to help my students gain a deeper comprehension of the Spanish-speaking world. When a student achieves a deep understanding of a language, she or he starts to understand the cultural values from the point of view of a native speaker, without the need for egocentric comparative perspectives.

The teaching of language was the first step that brought me closer to my interest in multilingual/multicultural education. I started to reflect about student success and failure in my own classroom. I noticed that every classroom is a unique culture, similar to my own complex Jewish-American-Venezuelan–North American one. In the classroom there are the same subtle processes and the same social patterns of interaction that exist in other human groups. Comprehension or ignorance of unwritten rules of classroom process and conformity to or alienation from the school culture are basic factors in academic success or failure. My multicultural experiences with such unwritten rules and my own biography, full of alienation from and conformity to various cultures, guide my professional mission, the academic achievement of every student.

My youthful and idealistic goal of helping South African blacks fight the system of apartheid is not that far from my daily work of breaking barriers imposed by an educational system filled with hidden prejudices. As a multilingual/multicultural educator, my job is to assure the recognition and utilization of the cultural roots and the rich funds of knowledge that every student brings and contributes to the cultural world of the classroom (Moll, 1992). Every student is a complex world constructed by the sum of values and the way of life of his or her ancestors. My profession attempts to give voice to each one of these worlds, without the fears, without the sufferings, without the alienation, and without the persecutions that past generations of my Jewish ancestors and uncountable other religious and ethnic groups have suffered.

My diverse worlds—the Jewish, the Venezuelan, and the German—have interlaced to influence my work as a professor, researcher, and writer. The Jewish dialectical viewpoint, together with a deep respect for education, is the spiritual guide of my pedagogical work. The warm and generous hospitality and welcome given to Jewish immigrants by the Venezuelan people left in me the imprints of compassion and an acceptance of every student as a unique human being. Nevertheless, the omnipresent shadow of my German culture predominates; it dictates the perfectionism and pragmatism of my work. The critical tone in my father's voice has been an imaginary wall that has often imposed itself between my ideas and my writings. This is the reason that, until now, my publications have all been empirical studies and textbooks. They serve to analyze facts in terms of black and white; utilitarian works in which perfection is the goal, the goal of my German father.

Maybe someday I will be able to overcome this obsession, this feeling that my writings have to be absolutely perfect or not be written at all. Maybe the Jewish world of questions with no definitive answers combined with the flexible Hispanic world replete with understanding for inevitable human failings will help me overpower my own autocratic and despotic German upbringing. Till then, my Hispanic Jewish and German Jewish pasts, added to my North American Jewish present, will design my thoughts, my lessons, and my essays and weave my past dreams and my present dreams into my dreams of the future.

References:

Moll, L. C. 1992. "Bilingual Class Studies and Community Analysis." *Educational Researcher* 21 (2): 2–24.

Whorf, B. C. 1956. *Language, Thought, and Reality: Selected Writings,* ed. J. B. Carroll (Cambridge, Mass.: MIT Press).

Chapter 5

El Azar-Fate Put the Novel
Cláper *in My Hands*

Joan Friedman

EL AZAR-FATE PUT THE NOVEL *Cláper* in my hands. In this lyrical memoir, the Venezuelan-born Jewish Polish writer Alicia Freilich Segal not
only "spoke to me," she actually "spoke about me." As I translated the
novel into English, the words resonated in my soul. Through them, I
began to reconcile with my own ghosts and reconnect with what the
Venezuelan Jewish poet Sonia Choron calls an "hebraismo ancestral."

Webster's dictionary defines *translation* as, among other things:
"to change from one language to another" and "to put into different
words." To "change" this evocative novel was certainly not my aim.
To "put it into different words" turned out to be a true labor of love.
As a Jew, I have always been spiritually bound to the "word": to its
penetrating and occult powers, to its hidden variations and meanings.
Freilich's words disturbed and haunted me deeply; they reopened
wounds I had no consciousness of.

As I struggled with ways to convey the feelings and ideas of the work,
I was reminded of the "potential" translation that Walter Benjamin says
all great works have "between the lines." Between these mellifluous
renderings of our immutable ties to the past; between the Claper's

bittersweet Yiddish humor, sage Talmudic teachings, and ancient superstition; between the sophisticated, elegant, and literate narrative of his *criolla* daughter; between their voices chatting away in the timeless realm of the imagination, I unearthed my own "translation." The words led me to a safe space, a comfortable distance from which to rescue and reconcile the threads of my past. I understood how my passion for life and boiled potatoes with sour cream and onions came all the way from a shtetl near Odessa, how my passion for music and books was connected to an elegant salon in Berlin, and how my passion for dancing and talking were conceived and nurtured under the hot Venezuelan sun.

mis antepasados . . . those who preceded me . . .

The Beins were a large and prosperous family of accountants and lawyers who had been proud Berliners for as long as anyone could remember when, in 1939, one of them, my maternal grandmother, packed up her sixteen- and thirteen-year-old children for a long train ride. The Sorbonne-educated Erna Bein decided not to "wait and see what happens." Instead she got her children by train to Naples, Italy, and from there on the *Terukuni Maru* to the only port in the world that was welcoming Jews.

My mother Marion, her brother Werner, and their mother lived in the Shanghai ghetto where, for the ones lucky enough to get out of Poland, Czechoslovakia, Rumania, Germany, life was not too bad. Even though they did not have complete freedom of movement and had to show their papers every time they went in and out of the ghetto, many found work, had a degree of prosperity, opened restaurants and Viennese cafés, and established theaters. Fate had already decided that Marion, the "beautiful Berliner," would meet Abe, the "brainy editor" of *The China Press,* who, as the family joke went, "took her out of the ghetto" and all the way to Chessfield Park on Yuyen Road, and later to a bigger house on Route Kauffman with a pink camellia in the garden.

My paternal grandparents had never had fine food or been in elegant salons with artwork and music around them. Reisel Whitcob, born in Uman, Kiev, in 1891, and Moishe Ladar had only been lucky enough to, by their mid-teens, have survived half a dozen pogroms. Somehow, and I find it difficult to believe, these two young people managed to walk to Shanghai, where they married and where in 1916 my father Abe was born. Abe was followed in 1918 by his sister Esther and in 1914 by his brother Izzy. When my father was ten years old, his father died. Reisele, unable to live without him, died of consumption a year later. So the Ladar children were raised by Aunties Ethel and Gidalia Mochan, who only spoke Yiddish and Russian and who could neither read nor write. I remember so clearly reaching into their pockets, always filled with hidden treasures, especially rock candy tightly wrapped in a little cloth. I remember the little ring with a bright red ruby that Uncle gave me, which made it all the way to Madison, Wisconsin, USA, and then vanished from my life.

"The Beauty and the Brain" were married November 22, 1942, a year before Pearl Harbor and the war in the Pacific. I was born fifteen months later, on February 20, 1944, and was rocked to sleep to the tunes of Al Jolson, Enrico Caruso, and Jan Peerce, to Yiddish and Russian songs. I danced Scheherazade in front of company—which often included the entire Jai Alai team—and remember seeing my parents dance to Gardel's "La comparsita." With the communist takeover, my father, a visible journalist and a person involved in securing the safety of many European Jews, had to flee. The Venezuelan ambassador suggested his country, so, thanks to Mr. Ferrer, the Shanghai "boychick" who spoke several dialects of Chinese in addition to Russian, Yiddish, and German, ended up as a "musiú" (Venezuelan designation for all foreigners) who had to add Spanish to his repertoire. Neither of my parents managed that very well, which was a constant source of embarrassment to me. Among many examples: "No, Marion, no se dice *pusió* el libro en la mesa, se dice *ponió*."

My mother, my brother Morris (Moishe), and I stayed behind for a year until all the documents and enough money were secured. The rest of the family left for Palestine, except for my grandmother Erna, who ended up in Sao Paolo, Brazil, as housekeeper and French teacher in a very large mansion . . . but that's another story. . . .

As my people had walked over the Ural mountains out of Russia, in 1949 my mother, my two-year-old brother, and I were "sanpaned" out of Shanghai. Only sampans, which are a kind of light and low canoe, could come into the heavily mined port. I remember that night very clearly. Strange people lying all around me very still. We were covered with a smelly, heavy, oily blanket-like thing. My mother whispered that I could not make a sound once the movement started. She put her hand on my two-year-old brother's mouth to make sure he would make no sound either. After what seemed forever but my mother assures me was not very long, we were transferred onto a big ship, the USS *General Gordon,* right there in the middle of the ocean.

We had to climb up little wooden steps connected by rope. My mother carried my brother in one arm, her shoulder bag with all our precious documents over the other, and with her free hand held on to the rope. I would have to do this alone, she told me. She told me not to be afraid and not to look down. I did anyway and almost died. There was just black shiny water under my feet. It was hard for me because my short little five-year-old legs barely reached the next step. My mother was right behind me and kept saying that I was a big girl and was doing just fine.

Once we were on the ship, life seemed quite fun. Since my mother was so young and beautiful, all the American sailors gave me and my brother more ice cream and chewing gum than they did to other people.

At one point I remember my mother telling me to look out and pointing to a mountain she said was very important: the Rock of Gibraltar. In Honolulu, she somehow managed to get us off the ship and into a taxi that took us to the biggest store I had ever seen. There she bought me a straw hula skirt and plastic ukulele, which were my first, and for a long while only, toys in Venezuela.

primeras experiencias . . . identidad inmigrante/judía . . .
influencias de padres . . .

My first memory of Venezuela was of landing in Maiquetía Airport on a Pan Am flight from Houston, Texas, where our ship docked. As the plane approached the terminal, my mother pointed to a very dark man in a white suit with a white hat and said he was my father. I had not seen him in over a year. I had never seen a dark man before. I was frightened and did not want to believe that that dark man was really my father.

I remember feeling very hot during the long trip to Caracas, which in those days was a on a dangerous single-lane *carretera* built by hand by General Gómez's prisoners. As my parents spoke of important things—in Yiddish so I would not understand—I held my breath when we went around the curves and stopped breathing altogether when I looked over the precipices on the way to Los Teques. I will never forget the barefooted and big-bellied children standing at doorways of strange-looking straw houses with tin roofs. . . .

My father had "settled" in Barquisimeto, a small town where he ran La Pagoda China—a shop that sold frames, mirrors, and glass. We lived in a two-room apartment at the Edificio Ramos García, right on the Avenida 20. I remember a lot of noise. A few months later, we moved into a larger apartment in the same building. My mother always refused to consider buying a house, even when we could afford it, because she always felt there were "too many snakes" around.

The Yiddish, German, Russian, Chinese, and English that had surrounded me since birth were no help as I strained to understand the sounds surrounding me in the classroom I was thrown into. Later, the woman dressed in a long black tent with a starchy stiff white thing on her head who was the teacher told my parents that I seemed intelligent but distracted. The nuns at the Colegio de la Inmaculada Concepción—known to us girls as "los zamuros"—ended up having me for the rest of my schooling and treated me very well, except for one or two who kept trying to convert me. Why a Catholic school? It was the best school in town, and anyway, there were no Jewish ones.

As children will, I quickly learned the language, and even excelled at it. Never wanting special dispensation or to be treated differently, I even studied catechism, which was one of the subjects averaged into the final grade. So, at the end of the school year when the awards ceremony took place, I had deserved my *primer puesto* fair and square. We "chosen" ones went up on the stage, right in front of a beautiful statue of the Virgen de la Inmaculada all in white and blue, and walked down one by one when our names were called. At the bottom of the steps, sitting in the front row, bejeweled and wearing his beautiful purple cape, sat the bishop, whose ring we all had to kiss. From way back in the hall I could feel two sad black eyes drilling into me, so proud and yet . . . Then I would repeat the yearly ritual: I would bend respectfully and touch the ring to my forehead.

Because of my genetic programming, my *herencia,* even though I never had a formal Jewish education, I knew I had to be better in school, I knew I had to work harder, and I knew had to be tolerant of and fair to others.

I am and have always been invisibly and subliminally Jewish, and I knew that before, while, and since being called "hebrea" and "israelita."

Our family never felt any personal anti-Semitism. Quite the contrary: we were not only accepted, but warmly welcomed by the community because my father was such a larger-than-life figure. The Barquisimeto of the early fifties, which was still a sleepy, almost colonial town slowly coming out of a long and harsh dictatorship and about to go into another, anointed "El Chino Ladar" as the resident intellectual. Every night, in la Plaza Bolívar, right in front of la Iglesia de San José, the men gathered to play dominoes while "el Chino" pontificated in very imperfect Spanish on Marxism and Mozart, Maimonides and Mussolini, Romulo Gallegos and Mahatma Gandhi, Truman and Turgenev, Sun Yatsen and Yevtuschenko, Helen Gahagan Douglas and Claire Booth Luce. . . .

My mother, "la bella Ladar" was admired for her beauty and elegance. I remember her being ill in bed for quite a while soon after we arrived, but, as she had done and would continue to do throughout her life, adapting very well to the heat and slower pace of life of the tropics. What she never got used to was seeing men spit "blood" on the streets, even after my father explained that it was chewing tobacco. Yet it was as "la Alemana" as she was known in some circles, that she sent the bill collector to people my father was too embarrassed and proud to collect from. No matter what or where, my mother always managed to pay the bills.

Being Jewish in Barquisimeto at that time meant not eating bread for Passover and sharing our matzah with all our Venezuelan friends. I remember Passovers as being such fun. Not because we had big Seders. The first real Seder I ever had was in New York when I was nineteen years old. Passover was fun because, since we could not just go into a supermarket to buy matzah, my father had it imported directly from the United States. When it arrived at the local post office, the word would spread pretty quickly that "llegaron las galletas del Chino." Boxes of matzah were shared with all who wanted.

To me, being Jewish meant: "Don't ever forget you're Jewish!" and that we had to help the ones living in a place called Palestine by putting coins in a little blue tin can and by sending monthly care packages because: "They need it more than we do."

Being Jewish meant being unable to follow the Hebrew in the Caracas *shul* we went to for Yom Kippur, and being Venezuelan meant that in chapel at school, I could not only follow but participate fully in the entire Mass in the original Latin!

el viaje final

Part of me walked over the Ural mountains out of Russia; part of me trained in Germany; I was sanpaned out of Shanghai in 1949; and, in 1960, as my parents added another journey to their peregrinations, I added another devastating chapter to the befores and afters of my own history. There are *parrilladas* to go to, pictures to be taken, and presents to be received before we are jetted out of the sun with the heartbreaking certainty of an ending. The Pan Am jet landed at Idlewild airport in New York City, where my elegant and white-haired Granny Erna waited with Ludwig Rosenberg, my mother's father, who had turned up alive on a list of survivors.

Again I was estranged from the sounds around me. Although I spoke English without too much of an accent, I could not read or write it. I had to learn a new language and start again from the beginning.

I enrolled in Hunter College on Park Avenue, where I remember a person in the admissions office looking up after I said "Jewish" because she knew that in South America "everyone speaks Spanish and is Catholic."

As always it is not my religion nor my ethnicity that causes my pain and isolation, but "the word." For the world history course, my mother and I read the texts together, after which she basically explained what I needed to know. The math was easy, the required English lit course wonderful! I loved reading William Faulkner's short stories, looking up the words and saying them out loud. I worked hard. So why had I gotten so many red markings on my paper, I wondered?

"Miss Ladar, I feel you are not taking this course seriously," said Professor Goetthals. Seems my "The hole story deals with . . ." was sloppy work. He wanted to know why I had not looked up the words if I didn't know the difference? What difference? Why look up something you know? Whole/hole? Same *sonido* . . .

My mother began working in the mail room of Blue Cross/Blue Shield on Park and Thirty-Second Street. I helped with the cleaning and cooking. My father's sister Esther, who had gone from Shanghai to Palestine and then San Francisco, came to live with us at 875 West End Avenue at 103rd Street on the Upper West Side.

"La Chinita" or "la hija del Chino," who, in the delicious tropics flourished epiphytically, like an orchid, became totally disconnected in the North. I withdrew into myself and dealt with my isolation and loneliness by deepening it. I broke with the past, cut myself off completely from any association with Venezuela. I wrote no letters and answered none. Eventually they stopped coming. It would take me twenty-eight years to make the journey back "home."

My father joined us the following year. Now in his late forties, it was impossible for him to find work. My mother continued to work and he continued to look for work. But he read voraciously, saying that after ten years in an "intellectual desert," being in New York made him feel alive. Over time he became very bitter and blamed fate for being unfair to him and life for passing him by. Venezuelan friends came to New York and he wined and dined them, never admitting he had no money. Eventually his friends made it possible for him to be the "attaché" to the Venezuelan consulate in New York, later in Hong Kong, and eventually in Jerusalem. That was the happiest period of his life.

My mother became a complete American success story, though, and by the time she retired, the captain of the high school swimming team, who had been prohibited from using the pool because of her yellow star and prohibited from graduating high school, was head of the accounting department at Blue Cross/Blue Shield, New York, USA.

My love for language led me to a degree in Italian literature and eventually to graduate work at the University of Wisconsin at Madison. There, Fate arranged it so that I would meet a nice Jewish boy from Chicago. We have been together ever since and share two lovely children born in Media, Pennsylvania, who laugh when I slip now and then and say things like: "Don't molest me! I'm working!"

objetos traídos

An *Adventures of Pinocchio* with the inscription "Shanghai Jewish School. Recitation Prize to Joan Ladar. 22nd Dec. 1949" has a special place on our bookshelf, as does a beautiful King James version of the Bible dated in my father's hand: Shanghai, 1943. I treasure a yellowing

"Foreign Correspondent's Club of China" card dated 1948 and two extraordinary little brownish books: *Prayer Book Abridged for Jews in the Armed Forces of the U.S.* and *Readings From the Holy Scriptures for Jewish Soldiers and Sailors,* dated March 6, 1941, and signed by FDR, both of which never left my father's side until the day he died in Miami, Florida, in 1987.

My mother tore up her German passport marked with *J* and a swastika as soon as she set foot in Venezuela, but fiercely holds on to the little black cast-iron frying pan that belonged to her grandmother Elsbeth Bein (née Brauer). Sometimes even I find it hard to believe that something used in a kitchen on Prinzenallee—next to the synagogue my great-grandfather helped found—and later in a kitchen on Bötteger Strasse is still used to make *riquísimos* crepes and omelets on Kendale Lakes Drive in Miami.

It seems I've always been trying to fit in (where?), to be like everyone else (whom?). People are still surprised to learn I'm Venezuelan *and* Jewish. In 1974, when I told a colleague at Harvard that I would not be in class on Yom Kippur, he made some remark about how "converts" were more committed than "real Jews." Obviously he assumed I had converted when I married a Friedman! It is true that although I consider myself Venezuelan, I am not like the Venezuelans many people know or have read about and I certainly am not like some Jews they know or have read about. I often felt neither Venezuelan nor Jewish in New York. By now, in my fifty-seventh year, I have forgotten the Chinese I spoke when I was six, I understand only a little Yiddish, I don't like German, and I speak no Russian. When asked what is my mother tongue, I say Spanish, even though I have lived longer in the United States than I did in Venezuela.

As I read *Cláper* and began to *ladinar*—translate—I reconnected with my past, with my Jewish *herencia*. Deciphering the hidden meanings of words, I uncovered and recovered an identity buried in long-dormant memories.

Now I know that my identity is the goose bumps I feel when I hear a sweet eleventh-century song sung in Ladino; it is my hips swaying and my total inability to sit still when I hear good Salsa music; it's how

Hannah Arendt, Isabel Allende, and Anna Akhmatova's words affect me; it is what binds me to the Jewish Diaspora begun at the time of the Fall of the Temple in Jerusalem; it is what connects me to the Inquisition and Sepharad; it is what makes me shudder at the height of the houses in the Venice ghetto; it is what makes me cry and be moved by Isaac Bashevis Singer; it is what makes me understand why my mother never wants go back to Germany; it is what makes me so proud that the Fonseca, De Lima, Lopez, and Henriquez families in Coro helped sponsor the Venezuelan War of Independence and Simón Bolivar's exile to Curacao; my *herencia*/identity makes me so proud that my children were bar and bat mitzvahed.

My identity is my *herencia* and comes from long ago and far away; it follows and accompanies me always. It is why I call my daughter "girlschen" and "mi amorcito," and my son "boyschen" and "Danielschen"; it is why I call my mother "liebchen"; why my father called my brother "boychick," "pisher," and "goniff" and me "fishkele" and "tzasynka"; it is why my nickname is Tzasy—"little doll" in Russian; it is why Granny was always "Mutti," why my husband is called "Pappi," and why my brother and I were "kindele" and "hiasels" who "Oh Gottenuy," should have "mazel" and not all the "tzures" they had had. Because of my *herencia* I prefer to drink hot drinks in the summertime like the Chinese but will, at the drop of a hat and at any time and anyplace, opt for a Venezuelan Ron Pampero Añejo straight up.

My identity is my birth certificate with the Chinese character for none next to the line for "Nationality."

My *herencia* is the sweet pain and pride I feel over the following piece, written by my daughter Ruth on the Passover of her nineteenth year and included with her permission and my eternal gratitude.

open door

One day in Shanghai, China, a little Jewish girl is born. Stateless, her birth certificate proclaims. One whose mother tongue never cries communism's mandarin, only huddles below bombed declarations of despotism soon to be. In sampan-rustled water, the little girl watches her city alive, fire long after aurora's glow. She holds the hand of her mother . . . a hand somehow wrinkled even as one so young and beautiful. Perhaps her hand remembers with its lines how dirt smells, falling upon her father, uncles, cousins, aunts. Stone, shadowed by spider-emblazoned red flags; as if German soil alone had the malificence to hold their souls.

In the crest of thunder sea of night their sampan rides. On some banked ellipse a husband and father awaits. The little girl's brother cries, even a baby could smell his father's soap from across so many continents. The editor always should smell nice, especially when fleeing from the land he has always known. Her father the editor, with his laughing hands, hands that scare even big red armies in the power of their words.

Well, now there are Catholic schools, and bishops' rings to be kissed by the highest in the class. Not your lips her father says as he opens his matzah shipment from New York City. Heh, the strange crackers are in. Chino, can we have some? So everyone eats of our bread, of our culture's song, and the little girl's father smiles and shares. Some people never will be good businessmen. The little girl cuddles her doll in her hand as she stands before walls of playthings and feels the breath of another girl on her back. Amid so much glory, in a room of so many riches, her hand only feels a callused eye. One who dances in golden bliss and never thinks about how she will tell the bishop she cannot kiss his ring.

Then one day the little girl has her own children. She thinks back to palm-treed days and Latin rhythms hummed, but has long begun anew. The here of now is her state, her children, her husband, her job . . . but sometimes her hands shake when her father tells her to return to Venezuela, to look back. She shudders and dreams of salt.

Now my mother sees part of her alma, her state in America del Sur. Maybe the same part that in the back of her mind remembers a

Roosevelt who didn't really want his land to be Jewland. She invites poets to speak at the college who define themselves as Chilean Jews, and I watch them and my mother, from the back seat of the car, as we drive them to the airport. They touch each other with hands ripened in Spanish that doesn't seem quite so rapid to me anymore and the glow of having fought to be. My mother cries. I know she is remembering the sampan and hearing her birth certificate shout.

Here I sit, never knowing what taking college literature courses was like at Hunter not speaking a word of English, translating each word of each book before writing paper after paper. But someday down the road teaching at Harvard and Swarthmore, living in middle-class suburbia and driving a Ford Taurus with front-wheel drive, I read biology and wonder what a polypeptide really is. They have things called communities here. I go and sit amidst other Jewish students. I let my hands brush words in *siddurs* that seem useless to everyone else as they sing with fervor and closed eyes.

And then it's Passover and I open my own box of matzah from Philadelphia. I too share, with people who "really want to learn about our culture." With wide eyes and exclamatory delight they eat of my people, of my history, of my hopes and my identity like crumbs left for some Seder that might never be. Let all who are hungry come in and eat. Make Passover. I kinda don't feel much like it anymore. But my hands shake too. Too much caffeine or belonging left to dreams and those who have forgotten. Like the girl with too many dolls, they will always be happy. Do you hear my voice from Venezuela to Germany, the United States, Israel, and Russia. Do you hear me sing with Diaspora's laughter and all her fury. I think of all the colors inside of me of my skin of my heart of my hands and with pride, I too am happy.

—Ruth Friedman, 1999

Chapter 6

Memories of Comings and Goings

Ethel Kosminsky

For my dear daughter Claudia Kalili Ortiz,
companion and wandering friend of New York

AS A SOCIOLOGIST, I AM accustomed to interviewing others, to collecting their life stories. This time I am interpreting the role of the other, the interviewer who has vanished inside the interviewee. An experience that is curious, happy, and anguishing all at the same time.

My grandmother Maria used to talk about how, one day, she would write a book about her life. My mother Anita has written about my Grandmother Maria and Grandfather Leon. Now the job of linking the chain of memories between generations, those that were, those that are, and those that will come has fallen upon the shoulders of Maria's granddaughter and Anita's daughter.

Jo and the Girl Who Did Not Want to Eat

"Ethelzinha, open your mouth."
"No."

"I'll tell you the story of Fia. Did you know that Fia goes to school? She knows the alphabet; she has a workbook."

And that's how it was: the young girl would eat while she was engrossed by stories of Fia, the neighbor's dog. Why didn't the girl like to eat? I don't know. I don't have the slightest idea. I only know that until today I carry with me the stories of Fia, told by Jo our maid. I must have been only three years old, and the year was 1949. I remember I liked Jo a lot. She was really black and her skin shined. I liked to look at her, touch her, stay near her, watch her eat lunch. She ate different foods than we did. I remember she used to place black beans and cassava flour on her plate and then add boiling water. She cut *charque* meat (dried, salted meat) into strips, made a ball of it with her hand, and with a quick move popped one ball after another in her mouth with great pleasure.

I wanted that food too, but my mother didn't let me eat it. I found our food to be tasteless—rice and fresh meat every single day, plus a vegetable: okra, *lingua de vaca* (a spinach-like vegetable), and squash. Sometimes we ate fish, liver, or cow brains. "Brains are good for the intelligence," my mother said, but was liver good for the blood? I don't remember. All I know is that I didn't like brain stew with potatoes. But I had to eat it. However, while my mother rested after lunch, I would secretly look under the sink where Jo kept her dry meat wrapped in newspaper and cut myself a little piece, sometimes two or three, and I would eat it while hiding in the bathroom. Oh, how I wanted that food.

Jo ate with pepper. There were pepper plants behind our house in the yard. There was red pepper, green pepper, and malagueta pepper. I was also told not to eat pepper because it was bad for my health. One day, I went to the pepper plant and got some peppers and put them in my mouth. Why? Oh, how it stung. It felt like I was going to burn a hole in my mouth; tears jumped from my eyes. Jo said, "Put a little bit of sugar on those lips. The pain will pass." Said and done. It really passed. She seemed to know everything.

In Poland we ate our meals with a knife and fork. Yet Jo ate with her hands. And not only Jo. We had some neighbors and I became friends with their daughters, Teco and Ju, while my mother befriended Dona Zizi. That was the nickname of Dona Edmea. Everyone called her Dona Zizi, just like I was known as Ethelzinha, the dimunitive of Ethel. Dona Zizi also ate with her hands and ate that same kind of food that fascinated me, as well as other forbidden foods like pork, watermelon, cucumber, and peppers. I couldn't eat pork because, aside from being Jewish, it gave me indigestion, just like watermelon and cucumber did. I wanted to be like all the others, to eat all those foods. Why did I have to be different from other people?

Jo and the Festival for the Saints

Jo had very dark skin. She wore a cloth around her head like a turban. From time to time she would press her hair with an iron that was actually large pliers that had two plates rather than two claws. She would warm these two plates in the fire and then stretch tufts of hair with them. The smell of burnt hair rose into the air. This was how black people "straightened" their hair, as they themselves described it.

When my parents would leave the house at night to go visit someone, Calu, Jo's sister, would spend the night with us. During that time it was entertaining for me to hear them speak. I used to dress up in my mother's clothes and put on lipstick, Cilion, and blush. Cilion was a cream that we applied around our eyes to give them a languid look. Of course, I also wore my mother's high heels. "Look, even Ethelzinha doesn't look ugly, with that makeup, with those things," Jo used to say. And then I had to go to bed, while they would stay up talking. What did they talk about? About the bosses, whether they were good or not. Jo used to say, "I like Seu Abrão a lot, but D. Anita . . ." Calu would talk about her problems, like her hair falling out, or what she ought to put in her hair, perhaps some special leaf? They had to stay up until my parents returned. A tyranny, I think, from today's perspective. At that time, I felt it was just something that wasn't right.

At night, noises could be heard from down the hill beyond our backyard. Our house was on Rua Alvaro Adorno, number 53, in a neighborhood called Brotas. The whole side of the street led to a steep drop. The yards of the houses were like ramps. Down there was a mystery. What down there produced that sound, like a cry for help? It was a mystery and at the same time scary, but not for my mother. One day Dona Zizi came to tell my mother that Jo frequented those places below the hill. My mother wasn't bothered. Jo was "a very good maid, she cleans and cooks well and has all my confidence." My mother said with pride, "I don't know how to make coffee, nor rice either, so don't count on me."

But in the end what was down there, down that deep embankment? It was those "black people." Doing what? "Doing Candomblé," said Dona Zizi, who was very Catholic and kept a bunch of saints in a type of closet in her house, as if it were an altar. Jo didn't lose her job, she continued "raising" me and maintaining her saints, Cosmos and Damian, in a corner of her room. One day when I was four-and-a-half years old, my mother went to the maternity ward of a hospital and gave birth to Nilton, my brother. Jo continued to care for Ethelzinha. I remember her bathing me in an aluminum bathtub. Since the shower only had cold water, the water had to be warmed for people taking a bath. Adults would take baths with cupfuls of water and the little ones would sit in a bathtub. During the rainy season, or "winter," as it is called in the northeast of Brazil, winged ants appeared in great numbers. And wouldn't you know that during one of those baths, one of these ants would fall in the bathtub? I was scared and at the same time enchanted. I played with the ant, trying to hold her in my hands.

Another, still more sensational, memory was the *caruru* that Jo made for me. The *caruru* was a party in honor of Saints Cosmos and Damian, twin brothers revered in Candomblé. Dohum, Crispim, and Crispiniano are their cousins. Like a good devotee of Saint Cosmos and Saint Damian, Jo, offered a *caruru* to ease Ethel's anxiety about her entrance exam to high school. This could only take place while Dona Anita was visiting her family in Recife. It was a small, but pretty, party. She prepared the saints' favorite food: dry *caruru,* made of okra and dry shrimp; and *vatapá,* made of bread flour, fish, dried shrimp, cashews, and peanuts. Everything was done with African palm oil, which gave the food a yellowish color. We also ate *efo* (a sour vegetable), white rice, popcorn, sugar cane cut up into little pieces, and candy. A lot of candy, because the saints were children. Jo placed a little bit of each food in a small ceramic bowl and guaranteed me that the saints would come to eat it later. Since the saints were children, all the guests were children from the neighborhood and we all ate with great pleasure. Jo was an excellent cook.

What happened to Jo? Twice, my mother had ugly fights with her. Maybe my mother felt that she had too much power inside the house, that her own authority was being threatened. I don't know; I only know that one day Jo left our house. The house became chaotic and my mother nervous. Every day my father came home for lunch, but now he had to stop at the bar of Seu Manoel in Cidade Baixa (the downtown section of the city, located at sea level) to pick up rice, beef, french fries, and manioc flour for us to eat. The food came wrapped up and tied with a string. At that time we ate all our meals at home; there were no restaurants; everyone ate at home. Seu Justo, who worked at a government bureau with my father and was Jo's godfather, was asked by my father to intervene in the dispute, and as a result Jo returned, and I became happy. That happiness, however, was short-lived. One more fight and Jo left our lives forever. Sometimes even today I miss her. Where is she? Is she still alive? If she were alive, she would be around eighty years old. Much later, we heard that she had found a nice house to work in and that her bosses had registered her as a hired worker—during that time there wasn't any social security or pension plan for domestic employees—so that when she became much older, she could retire. That is the story of Jo and little Ethelzinha.

Alvaro Adorno Street and Tuti, Teco, and Ju

Alvaro Adorno Street was a narrow street, "a dead end," Dona Anita used to say with distaste. Leaving the main street, one would go up a hill that was shaped like an arch and go down the next hill. That arch was Alvaro Adorno Street. The houses were small, almost glued to each other. However, there was one good thing: each house had a yard with a steep drop and we children used to play there or on the street or in our friends' houses. The only car on the street belonged to the husband of Dona Zizi, "Uncle" Carias, as he liked to be called. At that time, few people had cars. Everyone knew who had a car. People would take buses, streetcars, or small vans to work, although not every street had a streetcar.

Since I began this story by talking about Fia, it's only just to return to her. Fia belonged to Seu Manoel's family, which had emigrated from Galicia, a region of Spain that sent many immigrants to Salvador, the capital of the state of Bahia. Africans, Spaniards, and Portuguese made up the principal immigratory contingent to Bahia. Dona Maria, Seu Manoel, Tuti (a short, chubby boy my age), and Maria Eliza (a pretty girl) composed the family that lived at number 51, between us and Dona Zizi.

Seu Manoel's bar in Cidade Baixa, an area with government offices, a port, wholesale and some retail commerce, and the main post office, served food and drinks and sponsored conviviality among local clerks, office workers, and government workers. All government offices and retail stores closed from noon until two, prompting many people to go home for lunch. After eating lunch, many people took a short nap.

Seu Manoel and his family were very quiet, very reserved. Seu Manoel died very young from throat cancer. I remember him walking slowly on the street in the afternoon with a piece of cloth wrapped around his neck. Tuti had to take over his father's bar. I think he must have been only twelve years old then. He stopped studying in school and went to work full time. From that day on, Dona Maria never stopped wearing black; she was always in mourning.

Since Maria Eliza was very young and never left the house, my friends were Ju and Teco, the daughters of Dona Zizi who lived at number 49. The sisters were much older than I—Ju was five years older and Teco ten. I remember them as if I had last seen them yesterday. Every afternoon I would go to their house, eating my cookies, and watch them studying and doing their homework. "Uncle" Carias was the son of Portuguese parents, and I think Dona Zizi was also of Portuguese origin. There was always something new and exciting going on in their house. I remember when they bought a Victrola and, for the first time in my life, I heard records. It was incredible to listen to music of one's own choosing. In my house we had a dark, pretty radio. Every day at 5:30 P.M. my mother and I listened to the Gessy Theater's soap opera, enchanted by the sound of rain and wind on the radio. How did they do that?

I miss Ju and Teco. I remember Ju's notebooks, decorated with magazine clippings, and the care with which they cleaned their house, and the ribbons they put on the keys to their closets. On cleaning days, Ju and Teco placed their furniture on the walkway leading to their house so that their maids could clean and wax the floor.

"Uncle" Carias also bought the first kerosene stove on the block. The gas stove had just been introduced, but he was afraid of explosions and so he bought a kerosene stove. We continued to use a charcoal one for a long time after this. Our enormous brick stove occupied a large part of the kitchen. Sometimes I would buy charcoal at a depot near our house and Jo would fire up the stove by placing some alcohol-dampened charcoal in the stove, lighting some rolled-up newspaper, and then throwing the flaming newspaper onto the charcoal. In order to maintain the flame she would occasionally use a fan made of braided straw. The charcoal would blacken the bottoms of our pots and she used to clean them carefully with sand and a *bucha* (a hard vegetable) or sometimes with steel wool. We bought the sand from a man who collected it at the beach and delivered it by leading a burro on the street. "Uncle" Adolfo, another neighbor, made the steel wool pad.

The House with the Niche of Our Lady of Lourdes

Uncle Adolfo and Aunt Celia were "contra-relatives" of my mother; they were Sephardim. Aunt Celia's brother, Uncle José, married Aunt Dorita, my mother's sister. Adolfo had come to Brazil from Turkey, and Celia was probably from Turkey as well. I only know that all of Celia's brothers lived in Recife. Only much later did her sister come to live in Bahia. They had light-brown skin, a very pretty color. They lived in a very large house facing the main street in Brotas. Their beautiful house sat at the top of a long marble stairway. Midway up the stairs on the left side there was a niche that contained a statue of Our Lady of Lourdes. The gate to the street was never locked, so that people could enter and go up the stairs to light a candle to the saint. Sometimes I heard my mother comment to my father "How can they keep the saint if they're Jewish?" It seemed inexplicable to my parents. Had they found the saint when they went to live in that house? It seemed so and they didn't want to remove her.

Uncle Adolfo's living room had painted ceiling panels that resembled Italian masterpieces of the Renaissance. Its floor was made from long, dark planks of wood; its furniture was dark and heavy, with table and chair legs twisted in a decorative manner. How many times did I sit in that living room, waiting for the telephone—the only telephone on the street—to secure a dial tone so that my mother could call someone? In one of the rooms, Aunt Celia had a piano, and sometimes, at my request, she would play some classical music. I remember the delicious aroma of food; sometimes I ate lunch there. They ate a lot of grilled mutton, a lot of cucumber, and watermelon. A skinny poor man sold them the mutton. The customers used to order beforehand, and he would carry the meat wrapped in leaves in a straw basket on his head. Sometimes my mother also bought some pieces of mutton, which Jo would grill on a bonfire in our backyard.

Uncle Adolfo's factory sat behind his magnificent house, but its entrance was located at the end of a dead-end street near our house. In order to reach Aunt Celia's house from my own, I had to walk through the factory. Since the factory was dark, I was always a bit afraid to walk through it.

His factory made steel wool pads—thin pads used to clean pots, and rougher, more abrasive pads to remove the old wax from wooden floors before a new coat of wax was applied. Aside from steel wool, Uncle Adolfo made adornments for coffins out of silver-covered cardboard. I remember two chubby silver angels. I don't know if he also made the coffins. The factory workers were mostly black; some were mulattos.

Celia and Adolfo had four children, three boys and a girl, who were all older than I. One day, I heard an unexpected conversation about Edna, who was their daughter, and a female factory worker who was her biological mother. My mother used to say, "Adolfo is a good man. He had that daughter before marrying Celia and since she only had boys, he went to look for that girl. She was already big when she came here, she must have been ten years old. And Celia accepted that. Edna was really dark and had nappy hair. Dona Zizi confirmed this telling my mother, "Nita, did you see how dark her knees are?"

Edna grew up, married a Jewish doctor, and had children. One day I asked my mother whether Edna had ever gone looking for her real mother in order to help her? "Stop being stupid, girl," responded Dona Anita, in that tone of voice of someone who knows everything about life and everything about human character, primarily in regards to money and skin color.

Our House on Alvaro Adorno Street, Number Fifty-Three

I was born in Natal in the state of Rio Grande do Norte because my mother wanted to be close to her own mother when she gave birth to me. She stayed there six months, and when she returned to Bahia she thought that my father would have already found a house for them to move into. Until then, they had been living in a single room rented from a Jewish family. Dona Anita remembers that, "Everything was done in that room, even the food was cooked on a small antiquated stove in a corner of the room." She had hoped that my father would have found a house, but "What a joke. Abrahão lacked initiative." We finally bought our house from Uncle Adolfo after I was born. Adolfo had built a small house near his own home, and I remember that my father got a long-term loan from the Caixa Economica bank to pay for the house. This represented a real financial sacrifice, for the last payment would only be made when I reached the age of fifteen.

Like all the other houses in the neighborhood, ours faced the street and lacked a front yard. It had a small living room, a small dining room, and two bedrooms. Since it was shaped like a square, it didn't have a hallway. One bedroom could be reached only by walking through the living room. Likewise, the dining room led to the kitchen. At the far end of the kitchen stood our bathroom, which contained a toilet, a small sink, and a shower. From the kitchen one walked down a stairway to the backyard. There it was heaven. In the lower part of the house, there was a walk-out basement, a big room with a cement floor and a bathroom. My father divided this room into a maid's room and his study, where he worked nights at his drawing table. In the maid's room, Jo slept on a canvas bed, kept closed during the day. I kept my toys in a trunk placed in a corner of the room. The room's door and window opened to a cemented part of the yard where Jo would scrub our clothes clean. She used a big, wire-enclosed wooden frame to stretch our white clothes under the strong sun so that they would retain their color. We also kept a hen house, where my father raised chickens.

Our backyard led to a deep descent. To the left, some sugar-cane plants dotted the hill. Farther down, an enormous genip tree grew brown fruit that resembled softballs. I used to retrieve the genipap fruit which fell around the tree, peel it, take out the seeds, cut it into little pieces, and mix it with a bit of water and sugar. In the afternoon, I would prepare a glass of this fruit and would eat it on my way to Teco and Ju's house. Behind our yard there were several banana trees. "Uncle" Carias would tell my father, "Abrão, you need to build a wall at the end of the yard because the blacks are entering your yard to get bananas and the earth is sliding every time it rains." For whatever reason, my father never built that wall, whether because he didn't care if the poor people took some bananas or because he didn't have the money to construct a wall.

Reveca, Our Teacher

When I was five years old, I entered kindergarten at the Escola Israelita Brasileira, located in the Sociedade Israelita da Bahia. The building was used for all the activities of the colony: synogogue, school, youth groups, and parties. The school taught kindergarten and the first five years of elementary school. Set back from the street, the building stood, like so many others in Bahia, on the top of a hill, and its four floors included two which were below street level. When I was a child I had the impression that the building was very large. Now, I think that I wouldn't find it that big.

Located on the first subfloor, our kindergarten classroom looked out to the stairs outside the building. Only a few years ago, I learned from my mother that my father had designed the blueprints for the building. Our teacher, a young woman called Reveca, taught nine of us in the class. Every day my father used to take me to school and pick me up at lunchtime to take me home. I remember that I had a small brown school bag, a present from my paternal grandfather, Mauricio, who lived in Recife. For my morning snack I used to eat a banana, some buttered bread, and lemonade. During the school day we played, drew, and sang songs in Yiddish, Hebrew, and Portuguese. I still remember some of the songs: "David, melech Israel . . ."

Ms. Reveca was a "poor young woman," my mother used to say. She had a brother, who became a doctor, and an older sister. They lived on the first floor of an old house on a hill that connected Nazare, where the school was located, and Brotas, where we lived. I remember,

I don't know why, that I once went to her house, which appeared dark and very poor. Her parents looked very old. Being poor makes people look old very quickly. I liked Reveca. How old was she at that time? Maybe fifteen or seventeen years old. Occasionally, I still see her when I visit my mother in Rio de Janeiro, where she has also moved. And she always says, "Ethel was the most intelligent of all my students," which still embarrasses me today.

Seu Abrahão, My Father

Seu Abrahão was really Abraham in his official documents, but in Bahia his name became Abrahão. The *ão* in Portuguese has a stronger sound than the *am*. He was thin, with blond hair and blue eyes; his face always had a worried expression on it, and he rarely raised his voice. "The house could fall and Abrahão wouldn't lift his head from the newspaper," my mother used to say impatiently. A few years later she would say the same thing about me: "The house could fall and Ethel wouldn't let go of that book."

My father was introverted, perhaps even sad or melancholy, and he used to work at his drawing table past midnight. An accomplished painter as well as draughtsman, his works adorn the walls of our family members' houses. For relaxation he liked to read and listen to music. When he was finally able to buy a used Victrola, he would listen to classical music from the few records that he had. He did this when my mother wasn't home, since the sound made her uncomfortable. I was already fourteen when we satisfied my mother's dream and moved to an apartment in Nazare near the Sociedade Israelita da Bahia, and could finally live among people who had a little bit more money. My mother says that the move wasn't good for him. He lost his space, his place to be alone with his drawing table, his books, and his canvases, paints, and paintbrushes. In the apartment, he had to share all of this with my brother in the same room.

My father taught drawing at the Escola de Belas Artes da Bahia, today part of the Federal University of Bahia. His landscapes and characters show a delicate stroke. Today, his paintings remind me of the work of the French Impressionists. Some are sad, like the one of a couple on a city street walking and hugging each other under the yellow light of a lamppost. That is my favorite. Another painting depicts a street in the old part of the city, which probably dates from the eighteenth century. Called Pelourinho, this neighborhood housed poor people at the time of my father's painting, but today has been transformed into a tourist attraction.

Today I wonder: how did he paint so beautifully with so few resources? He had few books about painting; some, translated from Spanish, had been published in Spain or Argentina. The only museum in Bahia at that time was the Museum of Sacred Art, which contained Christian religious art. He never had the money to travel to museums in Paris or any other place. The only trips he made were to visit his family in Recife, Porto Alegre, Rio de Janeiro, and later Sao Paulo after I had moved there. I think that the trip to Rio with my mother was the only vacation he ever took. When he died in 1971, the school exhibited his paintings in connection with its own sesquicentennial.

In addition to teaching, my father worked as a designer for the Federal Department of Public Works Against Drought, an agency that constructed immense reservoirs to combat drought in the arid Northeast. I can remember him as an architecture student, staying up very late designing projects for school on his drawing table. I was already twelve years old when he became an architect.

Sadly, we lost him so young, at the age of fifty-four. He had been sick for seven years with leukemia and wasted away little by little. I remember the last time he went to the hospital. The doctor said, "It's better to put him in the Hospital das Clinicas, because at least the doctors there know how to give the right prescription. In the private hospitals they only know how to give aspirin." It couldn't have been any other way because we didn't have money to put him in a private hospital.

I remember him lying in a hospital bed, in a poor room, my mother beside him, trying to talk to him. A tube inserted into his arm delivered his medication and serum. The iron rails that held the plastic bag with the serum had such rusty feet that the nurses had put cotton around them so that ants wouldn't climb up. How I wanted to run out of there. Meanwhile, on my uncle's insistence, I had to ask my father to sign a check so that my uncle could take out the little money that my father had in the bank, or else the money would have stayed there until his will was filed and nobody could say for sure when my mother would be able to receive it.

Why did my father always seem to me to be such a sad, melancholic, introverted person? I imagine that my father's childhood must have been very sad. Now, I regret not having talked to him about many subjects. My father was born in 1914 in the Quatro Irmãos agricultural colony, located in the interior of Rio Grande do Sul. This was one of several colonies sponsored by the Jewish Colonization Association, an organization founded by the philanthropist Baron de Hirsch. My father's father, Mauricio Kosminsky, or Moishe as he was called in Yiddish, and his mother, Eidel Milman (after whom I was named Ethel, following the Ashkenazi tradition of naming children after deceased relatives), both emigrated from Bessarabia as single young adults with their parents and siblings.

My Paternal Grandfather Mauricio Kosminsky

The eldest of nine children, my grandfather emigrated with his parents and siblings to Brazil. The family traveled on the *Captain Vilano* out of Hamburg and arrived at Ilha das Flores in Rio de Janeiro on May 17, 1913. The Kosminsky family comprised Ioss, forty-two years old, Scheine, thirty-nine, and the following children, all single: Moishe, twenty; Machlo; sixteen; Itria, fifteen; Fradel, fourteen; Iankel, twelve; Level, eight; Avarum, six; Chapke, three; and Bluma, one. The ship's register lists them as "Agriculturists." Maybe a claim to this occupation was necessary to leave Bessarabia. Families like the Kosminskys had their ship passage, land purchase, and initial capitalization for tools and seeds paid for by the JCA. They were expected to repay this loan from the proceeds of their crops. According to Moises Agranionick, a former resident of Quatro Irmãos, all the immigrants who arrived in Rio de Janeiro were quarantined in Ilha das Flores until they could prove that they weren't carrying any contagious diseases. What happened to the Kosminsky family during their enforced three weeks' stay? The ship's register reveals that little Bluma was put in a São Sebastião hospital on May 30 and died that same day. I imagine that Ioss and Scheine must have suffered greatly from their loss. Little Bluma didn't survive the long, tiring journey from Bessarabia to Hamburg and then to Rio de Janeiro. The ocean voyage itself lasted twenty days. The Kosminsky family finally left Rio on June 9 and traveled fifteen hundred kilometers by boat to Porto Alegre, Rio Grande do Sul, on the *Orion*. From Porto Alegre, the family took a long train trip to Quatro Irmãos. What did they discuss as they looked out the train's windows at the mountainous countryside? Were they hopeful, scared, or anxious?

My grandfather Mauricio didn't spend many years in Quatro Irmãos or in Porto Alegre, where many other immigrants later went following the colony's failure. Instead, he traveled a great distance to Recife, the capital of Pernambuco, in the northeast of Brazil.

My Grandmother Eidel Milman Kosminsky

The Milman family consisted of Ioss and Chaie (in Portuguese, José and Clara) and their children Eidel, twenty; Liber, eighteen; Idenkel, sixteen; Sury, twelve; Ity, ten; Itzig, eight; and Sezel, six. Like the Kosminskys, the Milman family had lived in Bessarabia and emigrated on the same sailing of the *Captain Vilano* from Hamburg. They continued on to Porto Alegre on the Saturno railway on May 25 and from Porto Alegre took the train to Quatro Irmãos where they also would become farmers.

I imagine that during the long trip from Europe to Brazil, young Mauricio and Eidel fell in love. Eidel must have been a pretty, blonde-haired, blue-eyed girl. Their son Abrahão, my father, had those features. Mauricio had dark hair and dark eyes. They probably fell in love quickly, for they married soon after arriving in Quatro Irmãos. And it was there that my father Abraham was born on April 4, 1914. Tragically, Eidel died while giving birth to her second child, who also died. Was it a boy or a girl? The doctor at the colony was at fault. It appears that the child was in a sitting position. Eidel screamed for hours and hours. I heard these memories from Aunt Sara's own lips when I visited Porto Alegre with my father thirty-five years ago.

Eidel's younger sister Sara raised little Abraham and taught him to write in Yiddish. The two wrote to each other in Yiddish throughout their lives, although they didn't see each other for thirty-five years. Mauricio remarried some years later and took little Abraham to Recife. Neither Abraham nor Sara ever had enough money to buy a plane ticket to fly between Salvador and Porto Alegre.

Sadly, my father never got to know his mother and no one even has a picture of her. Therefore, I've never been able to visualize her. The only material reminder of Eidel is a samovar that Sara kept. Aunt Sara wanted to give the samovar to my father when we visited her in Porto Alegre, but Aunt Sara's son refused because the samovar had been in the family for so many years. Thus my father was left without the only object through which he could connect to his mother. However, he gave his mother's name to his daughter.

One day a rich cousin of Abraham's from Porto Alegre visited us in Salvador. I still remember that visit. It could be that I'm confusing one cousin with another, because I remember the visit of Aunt Sara's son and not that of the rich cousin. Anyway, this rich cousin told me that he gave my father the money for a plane ticket to visit his dear Aunt Sara in Porto Alegre. I made the trip by bus. It was a long trip, maybe four days or more. I left before my father and I was waiting for him when he arrived at Aunt Sara's house.

Aunt Sara

Aunt Sara told me that Abraham had polio when he was little. Her mother, grandmother Clara, saved him. Clara was a very intelligent woman, short and full of energy. Day and night she took care of her grandson, wrapping warm cloths on his little legs and massaging his limbs. That was how she saved the blonde, skinny, blue-eyed boy Abraham. However, he was left with one leg a bit shorter than the other and one foot more arched than the other. I remember him making a type of arch support by folding a piece of cardboard and placing it in his shoe. He limped slightly when he walked. Yet despite his tired expression, he never complained and, after dinner, he would go down to his study to work late into the night.

Aunt Sara was of medium height and a little overweight. Her nose was rather long and her eyes always shone with kindness. She wore her hair in a tight bun. Uncle Pedro was much older than she and was very tall. While I stayed at their home, I remember waiting on Friday nights for Pedro to return from the synagogue; after the first star appeared in the sky we would eat dinner: chicken soup, gefilte fish, and many other delicacies that Aunt Sara could cook like nobody else.

More than forty years later, I heard the details of her life from Aunt Sara. "Before Seu Pedro, I was married to another man for ten years and never had children. One day he came to me and said, 'I'm going to divorce you. It's the law.' According to Jewish religion, if a woman doesn't bear any children after ten years of marriage, a husband can reject her. And that's how it was. So I took a train to Santa Maria and I cried during the entire trip. A gentleman came up and began talking to me. It was Seu Pedro. He was a widower with four children. That's how we met and we married soon afterward. A few months later my stomach began to grow, and Djarna was born, then Moishe arrived. What happiness! I found out that my ex-husband had also remarried and his wife's stomach became swollen as well. But it wasn't a child; it was a disease. He never had children."

The Quatro Irmãos Cemetery

In December 1996, my second husband Stephen and I decided to go to Porto Alegre to visit my father's maternal family and the old colony of Quatro Irmãos. We asked my cousin Moishe to help and he gave us the phone number of Clarice Agranionick, who lives in Erechim. So we traveled six hours by bus from Porto Alegre to Erechim, passing through a mountain range, some small cities, several soy and wheat plantations, and some cattle ranches. It was a green trip that inspired a certain peace. Finally we arrived at our hotel, put down our bags, and called Clarice. We decided to see the remains of the colony of Quatro Irmãos the next morning.

When Clarice arrived early the next day, she was younger than I, but appeared to be older from the expression on her face, her posture, and her clothing. We talked, and I learned about her struggles as a widow. She runs a farm that grows soy, wheat, and corn, and told us that the Jewish community is very small and that her brother-in-law is in charge of the synagogue. He needs more money to maintain the cemetery, but all the "Yidn went leaving" and only a few remained from the old colony, perhaps because they had had some previous farming experience. Indeed, Clarice said that her father-in-law had worked the land in Europe before immigrating to Brazil.

As we got in her old Volkswagen Bug, Clarice said, "We're going early or else we won't be able to stand the sun." We took the main road that links Erechim to Passo Fundo, then a secondary unpaved road. The car shook, and Stephen, who was in the front seat, held on the best he could. Meanwhile, I tried to take mental notes of everything I saw. When we arrived in Quatro Irmãos, Clarice stopped at a gas station to ask for the cemetery key. Yes, the cemetery stays locked, surrounded by a wall and located within the borders of a farm owned by some ethnic Italians. Clarice spoke of the cemetery's condition: "We're trying to see if the cemetery can be transferred to the city, so that we'll have more guarantees and some money to conserve it. When the people leave here, they forget that some of their dead are buried here. We had a problem with the care-taker of the cemetery and now we don't have anyone. Sometimes we pay someone by the day to come here to clean and weed. Even though its locked, people jump the wall to steal metal from the gravesites."

We entered the cemetery—on one side were the graves of men, and on the other those of women. In my hands I held a copy of the cemetery map, which I had obtained from an eighty-year-old former administrator of the colony. We tried to locate Eidel's grave. Under a scorching sun we walked from one side to the other, looking at the ancient tombs. Finally, we had to decide between two very ancient sites made of deteriorating bricks whose inscriptions had faded away. The desolation made us sad. With doubt in our hearts, we concluded that Eidel's grave was one of these two. I gave some money to Clarice to maintain the tomb and she offered to find someone. Clarice promised that, if possible, she would take a picture of the tomb. On our way back to Sao Paulo, my thoughts wouldn't leave Eidel, who lost her life in such a cruel way at the age of only twenty-two or twenty-three, in a strange land, leaving behind a young son. I also thought of my father, who was never able to go to the cemetery where his mother is buried. I decided to buy some letters for her tomb. When the letters arrived, we took a picture and mailed them to Clarice, who offered to get someone to put them on the tomb with the comment, "I hope nobody steals them." She finished by saying, "If it's possible, I'll send you a photo." And that's how it was; we left for the U. S. and lost contact with her. What happened to the tomb, to the letters? Eidel's only remaining descen-dants are three grandchildren—my brother, my sister, and I—plus five great-grandchildren: my four children and my brother's son.

Grandmother Rosa

Grandmother Rosa, my grandfather Mauricio's second wife, was a short woman with straight, evenly cut, graying hair combed to one side and held in place by a hair pin. Her face radiated kindness and simplicity. I remember her making pasta, cutting the pasta into strips, and then hanging them on a clothes hanger to dry. The yellow pasta was really delicious and we loved it. My mother used to refer to Grandmother Rosa as "my mother-in-law." Only later, while listening to my mother talking, did I find out that Grandmother Rosa was my father's stepmother. We used to visit my grandparents in Recife every year. We usually traveled by plane, but one time we went by ship. Today a trip from Salvador to Recife takes approximately one hour by plane, but at that time it was a long trip.

Grandmother Rosa was also an immigrant from Russia. Her family, the Letvins, arrived in Rio de Janeiro on the *Coburg* from Bremen on November 3, 1913. Her parents were Welhin, or Wolf, forty-five when he emigrated, and Sheine, forty-four. Their children were twins Simon and Aron, twenty; Riwa, seventeen; Chaya, fifteen; Zuvia (who would be renamed Rosa), twelve; and Itzak, nine. On November 19 they left for Rio Grande do Sul on a ship called the *Iris*. And from there they took the train to Quatro Irmãos.

Grandma Rosa and Grandpa Mauricio lived one flight up in an old building on Rua dos Coelhos in Recife. One had to walk up a dark stairwell to reach their long apartment, which included a terrace that was shaped like a rectangle with three open walls. That was where we ate our meals. In retrospect, I think that they were very poor. At the time I had some doubts, but I could tell the difference between their house, the house of their married daughter Clara, and the house of Aunt Rosita, my mother's oldest sister. Grandfather was a peddler, a *klientelchik* in Yiddish. In one of the rooms he had a closet full of fabric remnants, and he would always give my mother one of these samples as a present.

On the second story of the building lived one of my father's cousins, who had many young children. They were even poorer than my grandparents were. I remember my mother's note of contempt when discussing them. My mother never accepted poverty.

Grandpa Mauricio and Grandma Rosa had three children: Clara, Luiz, and Bela. The oldest, Aunt Clara, had two children at that time, Marcia, who was my age, and Israel. Afterward she had two more children. Years later I became envious of my cousin Marcia, who had the liberty to travel alone and could enjoy a more independent life. Aunt Clara's husband, Uncle Chele (in Yiddish) or Germano (in Portuguese), was a handsome man who made a fortune in the furniture business. It was whispered in the family that Uncle Chele had been a communist during Vargas's dictatorship.

Uncle Luiz, skinny and nervous, became a dentist. During the mid-fifties he was dating my future Aunt Clarinha (so named to differentiate her from his sister), who was also a sweet and caring person. Uncle Luiz liked to read mysteries and crime magazines translated into Portuguese. One title I remember was *X9*. I was forbidden to read this kind of book, but whenever I had the opportunity I would lock myself in the bathroom with one. It was a habit that I continued later in Bahia, where I read almost the entire works of the famous Portuguese novelist Eça de Queirós in my bedroom while my mother took her afternoon naps.

Aunt Bela, the youngest of the family and our most beloved aunt, was a pretty young woman with light skin and dark hair. Years later she became the protagonist in a major family argument when she decided to marry a *goy* who was much older than she and who had four children from his first marriage. It was a big scandal. The family didn't want to accept that she, a Jewish woman, would marry a *goy*. Grandfather Mauricio made her travel to the homes of relatives in other cities in order for her to forget her boyfriend. She even stayed at our house for a while. It didn't help, and they married. At about that time, Grandfather Mauricio got sick and died. Bela's brother and sister accused her of having killed him. Her half-brother Abrahão, my father, was the only one who supported her, and until today she remembers his support fondly and still misses him.

Years later, the story nearly repeated itself. I remember my discussions with my father. "Dad, why can't I date Eduardo? He's a good guy." And he, in his calm voice, explained to me, "Because, daughter, dating leads to marriage and marriage is a difficult thing if the two people don't share the same culture. And how are the children going to be raised? Will they be Catholic or Jewish? Each one will favor his own religion. It's like that, it's part of the human species, each one wants to raise his children in his own way." For my mother, there were no conversations. It was forbidden and she screamed, "What will the others say, my daughter dating a *goy*?"

I finally managed to satisfy my adolescent desire to rebel and left Bahia at the age of nineteen to search for knowledge and liberty in Sao Paulo, where I met and married a Sephardi Jew. My father was able to get to know his two eldest grandchildren, Claudia and Sergio. Unfortunately, by the time Marilia was born he was already very sick. Ana, my youngest daughter, was named in his honor. The marriage lasted seventeen years; ten would have been better. The same feelings that join people can later separate them. Maybe I didn't obey the principle adopted by my father: "It's necessary to know each other well before getting married. Marriage is a very serious thing." Looking back today, though, I see wonderful results: I have four beautiful children.

The City of Recife

Today I often wonder why I know so little about Recife despite having gone there so many times. When we used to go to Recife, we would stay in Grandpa Mauricio's house or in Aunt Rosita's house. Whether in one house or the other, our activities were dedicated to visiting— one day lunch with Aunt Clara, the other day at Aunt Clarinha's parents' house, the rest with many other relatives, both close and distant, and old friends of my father.

Uncle Luiz had a small black car, perhaps a Studebaker. It seemed amazing to me to ride in a car. On our small, narrow street only Uncle Carias had a car. If our relatives in Recife had a car, they would come to pick us up and take us to lunch at their home. If not, we would go by bus or streetcar. When I was eleven or twelve years old I used to visit the Circulo Israelita where I could meet people my own age.

The northeastern cities of Brazil generally lack plazas and greenery. The only large plaza I can remember in Recife had trees with lots of small monkeys hanging from the branches. This plaza was located in Derby, the neighborhood where Aunt Rosita lived. I liked to go there with my brother and cousins Dorio and Mario, Aunt Rosita's sons. Even though Recife has many beaches, I don't remember having ever gone to any of them. At that time it wasn't as common to go to the beach as it is today.

Aunt Rosita

Aunt Rosita lived in an immense two-story house, set back from the street and isolated on both sides by a large yard. The street was full of trees, which set it apart from the other streets in the city. Her husband, my Uncle Moises, was an import-export merchant and had become a very rich man. The story of how Uncle Moises became rich is worth telling.

During World War II, the Americans built an airbase near Natal, where the family then lived. Uncle Moises began selling cheap watches and jewelry to American soldiers and managed to get permission to enter the base. "It was like he went collecting dollars" and, by doing so, got rich. That's what is said in my mother's family. He was a very intelligent person, who read a lot and taught his wife Yiddish. He built a fortune that is still being enjoyed by his children and grandchildren today. My parents liked Uncle Moises a lot. Thanks to him, my mother opened her own small business at home selling ready-made clothing. He never asked her to repay the loan.

Their home was so big that a guard would sit on a bench all night guarding the house from robbers. I had never seen a guard before in my life. I remember seeing him every morning, short and skinny, with eyes red from lack of sleep. The first time I saw a private car with a chaffeur was also at Aunt Rosita's house. I still remember the chauffeur, Seu Valdemar, today. He was a well-groomed nice man with light brown skin. Rosita also had a gardener who would sing local songs like "Pisa na fulô, pisa na fulô, pisa na fulô / Não maltrate o meu amor" [Step on the flower / Don't mistreat my love]. Bica was the most important maid of the house. Black-skinned, short, and very old—undoubtedly the daughter of slaves—she had been the maid of my grandmother Dona Maria and, when Aunt Rosita got married and had Bessy and Beila, Bica came to take care of the girls and never left. When the boys were born, Bica took care of them, too. She had her own room and bathroom separate from the other maids of the house, and she used to say, "I'm a damsel . . ." Bica never married.

My Mother Anita

This is a long story that involves many countries and continents. My mother, or Mãinha, as mothers are called in Bahia, was born on October 19, 1918, in Recife, the capital of Pernambuco. She was the third daughter of Leon Volfzon and Maria Volfzon, called Mainie and, in Hebrew, Malke. It was a large family with seven children: Rosita; Jacob; my mother Anita, called Nitucha by her father, whom she most resembled; Dorita; Noya; Sarita; and Genita, the youngest and tallest. My mother Anita is now eighty-one years old. She's short, lightly tanned, with hair dyed light brown. She is still proud and elegant, restless and agitated; she likes to be in fashion and to have her hair done and her nails painted. Authoritative and intelligent, she's very good at giving advice. She really enjoys writing—maybe I've inherited that quality from her—and giving speeches. She lives in the Flamengo neighborhood in Rio and is the president of the local chapter of the feminist Zionist organization, the Pioneers.

Seu Leon Volfzon, My Grandfather

My mother is very proud of her father, Seu Leon. According to her, "He was an important merchant in the Northeast. He had the most abundant table of food in the Northeast. He was a Litvak. He didn't want me to marry your father because he said that they were from Poland and the Polish Jews weren't that great, that they were lower than the Jews from Lithuania, where he had come from."

Seu Leon was short, darkly tanned, and bald. He always seemed very agitated, giving the impression that he couldn't stop moving. He had a very funny way of speaking. "Oh, Anita!" he would call for my mother whenever he wanted something during his visit to our house in Bahia. He always arrived loaded with delicious things from the markets in Natal in Rio Grande do Norte, where he and Grandma Maria lived. He would bring *requeijão,* a type of cheese that is eaten fried; sun-dried meat; and cashews; as well as *pitomba* fruit. His arrival always made the party. The house would fill up with excitement.

Each morning during his visit, Leon would drink coffee and go visit his old friend Seu Miller in his furniture store on Ladeira dos Bombeiros. Had they come from the same city? I don't know. On Fridays and on Saturday mornings, he would go to the synagogue. Sometimes my father and I would go with him. I remember that after Saturday prayers we would eat herring with tomatoes, onions, and bread. It was a delicacy. I would peek in on the prayers, but I spent most of the time running around and playing with the other children.

Grandma Maria was taller than Grandpa, calmer, and spoke in a low, delicate voice. She was very white, and her thin white hair was mixed with some light brown strands. Her hair was brushed back, with the ends curling in, and held together by a pin. A thin hair net kept her hair in place. Grandma would often sit and talk with my mother while crocheting or reading a magazine. She dressed in a very simple manner, but she wore nylons. Because she was diabetic, she had to follow a certain diet. She would put small pills of saccharine, rather than sugar, in her coffee.

I liked Grandma Maria a lot. She always asked, "Ethelzinha, do you want to live with Grandma? You could study at the Escola Doméstica with the other girls." From that day on, every time I disobeyed my mother, she would threaten, "You're going to the Escola Doméstica." When I was nine or ten years old I really wanted to run away, and I thought of going to live with my grandmother. For a long time, I carried in my school bag paper, a pencil, and an envelope in order to write to Grandma. The Escola Doméstica was a school created by the state government with the objective of teaching middle- and upper-class girls the basics of cooking, taking care of children, and running a home. It was ironic, since these girls belonged to families that had many maids and they would never need to cook rice or change a baby's diaper.

My grandfather immigrated from Mogalev in Lithuania to Buenos Aires at the beginning of the twentieth century. He worked on the construction of the Buenos Aires subway and soon met Maria, also an immigrant, who was living there with her mother and two younger sisters. Maria Feldman was a beautiful young woman, tall, with very white skin. She was so beautiful that some years later a photographer in Natal asked my grandfather for permission to place a photograph of her in his studio window. Leon and Maria married in Buenos Aires and as they didn't want to stay there any longer they left for Recife, where Maria's brother was living. This brother, Isaac, bought tickets for the entire family to come to Brazil. Leon and Maria probably arrived in Recife in 1912 because Rosita, the eldest child, was born there in 1914. Leon kept the memory of the Spanish language and he named all his daughters with the Spanish language dimunitive ending -*ita*.

Once in Recife, Leon began working as a peddler, selling fabric from door to door on credit, just like my grandfather Mauricio would do later on. Leon was lucky. He prospered and opened a bridal store in the city. At that time, young women would spend years preparing their trousseaux. Truth be told, their mothers would begin preparing when their daughters were young girls. Everything was sewn by seamstresses; there weren't any ready-made clothes. Even bed sheets had to be made and embroided. Eventually, Leon became very well off and held an important position in Jewish society and a prominent place in the synagogue.

The family lived in a "large, good house," as my mother used to say. The children made friends with their neighbors, Jews and non-Jews alike. My mother's best friend was Clarissa, a non-Jewish girl, whose mother became friends with Grandma Maria. Clarissa's parents were wealthy and her father had an important job. I remember that he was the son of Father Rome. At that time, it was common for priests to have children. When my mother remembered her friend Clarissa, she used to say, "Clarissa of Father Rome." And that's how she continued to be known.

I think that it must have been right after World War I that Leon managed to bring his widowed mother, Reveca, his brother Nahum, and his sister Fanny, who was very like him, tanned and short, to Brazil. Leon told all his children about the pogroms he had seen in his childhood. In one of them, little Fanny managed to escape by hiding in a large jar used as a water jug. Leon also talked about forced servitude in the the Czar's army. These were the reasons he came to South America. Maybe as a result of all this suffering, Nahum "was never right in the head," as my mother used to say. She remembers him even now in his room at the far end of my grandfather's house. He died at a young age. Fanny married a prosperous furniture merchant in Recife and a few years later moved with her family to Sao Paulo. I went to visit her one day more than thirty years ago in her house in Sao Paulo. Fanny's move caused her brother to become more distant. Sao Paulo is very far from Natal, and trips at that time were less common because transportation was still very difficult.

As a result of the economic depression of the nineteen thirties, Leon lost everything. Uncle Noya, Leon's son, told me that his father had many invoices from peddlers who had bought large quantities of fabric in his store. Following the crisis of 1929, people didn't have any money to pay him, and he ended up with a bunch of worthless paper. Leon had already started a small furniture store in Natal, and that's where the family went. When their moving boxes arrived in Natal, all of grandma's dishware, all the beautiful English dishware, had been broken.

Behind their house in Natal they established a small furniture store. Some of the furniture came from southern Brazil, maybe from Paraná or Sao Paulo. In Natal, my grandfather never made as much money as he had in Recife. Natal was a small city whose economy depended on cotton production. It was far from the decadent abundance of Recife, which in the past had been a dynamic city, thanks to the wealth created by the overflowing sugar refineries. Life in Natal was much simpler. Leon, however, was a very dynamic person. He became one of the founders of the synagogue in Natal. Although the number of Jews living there was much smaller than in Recife, they managed to create a synagogue with its own building. Aside from that, Leon became a Mason and eventually occupied a very important position in society. He came to have many friends, both Jewish and non-Jewish.

Leon was an avid reader and subscribed to a Yiddish journal from the United States called *Zukunft,* meaning the future. He collected each issue, and I can remember the enormous pile of newspapers in his house. Always preoccupied with Jews who arrived in Natal without family, Leon frequently invited people to live in the house for a couple of days or to have a meal with his family. One of these guests never left. Seu Isaac stayed and lived in a room at the end of the house. He might have been a pharmacist in Europe—in any case he knew something about medicine because he always took care of Leon's children when they got sick. Often during family occasions like Pesach or the end of Yom Kippur, occasions that brought special treats from Dona Maria's kitchen, Leon would arrive with the "Yidn" he found alone in the city and would authoritatively tell the children, "Go to the kitchen, you're going to eat in the kitchen," and thereby make room for his guests.

Authoritative as he was, Leon had a big heart. A couple with whom he was friendly, probably from his hometown in Lithuania, died and left two children. They were very poor, but Leon didn't have any doubts. He got on a train and went to Recife and brought the children back with him. Just like that my mother got two more siblings, Liuba and her brother Isaac, as he was called by all. "Brother" Isaac studied history and geography and later became the principal of the Colégio D. Pedro II, the most famous public school in Rio de Janeiro, a post he held for many years.

Grandfather Leon sent his sons to college. At that time there wasn't a college in Natal, so Uncle Jacob went to Salvador to study medicine and Noya went to Recife to study engineering. Jacob became a very important opthalmologist in Natal. He was a socialist. I found out that he used to write about the country's public health concerns, but I've never read what remains from his writings. He died very young, only thirty-five years old, in a plane accident on the way to Rio de Janeiro. On board were the governor of the state of Rio Grande do Norte and other important people. Something went wrong with the plane, and it fell while over the state of Sergipe, killing all the occupants. It was a catastrophe for the family.

Uncle Jacob was the darling of Grandma Maria, as he was the most concerned about her. She never recovered. It was also very hard for my mother. Jacob had interceded on my mother's behalf so that she could go to the Ateneu, the state high school, since Leon thought that elementary school was sufficient for women because they had to get married. Later, when she went to Natal to give birth to me, Jacob said,

"You're not going to a hospital, you can get a disease. You're going to have the child here at home." And that's how I came to be born in grandmother's house on October 15, 1946. My mother has said that "it was D. Adelaide, the midwife, that got you. She was already on her third generation of babies."

The saddest thing of all is that Uncle Jacob left behind a son who never met his father. My cousin Jacózinho was born two months after his father died. Aunt Sarita, a pretty young woman, was left alone with a newborn baby. She stayed for a while in Natal with the child, but I think that she felt lonely and decided to return to her parent's home with Jacózinho. And that is where I first met her, thirty-five years ago, when I visited Porto Alegre.

When Jacob died, not only did I lose an uncle, I also lost my god-father. Even though "Jews don't have godfathers," as my mother likes to say, she considered him to be my godfather. It was he who took care of my birth certificate because my father was far away in Bahia. The hospital where my uncle had worked named one of its rooms in his honor, and Natal named one of its streets after him.

Grandpa Leon was a very active person. Every morning he would leave the house very early and go to the market to do the day's shopping. At that time no one had a refrigerator. He would shop at the market and then call a *moleque* (poor boy) who was waiting in hopes of earning some change, to carry the basket of food home, which he did, on his head. Leon had many friends throughout the city. If some-one couldn't buy a food-keeper, as we called the place where we kept food, he would make a deal. My mother remembers that they received milk and meat like this because of a deal that he had made with the milkman and the butcher. Many years later, as an old man, Leon earned the title of Norte Riograndense citizen, awarded by Natal's city council as thanks for his and his children's services to the city.

Grandfather Leon died in 1969 in Natal at the age of eighty, a few months after the birth of my son, Sergio, one of his two great-grandchildren. When he died, my mother said, "His masonic companions went to present him the last homage. They placed a sash with the number thirty-three on him, signifying his high position."

Natal and the Beach of Ridinha

It was delicious to go to Natal. My grandparents had a large one-story house and an immense backyard. My extended family spent many summers together visiting in Natal. All the cousins gathered there. There was Roberto Luiz, who was my age, the son of Aunt Genita, and cousin Ethel Rejane, the daughter of Aunt Sarita, who was a few years younger than I. Aunt Genita lived in her father's house in Natal with her family—Uncle Neto and their two sons, Nilton Sergio and Roberto Luiz. Years later, after having moved to Rio, Genita had a daughter, Elza Regina. Aunt Sarita lived in Recife and afterwards moved to Natal with her husband, Uncle Mauricio, and her daughter Ethel Rejane. Some years later, she had two more daughters, Neide and Doritinha, and she also lived a good while with my grandparents.

In the house there was a sense of freedom that came from the fact that my mother was very busy with her family. We would run around the yard barefoot and, as a result, would attract a parasite that penetrated the skin of our feet and had to be removed. The children used to sit on a big table in the yard and one of the maids, with the help of one of the aunts, would poke our feet with a sewing needle, remove the bugs, and then apply methiolate. At least we got to live outside much of the day and eat the fruit of the earth—cashew fruit, mangoes, and tropical fruits called *imbu* and *pitomba*.

The neatest thing of all was the trip to the beach of Ridinha, where grandpa had a summer house. We reached his house by boat, and conditions there were very primitive. We had to bring everything from Natal, even our drinking water. Grandma Maria and my mother complained about the hardship, but Grandpa loved it. The house was built on top of a dune. Actually, the beach seemed to be covered by dunes, and fine sand would often get into our eyes. Uncle Neto, Genita's husband, was a member of the military and he managed to borrow some canvas cloths to place under the roof, yet when we awoke our beds were always full of sand anyway. Each morning, a soldier under Neto's command would remove the sand that had accumulated around the house. I remember that during our stays there we ate crabs and pink mangoes and sucked cashews. Delicious.

Between the house and the beach there was a club called ABC, where we would play ping-pong and the boys would play soccer.

My father didn't like Ridinha very much. I think it was there that skinny little Ethel, who didn't like to eat, got very sick. She had bad diarrhea, the beginning of dehydration. That must have scared her parents, who had lost a newborn boy, Wilson, to heart problems years earlier. From then on they treated Ethel with special care. Her feet weren't permitted to touch the ground. Aunt Bela remembers that even in Bahia's mild winter, Ethel's socks were warmed in the oven before she put them on. From then on, she followed a strict diet and a long list of rules, more vast than the ones in the Deuteronomy. As a result, her desire to eat everything prohibited grew.

Dona Maria Volfzon and the Discovery of a Gigantic Family

Dona Maria—Manie Volfzon—was born a Feldman. I discovered this only much later, while I was investigating our family history. When I was a little girl in Bahia, I always felt the lack of a big family. My schoolmates and neighbors, all of them non-Jews, always referred to their grandparents, aunts and uncles, and cousins. All of them had family in the city or in nearby towns. They always spoke about gatherings and the vacations they spent in their families' homes. My lack of family hurt, and I envied those girls, such as Darilda, who attended the Colegio de Aplicação and always spoke of an aunt who owned a beauty salon in the trendy part of the city.

Meanwhile, we had family far away in Bahia. Almost all of Mauricio Kosminsky's brothers had left Rio Grande do Sul and moved to Recife, Sao Paulo, Minas Gerais, or Bahia. The lack of a big, close family hurt. Every once in a while, my mother would talk about her grandmother, who had gone to the U. S., and my grandmother Maria, who had never again seen her mother, nor her brothers. My grandmother's brothers were very tall, my mother would say. This always fascinated me. For someone living in Salvador many decades ago, the United States, or "America," as my Aunt Rosita would sometimes call it, seemed to be on another planet. Many years passed, yet those childhod memories, memories I wasn't even conscious of, remained like scars.

In 1992 I decided to take a vacation in Ottawa and Quebec, Canada, and, since the U. S. was so close, I asked Aunt Rosita for the address of my grandmother's family. Rosita was the only family member who still had the address of our family over there because in the late fifties or early sixties, she and her husband Moises and their children had visited with them for a while. Once I had the address, I wrote from Ottawa to my mother's cousin Goldie and she invited me to spend a weekend at her family's home in West Orange, New Jersey.

Goldie and her husband Rudy picked me up at the Port Authority Bus Terminal in New York and then drove to their house in West Orange. We talked excitedly in English, the only language we had in common, even though I lacked fluency. We only knew a few words of Yiddish, she more than I. After all, she belongs to the second generation and I to the third. We were so overcome with emotion that we stayed up all night, breaking down language barriers. When Aunt Rosita had been there, so many years ago, the only communication then possible had been through Yiddish.

The next day Goldie had a reunion, calling all her cousins from throughout New Jersey. They all came with their children and grandchildren. It was very emotional, many of them looked like my mother and her brothers—their skin color, their hair, their double chins. The physical similarities were stunning. Yet they were really very different, having been born and raised in a different country. These similarities and differences motivated me to start an investigation that would change my life.

On my way back to Sao Paulo, I wrote a proposal to do a sociological study of my family. The general outline was to compare both sides of the family in order to analyze the differences and similarities observed on first contact. I presented this project to CAPES, a grant-issuing agency of the Brazilian federal government, which then passed it on to the Fulbright fellowship organization, with whom they had an agreement. To my great happiness, my grant was approved in October 1994, and I went to New York. Goldie and Rudy picked me up at the airport and I stayed a week in their house. They helped my investigation a lot by contacting more family members and taking me to various Jewish archives in New Jersey. Goldie had a party to celebrate my birthday along with that of her brother Kieve, and I took advantage of the occasion to interview much of the family. I also interviewed some family members in their homes. In November I traveled to Cincinnati, Ohio, and spent six weeks there, researching in the American Jewish Archives and studying in the library of Hebrew Union College. Midway through December I returned to New York, where I rented a room in the house of "Aunt" Maria, as I called her, and started my research at YIVO—the Institue for Jewish Research.

The Meeting with Stephen and the Great Change

After getting the names of my uncles and my mother's grandmother, Bela Feldman (called Beila in Brazil), I went to the United States National Archives in New York on December 30 hoping to uncover information about their arrival. It was a cold winter day. As soon as I stepped into the elevator, a siren began to wail. It was the fire alarm. Everyone had to leave the building and wait for the firefighters to arrive. While I waited for the building to be cleared, I stood on the sidewalk with some other researchers and office workers. I saw a tall, white man wearing a woolen hat, who was leaning against the wall of the building. I decided to approach him and start a conversation. He was surprised to learn that I was a Brazilian Jew and was in New York on a Fulbright scholarship to research my family history.

After the firemen left, we entered the building and went to the eleventh-floor archives. He was very helpful and showed me how to use a microfilm reader. We spent the whole day working together and shared a horrible sandwich in the building's cafeteria. We exchanged addresses and telephone numbers, but I spent New Year's Eve alone with "Aunt" Maria, feeling very homesick for my children. A few days went by, and I don't know who telephoned first. I say it was I and he says it was he. The only thing I'm sure of is that it was the beginning of the great change in my life. In November 1995 I went back to Sao Paulo, but he arrived in January 1996 and we married on the twenty-seventh of that month. In the morning, we had a civil ceremony with my children, my mother and sister, my father-in-law, and my sister-in-law. That night we had the religious ceremony at our home, which our friend Nancy translated from Hebrew to English to Portuguese. Soon after, there was a great party, surrounded by our children and friends, including the family of my deceased former husband.

After so many years alone, it felt wonderful to be with a partner who spoke the same language of love and understanding, and whose background was so similar; we are both third generation descendants of Eastern European Jews.

My Grandmother Maria's Family

Goldie, a fountain of information about the American side of the family, showed me my first view of my great-grandmother Bela Feldman. In the photograph she wore a wig, a sign that she was Orthodox, and displayed a stern expression. Goldie, who was five when Bela died, remembers her as a very quiet person. This is not the impression that the Brazilian cousins have of their grandmother. They heard from their mother, D. Maria, that Grandmother was very authoritarian: she chose Berta for Isaac and forced him to marry her, against his will.

Grandmother Maria's family story is one of comings and goings, of losses and gains, of separations and reunions. People lost their original names and gained others; they established themselves in cities and countries, fleeing from pogroms and Cossacks or from the Czar. They were always fighting "to make a decent living" for themselves and their children. Some succeeded, others were left halfway there. Grandmother Maria's family left Ukraine bit by bit. There wasn't enough money for them to leave together. The first to emigrate was Fishel, the oldest son, who arrived in the United States in 1900 from Kupil, Ukraine. Fishel went to Elizabeth, New Jersey, where he had a cousin, and he started calling himself Philip. In 1901 Herz, the second son, emigrated to the United States, lived a few years in New York, and then established himself in New Jersey. Herz soon started calling himself Harry. After Fishel and Herz it was Dvoira's turn in 1907 to leave the province of Podolia, Ukraine, for the United States; she also settled in New Jersey. Dvoira changed her name to Dora. Fishel, the eldest son, paid for the ship passages of his two siblings.

Uncle Isaac, who, according to my Aunt Rosita, had been living in Siberia, probably arrived in Brazil in 1910. Unfortunately, it wasn't possible to find any precise information about the Brazilian side of the family because the archives in Recife had been destroyed due to inadequate storage. Things like that happen in Brazil because of the poverty and the lack of interest on the part of governmental authorities. Thankfully, we can depend on the memories of the family. Through these memories I found out the rest of our family saga. Isaac sent for his mother Bela and three more sisters, Maria, Gittel, and Rachel, who had been living in Proskurov, Ukraine. The ship couldn't dock at Recife because of a yellow fever epidemic, so the travelers were directed to Buenos Aires. On the way there, the ship must have stopped at Rio de Janeiro, maybe even at Santos, too, and the unanswered question remains as to why they continued to Buenos Aires. One possibility is that they had family there. Exactly how long they stayed in Argentina remains another mystery, although it was probably a couple of years. They stayed long enough for my grandmother to marry Leon Volfzon and for Bela to arrange for Berta to become Isaac's fiancée.

When Isaac sent tickets for them to go to Recife, they all left Buenos Aires: Bela, her three daughters, her son-in-law Leon, and Berta, Isaac's future wife. They probably arrived in Recife in 1912, since cousin Sito, the son of Isaac and Berta, was born in 1913, and in 1914 Aunt Rosita was born. Bela, Gittel, and Rachel didn't stay long in Recife. Bela didn't adapt well to the hot, humid climate of the city. In 1914, Fishel sent money, and Bela went to the United States accompanied by her youngest daughters, Gittel and Rachel. In the United States, Gittel changed her name to Gussie and Rachel to Rose.

Maria never saw her mother nor her sisters again. Bela died in 1935, and my grandmother Maria, a longtime sufferer from diabetes, died in 1963. My great-uncle Isaac had a little more luck. His American brothers sent the money for a trip in the late fifties so they could see each other again. That was the only time the six of them were reunited since they had left Ukraine. After Isaac returned to Recife, he became sick and died soon afterward. My mother would say later that he died "from the excitement and the cold he felt there."

Sometimes I think of my grandmother and wonder about the life she had with her parents and her siblings in Ukraine. They probably suffered from poverty and had very little contact with members of the family who had already departed for the United States. She used to tell her children, first in Recife and later in Natal, that her brothers were very tall. Fishel and Herz found the resources to survive, first in Ukraine and then on another continent. Their brother Isaac worked for a number of years in Siberia and the only thing I know about their father Israel is his name. Two grandchildren received his name, the oldest son of Aunt Dora, cousin Ira, and Uncle Isaac's son, cousin Sito.

One in the United States and one in Brazil. His grandchildren in the United States and Brazil say that Israel died in Ukraine from a lung disease, probably tuberculosis.

I have only a few tangible memories of my grandmother Maria, a few pictures and a pillow, made of the sorrows and what was left of her life in Europe. More important than the pillow, on which I sleep every night, is the fact that I am her granddaughter.

I would like to thank the Fulbright Commission, especially Professor Marco Antonio da Rocha; CAPES, the Brazilian foundation that sponsors research by professors; and FUNDUNESP, the grant-giving body from the State University of Sao Paulo, for their generous financial support from 1994 to 1995.

Chapter 7

My Cuban Story

Ester Levis Levine

—You're Jewish?
—I thought you were Cuban.
—You can't be Cuban and Jewish!
—As a matter of fact, aren't you a bit too white to be Cuban?
—And your English doesn't have a Cuban accent. . . .

AND SO IT GOES. . . . I have spent my entire second life trying to explain my identity to myself and to others. In my "first life," I knew who I was and so did everybody else. Yes, I did indicate I am in another life. I am neither schizophrenic nor did I die on an operating table and get resuscitated. I did have a "first life," but it died the day I left Cuba. For many years, that first life faded away in my memory to the point where I almost began to doubt its existence; with the nostalgia that comes with the passing of time, I have been clearing out the cobwebs, trying to catch glimpses that had long been forgotten. . . .

These glimpses only live in my memory. Unlike others who have left their native country, I have not been able to return to Cuba and search for my roots; unlike most adults, I have few photographs to remind me of my youth. As a result, I can only rely on my vague memories of my long-lost country and my previous life. Sometimes, I hear stories of someone who knew my family or of those who have been able to return to Cuba. These stories usually serve to confirm my previous existence and renew my nostalgia. And so, it is with this nostalgia and this flood of indescribable emotions that I will try to tell my story before it is completely lost.

Before my "first life" ended one day in March 1961, I had a typical happy childhood surrounded by family, friends, and comfort. My country was Cuba and my religion was Judaism. At the time, it never occurred to me that I was "multicultural" or that I was not a typical Cuban girl who loved school, family, friends, and dancing. I took for granted the few stories I heard of my parents' past and never really thought about them. It is only now that I realize that they, too, had a "first life" and that they had a chance to perfect their survival instinct as immigrants twice in their lives. Although I know that the immigrant experience made us stronger, I hope that my children, first-generation Americans, will never have it.

A first-generation Cuban, I grew up feeling that my family had been Cuban for generations. Some years ago, a Cuban friend of mine, upon meeting my mother, asked me about her accent. "What accent?" I asked in surprise. Sure, I had grown up with stuffed grape leaves alongside *plátanos chatinos,* but our soul had never been anything but Cuban. My mother, like my father, was a Sephardi Jew from Turkey. She was so "Cuban" in my eyes that it had never occurred to me that she spoke Spanish with an accent. Of a Sephardi family, she had come to Cuba when she was around ten and had adopted Cuba as her homeland. Likewise, my father had come to Cuba during World War I and had become totally "Cubanized." Rarely did my parents speak of Turkey, for it didn't hold fond memories for them. Although Turkey had been home to Sephardi Jews for centuries, it had never been a welcoming place for them. A resolution to survive compelled my father and my uncle to leave Turkey at the start of World War I. The

Turks had been known to place young Jewish men in the front lines, and my father and uncle were not prepared to die. They set out on a ship for the United States, but at its long stopover in La Habana, they had so fallen in love with the friendly people, the beauty, the warmth, and the similarity of Spanish to Ladino that they had decided to make Cuba their home. As my father passed through the immigration line, he even gained the "Cubanized" last name of "Levis." Apparently, the immigration officer had not been able to read his papers clearly and had mistaken the name "Levy" for "Levis"; this was only the symbolic beginning of my father's attachment to Cuba. For my mother's family, it had also been a question of survival. Opportunities for jobs and business had not been rampant for the Jews, and so my maternal grandfather had set out for Cuba with dreams of financial success. When he had saved enough money, he sent for his family. And so, the Cuban roots for both my parents had been planted. . . .

During my childhood, my father told of selling wares on horseback in the Cuban countryside. In his travels, he got to know the Cuban people and loved them as his own. They did not treat him any differently because of his Jewish religion or his Turkish background. As his business grew, he moved to La Habana, the big city with greater opportunity and a large Jewish community, and replaced his horse with a car and his traveling wares with a store. His claim to notoriety and patriotic allegiance—I remember seeing the newspaper clippings and the scar on his arm—was a brush with death during the Machado dictatorship when a bomb exploded under a park bench where he had been sitting. This experience, along with his adoption of Cuban citizenship, only served to reaffirm his love for his new country.

My mother grew up in the countryside of Santa Clara, where her family quickly adapted to Cuban life. Because her parents were not familiar with the schools there, they decided to educate her at home. In Turkey, her education had been in French rather than Turkish; all the Jews there had sent their children to the Alliance Française schools rather than Turkish schools. At home in Santa Clara, my mother continued with her study of French and read everything she could get her hands on; this included Hebrew books, which was not a typical pastime for Jewish girls at the time. Again, the family was treated like everyone else by the neighbors; she used to tell me about the woman next door, who was an expert in herbal remedies and often took care of the family's medical needs. The lack of good memories of Turkey or of the language, coupled with the welcoming atmosphere of Cuba, quickly founded in my mother an allegiance for Cuba. The family was happy in Santa Clara, but when the children got older, they decided to move to La Habana so that they could meet suitable young men and women from the large Jewish community there.

Cuba was now the homeland for both my parents but it went hand in hand with the Jewish religion. Eventually, their paths crossed in the Sephardi circles of La Habana. In the city, the Sephardi community, *los turcos,* and the Ashkenazi community, *los polacos,* each had its own synagogues and social organizations. At the time, the only interpretation of "intermarriage" was the rare occurrence of a Sephardi-Ashkenazi union. After a courtship, my parents married in both a civil and a Jewish ceremony in 1900. And in the next ten years, their finances improved and their family grew with the birth of four daughters: Reina, Carolina, Rosa, and Esther.

Our childhood always focused on the present and never on the past. Never do I remember any nostalgia on my parents' part regarding their "first life" or any desire to visit their youthful homes in Turkey. Never do I remember Ladino spoken, except with some older relatives, whom I thought spoke with a "funny accent." As the youngest of the four girls, I was not rushed into maturity. Spoiled by my parents and my sisters, I was always the center of attention. I loved to dance, and often did with my sisters' friends. I also loved to talk, and this often got me into trouble at school in spite of my excellent grades.

Family was the focal point of our lives. We often went in big groups with aunts, uncles, and cousins on weekend outings and vacations. Camps didn't exist, so my only sleepovers were at the homes of cousins.

Our home was Jewish and all our social gatherings were with other Jews, not because we wished to exclude the non-Jews but because they were not in our social circles. Judaism was not pushed down our throats but was just an integral part of our existence. My father went to the synagogue regularly and when we all went, the girls and women were upstairs, where there was often more talking and laughing than praying. Jewish charity events and Israel celebrations often brought the entire Jewish community together. My sisters socialized through la Macabi, a Jewish teen organization, while I attended some events held through la Shomer, a Zionist youth organization. I don't remember any serious discussions or speeches, but it was always understood that my sisters and I would marry Jewish men—and, of course, these men would be Cuban as well. Never was there a question of our Judaism versus our Cubanness. The two went hand in hand and complemented each other.

So that my sister Rosa and I would be in the same school, I was sent to a non-sectarian private school for my first four years. Once she finished there, I went to the Centro Israelita de Cuba, a Hebrew day school where there was instruction in secular as well as Jewish subjects. Always a good student, I loved school with all its academic and social opportunities. And I would have graduated at the end of sixth grade had it not been for the catastrophic events brought on by the reign of Fidel Castro.

Completely sheltered as a child and as the baby of the family, I had never been made aware of much of the political situation in Cuba. A few vague images come to mind, but the child in me never paid attention. Numerous bombings during Batista's last year, crowds cheering Castro's troops in the streets of La Habana on January 1, 1959, plaza executions of Batista's men by Castro's people, and anti-Castro leaflets thrown from an airplane during my sister Reina's wedding reception in January 1961 are some of the glimpses appearing through the cobwebs of memory. I loved my happy and carefree life and I thought it would last forever. . . .

And then our life started to change slowly. . . . In January 1961, my sister Reina married a Jewish Cuban man who was an American citizen. It was a big and happy Jewish wedding! Amidst the dancing and celebrations, I never thought that in less than three months my carefree Cuban life would come to an end. . . . By marrying an American citizen who worked in the United States, my sister had made the choice to leave our life in Cuba. Of course, the thought of her leaving enveloped us with sadness. However, this heartache turned into turmoil, as it was discovered that no way could be found for Reina to follow her new husband to the United States; since there were no diplomatic relations between Cuba and the United States, it was impossible for her to obtain a visa. And so, as my parents began to investigate other ways for her to go to the United States, we knew our family life would be disrupted any second. . . .

Another change in my happy routine occurred slowly. It seemed that every day someone would be missing from my school. . . . Nobody talked about it, nobody could talk about it—but we all knew. Each disappearance meant another family leaving Cuba. We sensed that the political situation was changing, but school continued as usual; children, especially, like to pretend that nothing is different, and, like all children, I did the same. I knew my parents loved Cuba and I was sure that my parents' optimism for change would never permit them to leave.

And then, one day, my life as I knew it completely shattered. . . . Discussions had never been a big part of my family life, but one day my parents told Rosa and me that they needed to talk to us about something important. We were totally unprepared for what followed. They first explained that Fidel had announced a program to eradicate illiteracy—Cuban schoolchildren were going to be sent either to the mountains or to Russia to be indoctrinated in the Communist way. Because of this government announcement, Rosa and I, the youngest children, were at risk, and although my parents said they hated to send us away, they felt it was better to send us to the United States than to Fidel's destinations. They had to act with haste to arrange first our departure and then that of our other two sisters. Again, my parents had resorted to their inherent instinct for survival. HIAS, the Hebrew Immigration Aid Society, a charity organization I had never heard of, was making all the arrangements for our departure, which, unbeknown to us, would be our exile. "What?" Rosa and I said in unison. "Just the two of us?" "Don't worry," my father replied. "Fidel will be gone soon and you'll be back in Cuba in less than six months." The child in me believed my father—never did it occur to me that his prediction might not be correct. Of course, the idea did not quite register in my mind, except that we would be following in the footsteps of our disappearing friends. . . . Since I could not grasp the thought of two young girls leaving for the unknown without their parents, I focused on the adventure of it. Although I had been on vacations to the United States as a young child, I did not remember "el norte." From that moment on, our life proceeded on two fronts. On the outside, we continued going to school as if nothing had changed—we were not allowed to tell anyone of our impending trip, except for the English teacher, sworn to secrecy, who would be translating my school transcript into English. On the inside, we were all busy with preparations. As a young child, I tended to focus on these—the purchase of a special suitcase that could hold forty-four pounds and new clothes, a special trip to the dressmaker to have a winter coat made, photographs for the new passport, choosing my favorite doll and book for the trip, and so on. As the day for our departure drew closer, all we knew was that HIAS had arranged for us and other Jewish Cuban children to fly first to Curaçao, where we would stay for a while until the American visas were procured. I certainly had never heard of Curaçao, and its mystery added to my adventure fantasy.

The infamous day in March came, and, truthfully, I remember very little. I am sure we all cried, but I don't remember. I am sure we were all heartbroken, but I don't remember. I have asked my sister Rosa about that day; she, like me, seems to have also blocked it from her mind. By forgetting the details of that day, we seem to have dulled our senses to feel less pain—I guess that was the moment that my family's instinct for survival was transmitted to the next generation. As I navigate among the cobwebs in my memory, all I remember is boarding a plane with numerous Jewish children and hanging on to Rosa for dear life. The minute the plane took off, my "first life" came to an end. Since that day in March of 1961, I have only returned to Cuba in my memory.

When we landed in Curaçao, we were met by Jewish families who were ready to take care of us. Thinking of this fills me with pride at being part of a caring global Jewish community. When called by HIAS, the Jewish community of Curaçao had been more than willing to take in Jewish children for an indefinite period of time. They were kind and generous and treated us like their own. There was no language barrier because they spoke Spanish, and there was no culture barrier because they were Jewish. Rosa and I, together with another pair of siblings, went to a large and beautiful home owned by "Uncle Bill." Hospitable and caring, Uncle Bill treated us like very special children and spoiled us. He never gave us his last name; he was not interested in recognition or thanks. The community had parties and picnics for us; they took us to the beach, their homes, the synagogue. By treating us in such a special way, they made us feel as if we were just on a vacation without our parents. And I guess that we tried not to think about our circumstances and just tried to enjoy the days while we waited for our American visas to be ready. After a week of this idyllic interlude, my sister Reina arrived on the island. HIAS had been working on her case as well, and had obtained entry for her in Curaçao. Needless to say, Rosa and I were thrilled to see her. Now there were three of us together; however, this reunion only served to remind us of the family we had left behind. A week later, our papers arrived; Uncle Bill told us we could stay longer in Curaçao before going on to Miami, but we were anxious to see what awaited us in the United States.

As the plane landed in Miami, my "second life" began. Again, HIAS had arranged for Jewish families in Miami to take in Cuban children indefinitely—until their parents arrived or until they were able to return to Cuba. Again, I am appreciative of the generosity of the Jewish community as I think of the many sacrifices made by all of these people in order to help other Jews. The first U.S. foster family was kind, giving, and very warm; with three children of their own, they were willing to take us in for a time. In the excitement of another new adventure, I suddenly realized that they spoke no Spanish. My solution to this obstacle was to use my sister Rosa as my interpreter—I decided that I did not have to learn English because she would take care of all my needs. To this day, I cannot imagine how Rosa took on this responsibility—after all, she was only five years older than I and her knowledge of English was minimal. After struggling for two weeks in this role, Rosa gave up and announced that I had to learn to fend for myself. My first response was to feel betrayed by my sister; eventually, though, the survival instinct in me told me to start learning. As I wrestled with being unable to understand the family, the customs, the language, the food, I yearned for my parents and clung to my father's promise that this would only be for a short time.

A few weeks later, I went to sixth grade with the daughter in the family. I was introduced to her friends and to other children, but they all looked on me as an attraction. In Curaçao, my Cuban identity had not been in question; it had just been accepted and understood so that I never noticed being different. In Miami, however, my differentness could not have been more pronounced. Nobody questioned my Judaism; I don't even know whether they knew I was Jewish. What I did know was that I hated being an oddity, the girl with the "cute" accent. Once again, my response was silence. The girl who in the past had been notorious for talking too much at school now resolved not to speak at all. I decided that if I never spoke, nobody would know I was different and I could just blend in. What I didn't realize was that even in silence, my clothes, my pierced ears, and my constant state of confusion would give me away. And confused I was. . . . The only person who understood me at school was a Cuban girl in my classroom. She was my guide, my interpreter, and my savior. The only subject where I felt any connection was arithmetic. In the other classes, nobody knew that I had been one of the smartest students in my Cuban school. I was now probably known as the dumb Cuban girl, who thought a fire drill was a real fire, a lesson on Hungary was about people being hungry, or that a girl's "passing out" in the cafeteria was the same as "passing away and dying."

And dying I was. . . . Every day, I came home and cried. Every day, I thought of our return to Cuba or the arrival of my parents in Miami. Every day, I longed for the days when I had been the center of attention in my family. I remember receiving very hopeful letters from my parents. To this day, I don't know where they found the strength to sound so cheerful. Now I realize what hell they must have gone through—the child in me then, however, never gave it a thought. I don't remember whether we were able to receive phone calls from my parents—that is another void in my memory. I do remember hearing that Reina made it to Chicago, where her new husband lived. We also heard that the American consul in Curaçao was no longer giving out visas and that Cuban Jews were now being routed through Jamaica and some Latin American countries. The news came that my sister Carolina's papers had come through, and she had left by herself for Jamaica, where again Jewish families came to the rescue. Carolina, whom we always called Lina, had hoped to reach Providence, Rhode Island, where the family of her fiancé had settled. Whenever Rosa and I thought about our extended family, it seemed as if we would never be together again, a prediction that is true to this day.

School soon ended, and I, thanks to the mercy of my teacher, passed sixth grade. Since our foster family's home was crowded and there seemed to be no end to our exile, it was decided that we move on to another foster family. I remember very little about this second family, except that it was not a good match. They were forever busy and seemed to have no time or patience for us. Shortly after, we moved to the third and last foster Jewish family. With only one child, this family was anxious to treat us as their own. Caring and very loving, they had the time, energy, and love for two forlorn Cuban girls. It was at this time that I became more confident in my English and regained much of my early gregariousness. One summer day, we heard that Lina had made it to Providence and would be getting married shortly. It had only been seven months since Reina's big wedding, where we had all been together in Cuba. Lina's wedding would be small, with Reina as the only family representative. I cannot even imagine how my parents must have felt not to have been there; I can only remember Rosa's and my heartbreak at not having the money or resources to be there with our sisters on such a momentous day.

September came, and with it my entrance to junior high school. Although I felt a little smarter, my sense of "difference" was overpowering. More than anything, I wanted to forget that I was Cuban; more than anything, I was reminded of it every day by my peers' and teachers' behavior. And then, one October day, the news we had been awaiting for over six months finally came! My parents were in Jamaica and would soon be in the United States! Rosa and I danced with joy! Finally, we would be together with our parents! Finally, I could return to being the baby of the family and be loved and cared for by my parents! Finally, I could return to my old life, or so I thought. . . .

Our happiness was indescribable as we met our parents at the Miami airport! A few days later, we said goodbye to our foster family and set out for a new life in Providence with my sister Lina and her husband and his family. Again, we were overjoyed to see Lina and have almost all of the family together. In Providence, something very curious happened—we became "refugees," a totally incomprehensible concept for us. The Jewish Family and Children's Service helped set us up in an apartment and enrolled us in school. There were many people in the Jewish community who offered their help to the first Cubans to arrive in Providence. However, they had no understanding of our background. Because we had no money and were at their mercy, many thought of us as coming from the shtetel rather than from a modern, sophisticated, and comfortable community. Many questioned our Judaism. "How can you be Jewish if you don't speak Yiddish or eat gefilte fish or matzah balls?" they often asked. It seemed that we were forever explaining who we were and where we came from. And since Rosa and I spoke more English than did our parents, the interpreting and explaining was often left to us. We were on a constant yo-yo between the Cuban and Jewish sides of our identity.

Junior high seemed to be a friendlier place in Providence than in Miami. This was probably due to my happiness at being reunited with my parents, but I just thought of it as a more inviting place. Interestingly enough, my memories from that time on are very fresh in my mind—there seem to be no blank spaces. Without the trauma of separation from my parents, I allowed myself to feel everything without the dam that had held those feelings back for the previous seven months. I completely plunged into school life and enjoyed every minute. Whereas I had previously shunned the label of difference, I now relished the notoriety of being "the Cuban girl who was a quick and avid learner." In school, I was still the only Cuban, but I liked the fame and the attention. With my peers, it was a bit more difficult. When my friends came over, I wanted to pretend that my home was not different from theirs. I was not comfortable with their hearing me speak Spanish with my parents or seeing different customs in my home. In this setting, it was my Cuban identity that was in crisis and not my Jewish one. I continued to work harder on perfecting my language—I guess my goal at the time was to be so fluent in English that nobody would know I had a Cuban past. In retrospect, I think that this was due to my immaturity and my lack of connection to a Cuban community. Little did I know that the time would come when I would go out of my way to assert my Cuban identity.

My academic accomplishments in junior high school were great. I spent my three years there winning spelling bees, science project awards, even the class presidency. It seemed as if everything I did was a success. When it was time to go on to high school, I chose the high school known for its academics and its large Jewish community. Again, there was no Cuban or Latin American community there. In high school, my academic success continued while I developed ties with other Jewish teens through Jewish youth organizations. At that time, my Jewish self blossomed while my Cuban one lay in wait.

Only when I entered Brown University did the different facets of my identity come together. For the first time in my "second life," I had the opportunity to connect with Jewish *and* Latin American students. For the first time in my "second life," I was proud to explain my heritage and I relished my roots. I went out of my way to speak Spanish with other students, and felt comfortable wherever I went. The major in Hispanic studies gave me the chance to continue where my Cuban education had left off and to discover the beauty of Spanish and Spanish American literature. At the same time, I equally cherished Judaic studies courses. It was during my college career that I became a naturalized citizen. I was ready to accept my American citizenship without relinquishing my Cuban roots. It had taken almost ten years, but I had finally come to a full realization of my identity as a Cuban American Jewish woman.

The story of my life here has a happy ending. I married a Jewish North American man who appreciates the many facets of my identity. My two children speak Spanish fluently and are especially proud of their heritage. For the last twenty-eight years, I have been teaching and guiding young people. I especially seek out Latino students and encourage them to succeed, to perfect their Spanish, and to be proud of who they are; I want to spare them the identity crises I once experienced. Hopefully, I succeed.

My Judaism continues to be an integral part of my life. In the last few years, the American Jewish community has become more aware of Sephardi traditions. I happily go out of my way to explain my roots and educate those who don't understand the Jewish-Cuban mixture. I devour information about Cuba, from newspapers and magazines as well as from people who have recently visited the island. Numerous articles have been written lately about the revival of the Cuban Jewish community, so people have become more aware of the possibility of being Cuban and Jewish at the same time. When I first realized that Fidel was there to stay, I had neither the opportunity nor the desire to visit Cuba. Now that I am older, I have become very nostalgic. Just the thought of seeing Cuba again brings me to tears. I know that the Cuba I knew no longer exists. I wonder if the Cuba I remember ever existed. As I get older, I feel the need to try to find out. Although my life is now in the United States, I feel that until I return to Cuba once more, I will not feel whole again. Several times I have talked to my sisters about planning a trip to Cuba together. I believe that some day we will go. And that will be my next story.

Chapter 8

Crossing Creative and Cultural Barriers

Natania Remba Nurko

IN THE UNITED STATES, people tend to label ethnic groups. When I filled out my application for admission to UCLA, there was a blank that called for "Ethnic origin." What am I? I wondered. I tried to pick one by excluding the others. The options included Caucasian, African American, Hindu, Asian, Latino, and Other. I thought: "I'm not Caucasian. I'm not Anglo-American. I don't have any African, Hindu, or Asian ancestors. Maybe I fit under Latino." Finally I picked Other and specified "Jewish Mexican." But what does it mean to be Jewish Mexican?

Jewish Mexicans: The Rembas

My paternal grandfather, Zeide Baruch Isaac Remba, used to get up at dawn to help his father milk the cows. The family had nearly a hundred cows, as well as oxen and horses. They took the milk they collected to Germany to sell.

The Remba family lived in Sczuczyn, a town of twenty thousand inhabitants of whom five thousand were Jews, located some eighty kilometers from Warsaw. Speaking a mixture of Yiddish and Spanish, my *zeide* told us stories about his shtetel (village): "The young people were educated, very *gelernt,* very *yiddish,* but not all of them were *frum* [religious]. On Shabbat they'd only attend *shul* [synagogue] to pray as a favor to the *eltern* [the grandparents' generation], *zol zei nisht filn shlecht* [so they wouldn't feel bad]."

When World War I broke out in 1914, my *zeide* Baruch's younger brother, Hershl, was arrested for deserting from the Polish army. Hershl managed to escape from jail and fled to Jedvabne, a town west of Bialstok near Sczuczyn, where he had relatives. He hid there in a basement for a few days, then he managed to flee to Köenigsberg, Germany, and eventually to Mexico. Since my *zeide* Baruch didn't wish to be sent to the front "as cannon fodder" either, he found some local healers and got them to perforate his eardrum. It was done without anesthetic. Because he was deaf, he didn't have to go to the battle-front. If my grandfather hadn't done that, we wouldn't be here.

At the end of the war, Polish towns tried to find ways to rebuild themselves economically. My paternal grandmother, *bobe* Rojl Grondowski, traveled to Szczuczn with a theatrical group that was trying to raise funds to reconstruct their town, Jedwabne. My *bobe* had a very good voice. She was assigned the lead role as Shulamis. My *zeide* was one of the organizers of the theater, and he used to tell me: "It was her voice that won me over. She was staring at me, and I stared back at her." Apparently, my *zeide*'s mother had a look at her, too: "Rojl vel zain dain kaleh, keiner nisht" (Rojl will be your bride, no one else), she said. My *zeide* never again wanted to hear about *shidduchin* (arranged marriage): "Geit gezunthereit, ich hob shoin a kaleh" (Go in good health, but I already have a fiancée). On December 31, 1919, my grandparents celebrated their *tnoim* (engagement) and they were married in Jedvabne, where Rebeca and Sarah, my father's older sisters, were born.

After World War I, the Poles used any excuse to have a pogrom, to get rid of the Jews. My *zeide,* like many Jews, decided to seek a better future in Amerike. By the mid twenties, the Immigration Quota Law restricted the number of immigrants who could enter the U.S. My *zeide* decided to follow his brother Hershl to Mexico with the idea of later entering the U.S. by land. He departed in 1924, leaving his wife and two daughters, and took the train from Warsaw to a French port where his month-long sea voyage began. According to my *zeide,* people had to be very determined: "They traveled all crowded together, without any comforts . . . there were people who couldn't endure the crossing and who died. They threw the corpses overboard to avoid epidemics." Their first port of call was in Cuba, and the second was Veracruz: "We couldn't disembark because of the Mexican Revolution, so the ship went on to Tampico. I stayed in a hotel until the local fighting was over, and then I got on a train for Saltillo, but in San Luis Potosí, the revolutionaries came on board." My *zeide* hid under the train until the shooting was over. "The revolutionaries came, and they searched our suitcases and bags. They took fifty dollars from me. But they never found what I'd hidden in the lining of the suitcase, where I'd put another bag, where I kept my *tefillin,* my *tallis,* and my *mahzor.*" Robberies were not the most difficult aspect of the revolution. My *zeide* was made to put on a cartridge belt and pistols, mounted on a white horse, and ordered to fight for the guerrillas like Pancho Villa!

As the revolution tapered off, my *zeide* went on to Saltillo, where his brother was. But when they met, his brother didn't recognize him and didn't welcome him. So my *zeide* decided to go on to Mexico City. "There I looked for acquaintances, fellow countrymen, and I began to work as a peddler, selling neckties, stockings, and handkerchiefs along the Calle de Cuba, where I lived. *Spanish, hob nisht ghekent ein finguer* (I didn't know even a finger of Spanish). I got along with a Yiddish-Spanish dictionary. When we were selling, we didn't say '*A cuánto?*'; we said '*A cwánto?*'"

From being a peddler, my *zeide* went to being an interstate religious trader. He got to know a fellow countryman who sold him *getches* (religious pictures of saints). His job was to transport this merchandise from Mexico City to Tlaxiaco, Oaxaca. He set it up with some country people and rented a hundred donkeys, at five dollars a donkey, including the driver. Along the road, he traded pictures of saints for the best Oaxacan coffee. He never accepted money, and that way he never got robbed. In his black clothing, with his religious merchandise and his Polish accent, the country people thought he was a Catholic missionary: "Un galaj, un heiliker." When he got to know the farmers well and told them he was a Jew, they'd say, "That's not possible! Jews have horns!"

It took my *zeide* four years to save up the money to bring my *bobe* Rojl and their two daughters to Mexico in 1928. I don't think my *bobe* had any idea how much my *zeide* Baruch had changed during their separation: he went from being a pale Pancho Villa without a mustache to being a dealer in Christian images and a coffee merchant near Popocatepetl. My *zeide* left behind his identity as *Tevye der milchiker* (Teviah, the milkman) herding cows in the winter forest of Poland, and had established himself in the tropical plains of the Valley of Mexico herding donkeys through the Oaxacan mountains like Benito Juárez. It may not have been sheer coincidence that he changed his name from Baruch to Benito.

The Nurkos

Similar lives in times of suffering found the same destiny. Both my maternal grandfather, Zeide Eliezer (Lázaro) Nurko, and my maternal grandmother, Bobe Jiene Gardinski, escaped from the anti-Semitism and poverty that afflicted them in the twenties in Lithuania. My *zeide* Eliezer escaped from jail, where he was being punished for refusing to serve in the Lithuanian army, and left Ukmerke, the town where he had been born. My *bobe* Jiene, who had been orphaned when she was just eleven years old, fled from her poverty, leaving her sister Sheinke and her brothers Shaike and Nathán in Raseiniaí. In their late adolescence, both from towns some one hundred kilometers from Kovno, my grandparents left for the New World without any relatives or material possessions. Neither could have imagined that in their new land they would found a family of nearly one hundred and a major textile company, Lanur (LA-zaro NUR-ko).

In Mexico City, my *bobe* had the good fortune to be adopted by her *shifshwester* (ship sister), who offered her lodging and work as a seamstress. My *zeide* used to work in a textile factory for thirty-six hours straight with only eight hours off between shifts. Their hard work enabled them to bring over a few of their relatives from Lithuania, but most of their families remained behind and 99 percent of them died in Auschwitz.

Little is known about the struggles of my *zeide* Luis (Lázaro) and my *bobe* Jiene; according to my mother, "they didn't like to talk much. Their first priority was to make money for their children. There wasn't much opportunity to talk to them. Maybe they wanted to forget the past, or reality had been so horrifying that they didn't want us to have to share that past . . . or they felt remorse that they didn't do enough, and that their families perished while they survived." What was always apparent was that both of them, having lost their parents in the old world, became parental figures for the rest of the family in Mexico—Lázaro always offering moral support, Jiene opening her house as a gathering place.

As the great matriarch she was, my *bobe* Jiene always felt a responsibility to observe the Jewish religion and preserve traditions in her home. She kept kosher, with the help of the servant Marciana, who, at age thirteen, had left her town of Zapotlán de Juárez in Hidalgo and begun to work for my *bobe*. Marciana was born on St. Marciano's day, and we called her Marcianita, so it wouldn't sound as though she came from another planet. What an irony, since Marcianita did come from a different background: her heritage was pure Aztec. She spent forty-three years with us, and became one of the dearest of our family members.

Marcianita had indigenous features and noble attitudes, but she was well acquainted with the rules of *kashrut* and the names of Yiddish dishes: "It's time to go to the *kich* and heat up the *gefilte fish*. Get out the *mandelachs* for the broth!" Marcianita had a gift for crossing back and forth across cultural barriers. She'd supply Aurelia Pineda, the second servant, with important information, translating Yiddish into Spanish. She'd tell her that the fish "in balls" was for the first course, and that the bread cubes were for the broth. She taught her the key words for each religious holiday: *A gut shabes!* (Happy Sabbath!), *A gut yor!* (Happy New Year!), *shikor* (drunk). Neither my mother nor I learned to cook as well as Marcianita, and she was the one who best understood the secrets of *kashrut* that my *bobe* brought with her from Europe.

Besides keeping kosher, my *bobe* Jiene felt it was essential to light the Shabbat candles in their antique candelabras, to go to *shul* during the *yom-tovim,* and to serve tea in her samovar. Jiene's metamorphosis was legendary: from a Lithuanian child, an orphan, living in poverty, she became a strong woman, middle class, professional, surrounded by relatives and friends. Six days a week she supervised employees at the Lanur factory; on the seventh, she did not rest, but rather derived great satisfaction from cooking her children's favorite food: "Enchilatkes!" And if her children did not eat well, up to her standards as a typical Jewish mother, she'd urge them: "Apúratele! Cómetele!" ("Hurry up! Eat it up!").

Natania Remba Nurko

In Mexico, when I tell people my name is Natania, they usually answer "What a pretty name, Natalia!" "No," I say to them, "I'm Natania, with an *n*." In Israel, my name is that of a city, Natanya. I was named Natania in memory of my uncle, who died in Auschwitz.

Natania is the feminine of Nathan. In Hebrew, *natan* means "gave" and *-ia* means "God." Gift of God. My paternal last name, Remba, is an acronym in Hebrew of *rabot mahshavot belev ha-ish* (many are the thoughts in the heart of man). We are descended from the rabbi Meire B'al Hannes, who signed his writings "Remba." It is uncertain but probable that my maternal surname, Nurko, comes from the Lithuanian town Nurkonas or from *nur*-Kovno (near Kovno).

Gefilte Fish Veracruz Style

Since childhood I've eaten gefilte fish Veracruz style. At home it wasn't seasoned too highly. It had olives, onion, chile poblano, and tomato sauce in it. Since childhood, I've felt that I am a *Mexicana de hueso colorado* (Mexican with red bones). I was born in the English hospital in Mexico City in the thirties, my first words were in Spanish, and I loved fresh hot tortillas. But, although I felt completely Mexican, my white skin and blue eyes betrayed me. I remember that when I was three years old, once when Marcianita took me with her to market, the women vendors would call out "Marciantita, what will you give me for the mangos?" "Look how ripe they are!" "How much for the little blue-eyed white girl?" My skin and eyes were constant reminders that I was different from the indigenous majority of Mexicans.

Although I grew up steeped in Mexican culture, because of my Polish and Lithuanian ancestors, I received the typical education of the Ashkenazi Jew. I went to the Colegio Israelita de México, Yiddishe Shule in Meksike, where Yiddish was taught with the hope of maintaining ties with the culture of our European roots, and the Hebrew language with the belief that it would connect us to our Biblical past. I learned arithmetic and science and history. I read the Tanah and Sholem Aleichem. I sang "Rodzhinken mit Mandlen" and I danced to "Hava Nagila."

I'm always asked the question: Are you Jewish or Mexican? The answer is not simple. To be Jewish and Mexican is not something mutually exclusive, since it is possible to form ties with both cultures.

Sometimes I answer: "I am a Mexican citizen of Jewish religion." But being Jewish Mexican is more complicated than a label or classification; it implies a dual identity. Both religion and citizenship form part of my identity. Being Jewish Mexican is a cultural hybrid, as rich as the experience of eating gefilte fish Veracruz style.

"Hollywood Style" Religion

I remember my first day in kindergarten, when the *lererke* (teacher) Elke had us repeat the days of the week in Yiddish: *zuntik, montik, dinstik, mitvoch, donershtik, fraitik, un shabes.* At three years of age, I already had a bifocal view of the world. I learned to live with two calendars—the solar and the lunar—and to celebrate two New Years— the 1900s and the 5000s. Although the school was secular, we studied the history and culture of the Jewish people; we celebrated both national and Jewish holidays.

At home we had a philosophy of life similar to the school's. We didn't keep kosher, nor did we observe Shabbat, but we went to *shul* on Rosh Hashanah, we fasted on Yom Kippur, we went to millions of bar mitzvahs, and, although we didn't think of ourselves as traditional, we were members of the orthodox Kehilá Nidje Israel.

In September of 1984, my family moved to Los Angeles, California. On our first Yom Kippur, we experienced culture shock: we found ourselves attending a Masonic temple rather than a synagogue. Rather than focusing on the rolls of the Torah or on *aron ha-kodesh,* the hall for prayer was a theater-like auditorium with murals depicting the Temple of Solomon. Instead of being on the second floor, women sat beside their husbands wearing *tales* and *yarmulkes;* and the *hazan* (liturgical cantor) did not sing "Kol Nidrei," but instead did an interpretation of it on the cello. It seemed to be a concert rather than prayers! In Hollywood, I learned that the Ashkenazi liturgy of Californians is very different from the Mexican Ashkenazi liturgy.

Yiddish with a Mexican Accent

I now live in Newton, Massachusetts, a city where English is usually heard. But when I travel from Massachusetts to California to visit my family, there is no need to speak English. On every side one hears a cocktail of dialects and accents: Mexican, Salvadorean, Guatemalan, Colombian and Venezuelan. When I take my car to be washed, I am asked "Where did you learn how to speak such good Spanish?" "I'm Mexican," I answer, and I see their skeptical reaction. I suppose they think that I am fooling them, since they can see that I look like a *gringa*. When I go shopping in Beverly Hills, I'm always asked, "Are you Russian? Because of your accent." When I reveal my Mexican identity, they don't believe me. They can't believe that Mexico has any light-skinned people. To speak Hebrew or Yiddish with a Mexican accent is odd. Once when I was visiting Israel, people in the street asked me in Hebrew, *"Aht drom amerikait, ken?"* (You're South American, right?) "No, I'm not South American. I'm from Mexico." "Lama aht lo ba-a lagur ba-aretz? Ze habait shelah" (Why don't you come live in Israel? This is where you belong [lit., it's your home]). And so I spend my life, everywhere I go—in taxis, restaurants, the post office, the grocery store—answering questions and explaining my accent, my hair, my eyes, and my complexion.

In the Artistic Sphere

In 1954, my father, Yehuda Luis Remba, graduated with a degree in mechanical engineering from the Escuela Superior de Ingeniería Mecánica y Eléctrica and began to work as a commercial printer with his father at the Santo Domingo Press. My *zeide* Benito had bought the Santo Domingo Press, complete with its Catholic saint name. Located on the Santo Domingo Plaza, the press was, ironically, just across the street from the building where the Inquisition had carried out its Autos de Fe and executed heretics.

In 1968, at the suggestion of the artist Pablo O'Higgins, my father enlarged his workshop and began to print graphic art with Mexican artists like Leonora Carrington, Gunther Gerzso, Alfredo Zalce, Carlos Merida, and Fanny Rabel. During the day, the press produced tax forms, wedding invitations, or calling cards, and at night it printed xilographs, lithographs, and seriegraphs. Eventually, my father worked full time making artistic prints. In 1973, he became acquainted with Rufino Tamayo, who challenged him to develop a graphic technique with relief. After experimenting in his workshop, my father received his first patent for developing a technique which combined a mixture of printing processes, hence its name: mixography. Since then my father has produced numerous limited editions, as well as sculptures, with a wide range of international artists, including Rufino Tamayo, Francisco Toledo, Mathías Goeritz, Henry Moore, Helen Frankenthaler, and Larry Rivers. In 1974, my father opened an art gallery, the Galería del Círculo, in the Zona Rosa, a prosperous area in downtown Mexico City. My mother, Leye or Lea Nurko de Remba, gave up her profession as a *lererke* of Yiddish in order to begin selling art, and the gallery became prominent.

Due to the context in which I grew up, since I was small I've participated in exhibit openings, visited artists' studios, announced art events in film shorts, and even on one occasion met Xóchitl, the queen of the transvestite community in Mexico City. My first awareness of myself as a participant in the world of art was when my father printed a collection of reproductions of pictures by Pablo O'Higgins, a North American artist who came to Mexico in the 1920s. On Teachers' Day, everyone else came to school with the usual gifts: perfume, soap, books, but I brought an album of artistic reproductions of O'Higgins' landscapes, which was my first step into the world of art and my first awareness that I was different.

Another early sign of my aesthetic inclinations came when I was participating in the Girl Scouts, the Guías Israelitas de México. "Be prepared" was the basic tenet of the Guías. To rise in rank, you had to earn merit badges. The majority of my companions chose camping survival skills to work on: putting up tents, lighting campfires, cooking without utensils, tying lots of different knots. I was the only one who chose to work on something totally impractical in the world of scouting: plastic arts. I didn't want to think about survival; I preferred imagination.

By the sixties, as I found out more about artistic spheres and the creative world, I joined a microcosm. As a Jew in Mexico, I was a minority. As a Jew and an artist, I was a minority within a minority. Except for a prominent Jewish subgroup of collectors, galleries, and art historians, it was not common in Jewish circles to enter the world of Mexican artists. According to my father, the Jew lived in his own world: "I grew up in a ghetto, and moving into the art world was a double shock." Crossing the barrier to that foreign world seemed momentous to my parents.

The ambiguity my parents felt was rooted in the nineteen thirties. The Mexican art world was dominated by communist tendencies, which did not concord with the commercial stereotype of the entrepreneurial Jew. For years, the Workshop of Popular Graphics held the leading position in graphic arts in Mexico and championed proletarian causes, unions, and leftist ideology. In contrast, my father, who did not grow up in the Jewish left of the late nineteen sixties, now found himself forced by circumstances to break with social and political limitations, and he established the Workshop of Mexican Graphics. My father's workshop attracted those artists who were interested in divorcing art from communist ideology and following a line of abstract or apolitical art. During the next fifteen years, my parents worked with Mexican artists, spreading the influence of contemporary Mexican art.

For my part, having been exposed to the Mexican artistic circle helped me to widen my visual field in order to see beyond my own community.

My Name Is Not Asher Lev

I was the only student of my generation at the Yiddishe Shule who chose an exotic career: art restoration. The Yiddishe Shule was located in the ex-convent in Churubusco. The conventional Jewish community considered me a "Bohemian," and my classmates thought my brand of Jewishness "interesting." Perhaps their perceptions had some truth to them—what kind of Jew would spend four years in an ex-convent studying Christian art and restoring old altarpieces depicting Jesus Christ?

As a restorer of Mexican art, one becomes steeped in the history of colonial art in which Christian themes predominate: paintings of the Virgin of Guadalupe surrounded by angels, the twelve apostles and Christ at the Last Supper. When I took a course on colonial iconography, I felt a great ambivalence, since my sense of being Jewish distanced me from Catholic art. During this era, I often thought of the main character in Chaim Potok's novel *My Name Is Asher Lev.* In this novel, Asher, an Orthodox Jew, constantly struggled against artistic instincts that drove him to paint a monumental oil painting of his mother on a crucifix. In my case, I never imagined that the process of exploring the symbols of Christian art would lead me to define my identity as a Jew more strongly. A greater understanding of Christian art allowed me to clarify what I am *not.*

On one occasion, when one of my cousins from Israel came to visit us in Mexico, I took her to visit the pyramids of Teotihuacán and the Sanctuary of Saint Mary in the church of Tonanzintla. I wanted to show her a Tequitqui mural I restored, in an artistic style that fuses pre-Columbian and Spanish iconography. Astounded, she said to me, "We Orthodox Jews cannot enter other temples!" I was puzzled, and I wondered, "How can it be all right for her to go see the Teotihuacán pyramids of the sun and the moon, but wrong for her to visit the Sanctuary of Saint Mary?" Like my cousin, the dichotomy I felt while restoring a pre-Columbian mural was not as severe as the one I felt when restoring a Christian painting, perhaps because Jews never had an antagonistic relationship with pre-Columbian cultures. In contrast, Jewish-Catholic relations have a history of persecution, including the Crusades and the Inquisition. Besides, the culture of the pyramid and the culture of the book have a parallel history of survival through millennia.

Jewish Aztec Princess

In a way, we fulfilled my *zeide* Benito's dream in 1984 when we immigrated to Amerike. From the ex-convent in Churubusco, I transferred to the University of California at Los Angeles (UCLA, sometimes nicknamed Jew-CLA). Compared with the ex-convent, I felt at home at UCLA, since there were no classes on Yom Kippur. "I belong here," I thought.

During my first weeks at the university, I was told that there was a structured system for socializing: clubs for women students. I was told there were even Jewish sororities, but that before being officially accepted I had to pass certain tests. The requirements included sexy clothing, stockings and high heels (no pants), and a triple layer of makeup, so I could look like a real JAP (Jewish American Princess). But I looked more like a JAMP (Jewish American Mexican Princess) or JAP (Jewish Aztec Princess), which is what Mexican Jews living in the U.S. were called. During rush, I kept smiling my Colgate smile. Nevertheless, I was not accepted. I thought that it was because I wasn't JAPy enough, but later I found out that they rejected me because I was Mexican. So outside Mexico, that identity as a Mexican intensified. In the U.S., where I no longer had to be defensive about my Jewishness, my Mexicanness became the issue.

The Voice of the Mexican in Diaspora

A way to keep up my ties to Mexico was to continue to study Mexican art. While I was working on a Master's degree at Harvard in 1990, I took part in a study of community art centers in needy areas. These organizations used art as a way to develop the social, economic, and cultural infrastructure of the poor communities. Because of my Mexican background, it was natural for me to focus on the study of the value of art in Mexican communities in the U.S.

"Art is the voice of the Mexican community in the U.S.," the executive directors repeated over and over again in my interviews with them. They constantly stressed that visual images gave Mexican Americans a way to express cultural pride in their monumental pre-Columbian past and their rich Mexican present. I discovered that following the steps of the three great muralists—José Clemente Orozco, Diego Rivera, and David Alfaro Siquieros—the Mexican American community had launched a growing mural movement in California. Through this artistic movement, the Mexican community in the U.S. had not only defined and redefined its bicultural identity, but also vigorously expressed its voice through the invention of its own aesthetic: Chicano iconography.

Jewish Iconography

In contrast with their place in Mexican history, the plastic arts have not had a vigorous voice in the history of the Hebrew people. Jews have distinguished themselves as the "people of the book" and producers of texts: the Torah, the Talmud, the stories of the Chelmers, and the novels of Isaac Bashevis Singer. Since antiquity, Jewish visual art has been defined by ceremonial or religious art objects and by domestic artifacts, which were exhibited only in Jewish homes or in museums of Jewish history. In terms of painting, the Jewish artist generally depicted themes from the Bible, the Diaspora, Zion, and the Holocaust.

Nowadays, artists of the plastic arts who work with Jewish topics are eager to transcend the Jewish cultural sphere. Even now, many of these artists are classified by museums as "artesans of Judaica," and these so-called artesans struggle to transcend the traditional art-world dichotomy between "craft" and "high art." Although there has been progress, no clearly defined Jewish artistic movement yet exists which is anything similar to the Chicano artistic movement. Plastic artists who might be labeled as "Jewish artists" are not categorized as such in collections in the most prominent contemporary art museums of the world, and thus lack collective international recognition. Impressionism, Fauvism, and Cubism exist, but there is no Jewish art labeled with an –ism. There are individual exceptions, respected on the international level by the artistic community, like the Jewish Russian artist Marc Chagall, who, in Paris, painted the world of his childhood in his shtetel, Vitebsk; or the Jewish American sculptor George Segal, who has many outstanding individual works such as *The Holocaust* (1983). With the birth of the state of Israel, many Jews have begun to express their Jewish identity more openly, stimulating Jewish artists to develop a Jewish visual language. This has contributed to an increased Jewish presence in the world of the fine arts, but it is still unclear whether it will result in a movement of Jewish art defined as such.

There is a historical and religious reason why there has not been a Jewish presence in the world of the plastic arts. The second commandment of the Hebrew Bible orders: "Thou shalt not make unto thee any graven image, or any likeness of any thing that is in heaven above, or that is in the earth beneath, or that is in the water under the earth." [Exodus 20:4] This paragraph prohibits the worship of God in any material form. From the beginning, Judaism taught that God is a spirit and made it an unforgivable sin to worship God in any external form that human hands could create, thus discouraging the free development of the plastic arts in ancient Israel. In effect, the Jewish religion has as a precedent the destruction of the visual image. The Hebrew Bible says that the first revelation of God to Abraham of Ur Cassdim was to instruct him to destroy the *getches* (idols) of his father Teraj. When the father saw that his son had destroyed the idols he worshipped, he asked him: "Who did this?" Abraham answered that the large idol had broken all the small ones. Teraj insisted: "Don't lie!

Don't you see that these idols don't speak, don't walk, don't think!"
And Abraham answered him: "Then if they cannot protect you, why
do you pray to them to protect you?" The Jewish God revealed himself in voice, not in visual image.

For years it was—and perhaps for many Jewish artists it still is—an
antithesis to function as a creative being and free thinker and simultaneously live regulated by religion. I remember that when I lived in
Mexico, I had a boyfriend who was a semi-Orthodox Jew. The central conflict in our relationship was how to decorate a Jewish home,
whether it could include figurative pictures or not. He preferred not
to have images on the walls of the house. I, having grown up surrounded by mixographic images, yearned to live amidst prints by
Tamayo, Toledo, and Rómulo. My boyfriend constantly insisted:
"Why can't you just have a still life, or get a flower vase?"

To Belong or Not to the World of Art

How then can the Jew justify the creation and appreciation of the plastic arts if religion prohibits the creation or appreciation of the material
image? Fortunately, this question did not dominate my parents' minds
during the eighties and nineties. Judaism had brought itself up to date
in the U. S., and, as a result, Jews had infiltrated the intellectual fields.
According to my mother, "One did not feel any immediate barrier in
the United States, since it's such a melting pot, with all cultures and religions. One did not feel out of place as a Jew. There were many Jewish
artists, collectors, and art dealers who were very involved in the art
world."

Having found a niche in the world of American art, my parents and
I had the privilege on one occasion of visiting the artist George Segal in
New Jersey. While we ate, he talked to us about how, a few years before, he had begun a correspondence with a German student. After
finishing his doctoral dissertation on Segal's art, the student came to

visit Segal at his house. When they went out for a walk, Segal showed him a chicken coop and told the student: "This is my studio; I inherited it from my father." The two of them walked though the hen house discussing each "environment," as Segal liked to call his sculptures, which included a man on the beach, acrobats in a circus, construction workers, and a breadline during the Depression. In the last room they came to *The Holocaust* (1983), one of the most outstanding contemporary art works of the twentieth century on this topic. Human beings of white plaster pay tribute to the six million victims who died in concentration camps. The bodies, in human dimensions, thin, indefinite, as if disappearing from the mortal world, do not seem earthly but rather tattered spirits who with their weak gazes cross the barbed wire seeking freedom.

The first words the student spoke to Segal were: "For years, I've tried to get my father to tell me what he did during the Hitler era. My father has never wanted to answer me." The student looked at Segal and asked him: "I wonder, what do you think of us Germans?" The visit ended. They said goodbye. Segal never heard from the student again. With this example, I became aware that it was possible to present Jewish topics in a universal context. Like Segal, my parents found the universality they sought in the U. S. American democracy, freedom of expression, Protestant openmindedness, ethnic interactions, and the aesthetic diversity of immigrants helped my parents to cross creative and cultural barriers more easily.

Crossing Creative and Cultural Barriers

I am now in the process of applying to become a U.S. citizen. When this happens, I will no longer be able to refer to myself as a Mexican citizen. Nor will I any longer be able to define myself as Jewish Mexican when I fill out forms. What category should I choose? Perhaps Jewish Mexican American or Jewish Chicana? I'll always belong in the Other category: Jew in Catholic Mexico, bohemian at a conservative *shul,* mainstream in the exotic world of art, a Mexican in the Boston suburbs, and a South American *galutit* in Israel. Separating myself as "Other" means for me that I'm transcending one sphere, entering another, transcending again, and going on until I define who I am. We also define ourselves by who we are not, acquiring perspective from the outside, participating from within.

My life is a mosaic made of a multiplicity of different experiences that reflect the history of a triple migration: enduring fear and suffering in an anti-Semitic Poland, a readaptation to a Catholic Mexico, and integration into a democratic America. The images that intermix represent Baruch the Polish farmer, Rojl the singing "Shulamis," Lázaro the Lithuanian-Mexican textile manufacturer, Jiene the typical *yiddishe mame,* Luis the promoter of Mexican art, Lea the Los Angeles art dealer, and the writer of the present mosaic text in Massachusetts. During our journeys we have been a family that has brought along with it from Poland to Mexico the *mahzor,* the *tallis,* and the *tefillin;* and from Mexico to the United States, the *zarape,* the *mole,* and the *mariachi.* I learned from my grandparents and parents that crossing over cultural and creative barriers is what makes us different and what makes us who we are.

Chapter 9

Growing up Jewish in Colombia

Cecilia Rosenblum

MY PARENTS WERE JEWISH, born in Siedlce, Poland. In 1923, my father was drafted into the Polish army. He swore that if he managed to survive the torment inflicted upon him by his fellow soldiers, he would leave the country. At that time, immigration to the United States was closed and, without the immediacy of the Nazi threat, his family thought that it was absolute madness to leave. Where would he go? What would he do? His options were limited—perhaps Central or South America.

He married my mother and departed from Poland without any fixed destination, against everybody's advice. The plan was to get settled and then send for my mother. His first stop was Mexico, where he knew some people from his hometown. After a short stay, he decided that it was not the right place for him. He continued on to Cuba, then Panama, and then northern Colombia, where he was overwhelmed by the tropical weather, the rainforest environment, the foreignness of it all. When he arrived in Bogotá, high up in the mountains, with its cool weather, its green surroundings, its people dressed elegantly in hats and gloves, and its glass-paned windows, he knew it was the place for him! A few Jews had already settled in Bogotá, and together they laid the foundations for what was to be the "Jewish community" there. After working for a year, doing any odd job he could, but mostly peddling, he saved enough money to send for my mother and his baby daughter, born while he was away.

For my mother, the journey was an ordeal: more than three weeks at sea, constantly nauseous, homesick, afraid, taking care of a baby, alone, heartbroken. She had left behind her entire family—parents, five siblings, nephews and nieces—all she knew, all that was familiar to her. Her greatest fear was that she might not see her family again. She never did. They all perished in the Holocaust. My father never saw his family, either. They were also all killed in the Holocaust.

My parents were very well received in Colombia, and, in spite of their longing for their families, they fell in love with their new country. From the very start my parents realized how free they were to do as they pleased, what a blessing it was not to be persecuted. As the political situation got worse in Europe, they appreciated more and more what they had. They swore they would never leave Colombia, not even on vacation, a promise they kept until two of their four daughters decided to come and live in the United States, many years later.

I was born and raised in Bogotá in the fifties, the fourth daughter in a middle-class family, living in a small and close Jewish environment. My father became fairly prosperous working in the construction industry, designing and building commercial buildings. Our social and religious life revolved entirely around the Jewish community. The Jewish holidays and rituals were carefully observed. We wouldn't think of missing a Shabbat meal—Friday nights we ate together, regardless of what was going on around us. The language at home was Yiddish, which my parents spoke exclusively to each other and to the children. The language around us was Spanish. It was a happy household, in spite of the horrors of the Holocaust. It puzzles me how, even though they must have known, at least partly, what was going on in Europe, they managed not to inflict their sorrow on us. Even years later, when we were all grown-ups, the topic was never discussed.

When the time came for me to go to school, I followed in the footsteps of my sisters—I went to the Lyçée Francais, considered to be the best school in the city at that time. There, I was immersed in a third language, in a third culture. School was all in French, and I had never heard a word of French before. I assumed that in school people talked in this strange language, and that it was up to me to learn it as quickly and as well as possible. It was in this French environment, among Catholic schoolmates whose mother tongue was Spanish, in a Jewish home where Yiddish was spoken, that I grew up.

I can say unabashedly that, in all my years at school, in fact, during my entire life in Colombia, I never experienced anti-Semitism. It was just the opposite; it was "pro-Semitism," if I may invent such a word. We Jews were a mild curiosity to Colombians; we were "whiter" than they were, we were generally the smartest kids in school, and we caught on to French very quickly—after all, most of us grew up already hearing several languages. Our French teachers identified with us more than with the Colombian kids, they liked the fact that we were such good students, that we were validating what they were trying to do. Our schoolmates looked up to us. It was "chic" to be Jewish, to have Jewish names—Sara, Raquel, Lea, Esther, Naomi. I was mortified trying to cope with my "non-Jewish" name—Cecilia! Why couldn't my parents have given me a proper Jewish name like most of my friends'? I thought to myself.

At home, we followed the Jewish tradition. We had a kosher home, our life revolved around the Jewish community, we had Jewish friends exclusively, a Jewish social life, a Jewish support network. In a small Jewish community such as ours, virtually everyone knew who was Jewish, and everyone knew if you were socializing with a non-Jew. This was a major taboo, one of the major paradoxes in my life. I could not understand how on the one hand we could praise and laud Colombia the way we did, and on the other hand go to school, work, etc. among Catholics, but not be allowed to socialize with them. We were never allowed to have Catholic friends in our house! And we were not the only ones.

All the other Jewish families we knew behaved the same way. The few
Jewish families that dared brake this taboo were considered "extrem-
ist," too liberal, maybe even communists! The fear was that their children would end up marrying a non-Jew. Ironically, a fair number of
Lebanese Christians attended the French school. They were "foreign"
like us. We had a lot in common. We could befriend them!

When I finished my schooling and entered the working world, my
trilingualism opened a lot of doors for me. I got a wonderful job with
a world-renowned ophthalmologist, translating the articles he wrote
into English and French, interpreting for foreign doctors while he was
operating, editing a magazine he published monthly. My involvement
with work grew; I met wonderful, interesting people, and yet, grown
up as I was, I still knew that I could only befriend non-Jews up to a
certain point. I still could not bring them home or go to their homes.
I certainly could not dare imagine falling in love with a non-Jew. My
world was opening up, my non-Jewish friends became more interesting, and I became very conflicted. How could I go on? How could I
pursue these friendships? How could we constantly blame the world
for discriminating against Jews and then behave the same way?
Weren't *we* discriminating against the very people who had welcomed us, helped us, given my parents the freedom to be what they
wanted to be, to prosper, to live in a non-discriminating environment? When I started to question my parents' values, the Jewish community's values, my parents became very concerned. Would I go so
far as to marry a non-Jew? Some of their friends' children had, and the
families mourned them as if they were dead. Could I do this to my
parents? Would I be able to live with my conscience if I did?

My parents were passionate about honesty and integrity. These
were the values that were discussed at the dinner table. How then
could they denounce anything that was not Jewish as being not as
good as what was Jewish? How could they tolerate racial injustice,
human inequality? Wasn't this a form of racism, of bigotry? My very
essence, my absolute inability to understand discriminating against

other people, the concept of superiority on the basis of race or any other reason, led me to consider taking a year off, getting away to another world to broaden my horizons, to have the freedom to decide for myself what was good for me, where I wanted to be. I came to New Jersey with my older sister in 1965. It was an adventure. We were going to be on our own, in an anonymous atmosphere, away from the watchful eyes of Bogotá's entire Jewish community. What an extraordinary experience to have that freedom, to really decide for myself where I belonged, whom I belonged with, to explore, to learn, to grow, to be independent. Within a week I had an apartment, a job, and a couple of Colombian friends. As I started to function in this American world, to understand it, to work, I experienced anti-Semitism for the first time in my life. Suddenly it wasn't so great to be Jewish, it wasn't something you bragged about. If anything, I soon learned that it was better not to talk about it. With my Spanish accent, it wasn't difficult to do. My identity had suddenly changed. I was now seen as a Latin American. I had another persona. I was now interesting not for being Jewish, but for being "Hispanic." Was I really Hispanic? What made me Hispanic? Was it the language I grew up with? But I grew up with two other languages! Where did I really belong in this American world?

I started to meet a lot of Latin Americans, people from other countries in South and Central America, countries I had never made the effort to learn about. These people were interesting, educated; they welcomed me, and they didn't discriminate against me. To them, my Hispanic identity was stronger than my Jewish identity. But was I really Hispanic? No, not really. There was a barrier there, there still is. I "discovered" the rest of Latin America through the many Latin American people I have met in the United States. I have come to understand the differences among the different countries here. I have become a lover of Latin American literature away from Latin America. At home, back in Colombia, other Latin American countries were not interesting; foolishly, I assumed that they were all more or less the same.

European literature, American literature, being up on everything American, reading *Time* magazine, memorizing American songs, that was considered being intellectual. Here, in the United States, trying to understand Latin America has become one of my areas of interest. Do I identify with Latin American Jews? Yes, if they share my broader view of the world. Do I identify with American Jews? Not really. I am still considered, after more than thirty years in this country, somewhat "quaint." The inevitable questions—where are you from, are you really Jewish, how come you speak English so well—become tiresome with time. Do I identify with non-Jewish Americans? Not really. I can't leave my past behind. I was really shaped in Colombia by all my experiences. I am a product of my environment and I don't really identify with any one country or culture entirely. Having grown up with several languages, I became interested in the culture behind these languages, in the worlds they were representing. Perhaps this is what shaped my personality, my interests, my broad view of the world, my "universality." I am both at home in many places in the world, among different people, and not really part of them. I am somewhat in the periphery. Am I subconsciously trying to fight against the notion of belonging only to one place, to one race? Perhaps. The fact that I chose Princeton, New Jersey, a university town, to settle in tells me that what I value is diversity, openness, intellectual stimulation. Princeton has allowed me to integrate my Jewish, Latin American, American, and even French backgrounds into my life. Could I have done that successfully in Colombia? I don't think so. When I go back to visit family and friends I enjoy reconnecting to the wonderful, secure feeling I grew up with, the feeling of being really special. I have traded that secure feeling for the ability to be independent, to continue to grow. I have paid a price; part of me will always long for the wonderful years I spent in Colombia, but, on the other hand, I could never go back and lead what I now consider to be a limited life. Can we ever have it all? I will always remember fondly my formative years. Colombia gave my parents sanctuary, and by extension, allowed me to become who I am.

Chapter 10

Found in Translation
On Becoming a Cuban Jewish Writer

Ester R. Shapiro

I USED TO THINK THAT I became a psychologist because I didn't have the courage to become a writer, my truest vocation. I chose psychology early in college, embracing an arduous career requiring long years of preparation, because I thought it would permit me to have it all: the life of a scholar, a reader and writer; the life of a creative artist; and a life of social commitment. Psychology would also make it possible for me to earn a secure income, an essential criterion for a young woman determined to live her one and only life on her own terms. Gravitational forces from my Cuban Jewish Eastern European family, thriving after successive transplantations from Belorussia to Cuba and from Cuba to Miami, pulled me toward practical certainties. My family offered a time-tested recipe guaranteed to produce the best life had to offer: marry a nice Jewish boy, preferably from the Cuban Eastern European community (a Sephardi or Turko could, if necessary, be substituted); have him join a family business or create one within the Miami Cuban Jewish network of mutual aid; start your family in your mid-twenties. Then, by the time you reached your vigorous forties and the twenty years invested in children and business had reached maturation, you could reap the bounty of grandchildren, the ease of business worries, and the devotion of the next generations. Of course, as a woman, you would work hard, with the children at home, maintaining an extensive network of family ties, while pitching in with the business whenever necessary—no shame for a woman to work hard to make a living, our family had done it many times before. Sadly, the idea that my generation should receive the text of our family lives like a well-worn prayer book, made beautiful by repetition rather than improvisation, did not suit my temperament or my historical place in time.

Did you hear the easy diplomacy in that last sentence? That is one of those cleverly crafted, purposeful illusions we can create with words. Let me tell you about my profound desperation: I dreamed once that my father had me jailed to prevent me from leaving home and attending college. Enraged and agitated, I requested paper and pen, determined to tell my story to an outside world which would surely understand who was truly the criminal here. But in one of those terrifying moments of dream-state paralysis, I found I could not produce a single word. Staring in despair at my cell's thick metal bars, terrified that words had failed me, I decided on a hunger strike, determined that if necessary my corpse would speak for me.

During my senior year in high school in December 1969, we went to Queens to visit my Tia Consuelo, my father's older sister, and her family. The visit offered a rare chance for our group of close-in-age first cousins to spend extended time together, which we hadn't done since leaving Havana nine years earlier. When we left Cuba in 1960, my father Jaime and his brother Noel recreated our extended family of twelve, headed by my paternal grandparents Berta and Lazaro, in Miami, Florida. From the time of her courtship at age seventeen in rural Bolondron, Cuba, the edge of the known world, Consuelo had lived her family life in the orbit of her husband's family. She had followed them to cold, exotic Queens, a vast, frozen, densely populated expanse, foreign to our generation's Caribbean sensibility. Together, we were the offspring of a nearly interrupted flow of life from my paternal grandparents, Lazaro and Berta, and the three children they saved from the coming conflagration. We knew deep in our bones how close Belorus 1936 had come in time and space to the incinerators at the end of the line. Now it was my turn to meet the man who would shape my future; Consuelo hoped she could make the match to her son-in-law's brother. If she could draw me close to her own family circle, perhaps the mingling of blood lines would bridge the distance from her parents, ending her own intimate exile.

At the time, I had already lost the battle to leave home and attend one of the prestigious colleges courting me. I appeared resigned to attending the University of Miami with my academically unambitious and consummately obedient cousins, but inwardly I burned with sedition. The courtship rituals and all the other certainties of shtetel life transplanted to Miami, Florida, and Queens, New York, sounded like quaint melodies filled with shmaltzy nostalgia. I listened affectionately to "Roshinkes mit Mandlen" while modeling myself on Grace Slick of the Jefferson Airplane as she flaunted her sexual independence with "Don't you want somebody to love?" I felt confident I could simply step forward and evade these obsolete family rituals, postpone marriage and childbearing before these roles closed with a heavy metallic clang on the life of my dreams. At seventeen in 1969, I was outspoken in my battles with my parents over my desire for personal sovereignty, determined to join my peers in creating a different world than the one our parents could easily imagine because it so closely mirrored their own. I look back now in a new millennium at that promising, immodest, rebellious young woman and wish I could have offered her some words of warning and encouragement. Not that she could listen to anyone back then; her generation believed they could reimagine the world and make it altogether new, unburdened by constraints of tradition. I know she will spend the rest of her life discovering the secret connections to family traditions hidden within the story of her hard-won independence.

So there we were, our group of cousins together on the threshold of our adult lives in Queens, 1969: Consuelo's son Leon, twenty-one and recently married, had joined his father's jewelry business; my father's brother Noel's son Samuel, twenty, was finishing architecture school; his sisters, Edith, nineteen, and Rebeca, seventeen, were dating the men they would eventually marry. Consuelo had already warned me that my cousins had been gossiping about me and calling me a slut behind my back. She wanted me to know they couldn't be trusted. I knew how contemptuously they regarded me, as even before sexuality came into the picture they had called me *podrida* (rotten) because I would lose myself in my reading and float far away beyond our cloistered family compound. They confidently assured me that reading was rotting my brain. My sister Rachel, sixteen, my close ally, disagreed profoundly with my strategy of open engagement, as she preferred to present the appearance of compliance while secretly safeguarding her private life between worlds. I can still see us sitting in a darkened basement family room, a television turned off in one corner, sofa and chairs forming a tightening circle as a casual conversation about values became a pointed, persecutory interrogation. Leon, befitting the authority of his new position as a married man, asked me angrily, trying to test the depths of my disloyalty: "If you knew your father killed a man, would you turn him in, or help him escape?" The intensity of my cousins' gazes gathered the room's light and turned on me like a spotlight. Looking around at my intimate peers, with whom I had grown up and loved and fought all my life, I reluctantly responded: "If my father was troubled enough to commit a murder, which I do not believe he is capable of doing, I would want to get him help." My cousins turned to each other in an angry uproar, disbelieving and outraged but not surprised that I had failed the loyalty test. Only one answer would do, and it was not mine.

Very early in my Cuban Eastern European Jewish childhood, I learned that books could save my life. In the hothouse Havana atmosphere of my transplanted shtetel family, deep immersion in text sheltered me from the emotional storms that swept through our twelve-person extended family, as closely knit and fiercely loyal as a Bedouin tribe. All our current conversations were shadowed by the living memory of family lives unfolding on the Russian-Polish border and entangling with the century's traumatic political and historical events. As a family, we were marked by politics and history the way a tree's rings show the violent paths of forest fires or the deprivations of drought. We carried these signs of suffering just as secretly, through the tight choreography of family relationships and careful construction of the family's foundation myths. I watched closely for the real action behind the curtains, for the contradictions and missing elements which linked our family past, with its secret losses, to our shared future as successful immigrants. I profoundly violated a shared oath of absolute filial loyalty by questioning the received knowledge from my elders as a complete, absolute guide to my own life. Books became a safe social world in which I could secretly explore the broken shards and ruptured connections of our shtetel lives transplanted in Havana.

Throughout my elementary school years, my family found my bookishness a welcome respite from my insatiable appetite for answers to questions best left unasked. It was only in my adolescence between cultures that my love of scholarship became a family liability, threatening my smooth progression through a daughter's obligations in a world made safe by increasingly stable material security and increasingly narrow family loyalty. No surprise when I tell you that the scholarly path I eventually chose required that I study family development in social and historical context. Perhaps it is also no surprise in retrospect, although I am always surprised at the time, that my evolving professional life, increasingly a writer's life, has been characterized by some of the same personal and political conflicts and contradictions as was my family life between cultures.

Psychology, which seemed to offer my soul a safe place for its complexity, is riddled with the conflicts and contradictions stimulated by its own struggles for intellectual identity. As a field between research and practice, between art and science, we try to characterize our human strivings for wholeness, our human struggle to cope with suffering and move forward with the flow of life. I teach a course on childhood psychopathology in an urban practice clinical psychology program. The course is officially called "Child Assessment and Treatment: Social Developmental Perspectives." Unofficially, I call it "The Poetics of Childhood Symptoms." When I had a full-time child and family clinical practice, I once worked with a teenager who slashed her skin with razors, between her thighs where no one could see. I learned that she always cut herself during nighttime dreams in which she obeyed her father's screamed instructions that she must be punished for her sexual transgressions. She had been raped, and considered herself at fault for having failed to see the warning signs, for having innocently enjoyed the pleasurable unfolding of her sexuality. As with any trauma, her rape took a life story with one set of themes and guiding images and recast them in its terrible light. Suddenly, her life also had to become the story of intergenerational transgression passed from a psychologically disturbed mother to her genetically doomed daughter, requiring punishment by a betrayed and unforgiving father. As I entered her world and joined her struggle to give words to her unspeakable suffering, we began to talk about problems of translation. Gifted at languages, she decided that English could not speak to the baroque world of passionate feelings with the accuracy of the Romance languages. She would speak to me in her fluent French when she dared speak of the rape. She encouraged me to consider, for the first time in my English-speaking life, what I had lost when my fluent Yiddish had vanished and my Cuban Spanish had atrophied from lack of use. We spoke of the losses of exile, which she experienced when her parents divorced and her father and stepmother gained custody rather than her fragile mother, and which I experienced when I left Cuba. She helped me become more humble about the limits of language in justly rendering her devastated landscape of suffering and loss. I helped her become more hopeful about the possibilities of language for restoring a more just, shared understanding in her family, one in which her corpse did not need to speak for her on her mother's behalf. At first reluctantly, because suicide beckoned seductively as a properly punitive end to her own suffering, she chose life over death, and walked forward on her life path. Ten years later, the same decade in which I had closed my practice to become a late-in-life academic, I ran into her as we were both trying on summer sandals. She brought me up to date, telling me about her work as a physical therapist specializing in trauma treatment. Working to make her own life whole, she had become a healer, just as working to make my own life whole, I had become a scholar, moving one step closer to my writing life.

During my childhood in Havana, Cuba, our family once again lived through the turbulence of another momentous revolution, with resonance to the past and portents for a transplanted future. My close-knit extended family had already experienced the Bolshevik revolution, World War I, and the violent preludes to World War II from front-row seats on the Russian Polish border. Thinking they had found a lasting home in Cuba's hospitable climate, they scattered across the island and settled into tiny rural communities as storekeepers. Within one brief generation they built the synagogues and yeshivas whose walls represented the commitment to an island which had so generously received them. I was an early and obsessive reader, fluent in Yiddish and Spanish, omnivorously devouring any texts I could get my hands on, from Yiddish storybooks of a lost shtetel world to official Batista newspapers depicting the barbarities committed by Fidel's rebel forces. I read *Uncle Tom's Cabin* in Spanish translation, and tried to understand what skin color–based slavery might mean on our interracial streets in Havana's Vedado neighborhood. When Fidel and his *barbudos,* the bearded rebels, entered Havana and nationalized all apartment rentals, my panicked and disillusioned family found itself publicly supporting their second socialist revolution while secretly packing their bags. Fearful that their children might betray their plans, they encouraged us to believe that we were remaining to build the Revolution, even as we packed everything in the house for a short Miami vacation.

Suddenly, in October of 1960, I was eight years old and struggling to absorb English as if my life depended on it, because my well-meaning third-grade teacher thought I would learn more quickly if I were placed in the classroom for the "retarded." I remember standing in the playground of the elementary school where we were still among the first of the newly arriving Cubans and struggling to replace the flow of Yiddish words with the requisite English ones. Grief for our lost Cuban paradise was a luxury we could no longer afford. Our family turned eagerly to the task of becoming assimilated North American Jews. Master storytellers, like all survivors, we re-wrote the story of our exodus as if Cuba had been a brief destination in our Diaspora wanderings and our passage to the United States, the true promised land for Jews, had finally been completed as planned. I learned English at record speed, but my once-fluent Yiddish was not the only casualty of my assimilationist survival strategy. The story of my own ties to Cuba, what I had lost in plain view, would lie dormant, appearing only in haunting dream fragments, until I discovered the need and the courage to return to Cuba. There, I was able to see for myself the island that had opened its ports to forty-five thousand Jews between the two world wars, fifteen thousand of us responding to the curious, generous, irreverent embrace of Cuban hospitality to become, joyously but briefly, Jubans. At the time we left Cuba, the wounds of exile still bleeding, the story's happy ending still unwritten, I was reluctant to give my struggling family anything else to worry about. I settled down to a bookish life because it permitted me to privately roam the widest unexplored world without disloyally challenging the family's fearful cloistered existence.

My beleaguered parents believed it was my adolescence between cultures that triggered my dangerous years of rebellion. I was simply following a path well traveled by my generation of United States peers, who refused to accept the mandates of social convention if they could order us to kill in Vietnam. I didn't have words for my own profound loyalty at the time, but I expressed it in my own fashion: I admired the creative inventiveness my grandmothers had shown when life handed them a guava and they cooked it in their kugel. I listened carefully to each and every family story and remembered them as vividly as if I myself had lived them, which in a way I did. Crossing time and space on an airstream of words, I have visited the shtetel in Rubyshevish, Poland, a town which no longer exists except in memory, its only gravestone a name etched on the translucent glass wall of vanished Jewish towns in the Washington, D.C., Holocaust museum. I have rebuilt the vanished town where my ancestors are buried image by image, out of the kaleidoscope of stories I have carefully gathered. I have visited Rubyshevish with my father, when I asked him to describe his childhood memories and he described the Polish town market he could see from their home, straddling the boundary between Jewish shtetel and Christian village. Brought reluctantly back by my curious questions, he described first the bustle of a rural market as the townspeople and farmers gathered, the ritual Friday night drunkenness as the profits from sales were celebrated with schnapps. As night fell the memories darkened, my father remembering that as the first stars of evening ushered in the Sabbath bride and our most sacred evening, the inebriated revelers turned a hostile gaze to their Jewish neighbors. Each fragment holds a whole world within it, a bridge of lives intertwined across space and time. These fragments have been passed on, our most enduring Diaspora legacy, through a chorus of voices carrying the piercing tonalities of sacred Middle Eastern chants, the bittersweet minor notes of Eastern European klezmer, now blending with the percussive African rhythms of Cuban rumba and my own formative rock and roll. I have listened carefully to the flow of voices, and have learned to discern both the overt sounds of the cherished and often told, and the undercurrents of the anguished or forbidden which must never be told. I gather them within my own soul's imaginings and forge fragments into a living whole, another generation's stories to live by.

When Abuela Berta died and we were sitting *shiva* for her, in the eight days of traditional ritual mourning, I lovingly prepared a family feast in Tia Elsa and Tio Noel's kitchen. Totally unprepared to appreciate my talents as a writer and scholar, and threatened by my storehouse of discomforting family stories, they could fully embrace my talent as a cook. I could offer a simple yet sumptuous repast, my dangerous excesses channeled into food prepared as a healing gift. As Abuela Berta's full-grown aging children sat around the kitchen table, I stood by at the stove, carefully choreographing Caribbean and Polish elements to the meal. I had selected a fragrant papaya at the supermarket, choosing one whose mottled orange skin, furry with patches of mold, covered firm, fully ripe flesh. Pairing the sweet fruit with the citrus acid of lime, I was rewarded with reminiscences of the Havana market's "frutabomba" or "fruit bomb" as Cubans distinctively call the slippery, voluptuous, dark orange flesh with its bounty of enzyme-rich black seeds. I prepared a chopped vegetable salad with cucumbers and fennel in which the sharp bite of radish and green onion was soothed by thickened yogurt and enlivened by fennel fronds and fresh dill. I received in response an unexpected story as Tia Consuelo reminisced about the cow which was always tethered to the backyard post at the boundary of the shtetel with the regional Polish market. Although she provided a year-round supply of milk, sour cream, and home-made farmer's cheese, nothing could compare to her springtime yield of milk after a long dark winter. Eating my Americanized version, my father, aunt, and uncle reminisced about Abuela Berta's chopped vegetable salad in its early summer splendor—the sour cream, carrying the subtle grace notes of tender green grasses consumed by their sated cow, paired with the garden's first yield of sun-warmed cucumber, radish, and green onions. Abuela Berta, who had suffered near starvation when their family home was made into an army hospital during World War I, had always rejoiced at a generously endowed table, and we enjoyed the lives she had made possible in her memory.

Sometimes I came upon a much-needed image altogether by chance, and it frightens me to consider how easily it might have slipped altogether from my reach, made inaccessible by time and distance and the realities of growing up on different continents and in different languages. I grew up with Abuela Berta, or Bobbe Bashe's, stories of Rubyshevish, her vanished shtetel town, which for her was the story of triumph over the many murderous attempts on her family's survival. She especially cherished the memory of the day in 1917 when, as a ten-year-old girl, she had outwitted the Cossacks, who swept murderously through their town and planned to loot the family's valuables. With emphatic amusement, she told me how she outsmarted them by standing on a chair and placing all their belongings of any value in a hidden storage area beneath the eaves of their home. The looters were forced to retreat empty-handed. My great-aunt Yochebed, who emigrated to Palestine when my family went to Cuba, spoke neither Spanish nor English until late in her life, when a retired New Yorker organized English classes in their apartment in Ashkelon, Israel. So, with thanks to an elderly English teacher, on my first visit to Israel I was able to ask for family stories. I was able to revisit with my great aunt a moment seventy-seven years in the past and still a compelling part of a timeless present unfolding into the future. Yochebed told me how she, the four-year-old youngest daughter, had seen the pogrom which had swept through their town in 1917. For little Yache, what stood out in memory was how recently her father and only brother had been killed on a flooded bridge, her mother forced to travel to Minsk to sell their remaining stock of furs, reluctantly leaving her three daughters alone in their home. Yache remembered well how she cowered in terror in a corner while Bashe, the eldest, who was in charge of the family, coolly climbed a chair and put away the fur-lined blankets which represented their remaining livelihood. The Cossacks did enter their home and left empty-handed. But Yache remembered one other detail even more clearly, and told me a story that she had not told for seventy-seven years. She took me to the place and moment when her returning mother, already warned that the pogrom had swept like a lethal storm through the defenseless shtetel, stood at their threshold and called out her daughters' names, her anguished tone betraying her terror that she might enter and find them dead. That fear, at least, was immediately put to rest by Yache's relieved cries. How a woman alone with three daughters would survive the coming world war became another family story, which, as my always practical Abuela Berta told it, rested on a foundation of the nutritive properties of potato peels.

After ten years as a practicing psychologist, I became a full-time college professor, lured back to early dreams of academic scholarship by the chance to help start a clinical psychology program dedicated to culturally informed work with disadvantaged urban communities. There I learned once again in a new way what it meant to live between cultures and struggle to reconcile the conflicts and contradictions of my new life. Our psychology department struggled with contradictions between practice and research. At the same time, the University of Massachusetts at Boston struggled with conflicts between ideals of the ivory tower academy and of the urban university which would join its communities in solving urgent social problems. So it was no surprise that both the psychology department and later the university regarded my sort of scholarship, dedicated to improving clinical practice, with the profound ambivalence which academics typically translate into devastatingly negative reviews of one's capacity for scholarship. What did surprise me were the ways my utterly negative reviews, which eloquently claimed that I had a good clinician's heart and a talent for storytelling but no sustained capacity for scholarly analysis, resonated with long-buried terrors. Shortly after learning that the College of Arts and Sciences Personnel Committee was determined to overturn my department's contested but positive tenure vote and vote to fire me, I had the following deceptively simple dream. A male colleague and I are standing up in a small motorboat which is approaching the University of Massachusetts at Boston Harbor campus. In reality, at the time, he was my partner and brother who had with me endured and survived similar bruising tenure battles within our department, but had unlike me been approved with glowing reviews by the personnel committee. In my dreamscape, our boat pulls up to a dock directly next to the brick-and-glass library building when in reality the docks end at a grassy slope some distance below. David is allowed to disembark, but I am not; I must remain on the boat, which now pulls away. Coincidentally, my friend and I consider ourselves on the broad continuum of families haunted by Holocaust survivorship, his family having escaped even later than mine and made their way to Canada. I have two associations to the dream, both linked to my Cuban Jewish Diaspora experience. First association: my family allowed only my male cousins to have a bar mitzvah, even though I was such a dedicated student that my teachers begged my parents to send me to yeshiva. They remained shtetel old-fashioned about what a poor investment a girl's education was, an education which moreover would make me nearly unmarriageable. Second association: when the *St. Louis* docked in Havana harbor in 1942, my maternal grandmother Abuela Adela, who had arrived in the twenties, traveled to Havana from the central province town of Cabaiguan to join Jewish protestors pleading with the Cuban government to let the boat dock. Havana was the port of last resort, but by that time Cuba was no longer accepting Jewish immigrants, fearing an unmanageable flood of desperate Polacos as refugees. My paternal grandparents, more recent arrivals, were too busy trying to get themselves established in a small town in rural Cuba to join a protest. The dream's symbolism shows starkly how my intellectual strivings represented profound issues of personal survival for me as a Cuban Jewish American woman.

My response to the negative tenure review had very little to do with whether I secured a steady salary and a great deal to do with whether I belonged, as a scholar and most fundamentally as a writer, in the places of learning I have learned to call home. I carefully crafted a statement describing the conflicts over academic values my tenure case had catalyzed, suggesting that our urban university required new creative solutions connecting scholarship and social needs. In doing so I spoke for myself as a woman, a Cuban immigrant, and a Jew whose life story had become an intergenerational saga shadowed by war, exile, and revolution yet flourishing in the light of family connections, shared hardship, and resilient hope. I spoke, too, for my urban students who discovered in my classroom the ways apparent barriers of race, immigration, or poverty instead offered vital, often untold stories of struggle, striving, and success. My positive tenure case became a focal point for an emerging intellectual community whose work bridged disciplines and breached the boundary between classroom and community. My own writing as a psychologist and healer has increasingly honored the important art of storytelling and the extraordinary opportunities our life stories offer, to ourselves and to each other, for shared affirmation and mutual learning. As a teacher, I continue to discover the rich tapestry of stories unfolding in my students' narratives. By offering the example of my own journey in a writer's life, I encourage them to discover the heart of their own true path toward knowledge. So concludes the never-ending story of a writer's life as a work in progress.

Chapter 11

Mosiacs
The Story of Her Life

Wilma Bloch Reich
as told to Jessica P. Alpert

Another Crossing

SPEAKING SPANISH, SPEAKING GERMAN,
ADOPTING ENGLISH

Our lives continued smoothly in Salvador for many years. I taught German, Ernesto enjoyed work, we spent time with friends and family. In the meantime, Ruth married an American and they moved with our twin grandsons to Texas. A year later, our first granddaughter was born. We visited them often and enjoyed their visits to our home in Salvador.

As the years passed, the situation in El Salvador worsened. The guerillas were terrorizing all of us, and our friends began leaving in 1979. The turning point was when one of our closest friends was kidnapped and later assassinated. Shortly after, a good friend of ours came over to visit.

Ernesto, why are you still here?

Always the same question.

In 1981 we finally left for Houston. We bought an apartment a mile away from my daughter's home and quickly furnished it. My second exile had begun.

Ernesto was depressed for some time and no wonder; he had lived in El Salvador since he was seventeen. Eventually he joined me in our effort to make friends and embrace our new country. We loved the new temple we belonged to; it soon became our constant. The prayers and the holidays never changed no matter where we went. I missed our help in Salvador and tried to simulate the wonderful Salvadoran dishes they had cooked for us. I turned all of this into a new adventure, a new experience, a new chapter.

Although we emigrated in 1981, we did not sell our beloved home in San Salvador until 1987. We accepted our new destiny and became American citizens in September of 1990. I must admit that I feel more like a citizen of the world. I have not one language, but three that I mix, or *mezcalo*. My grandchildren used to visit my small apartment and eat lunches of matzo ball soup, schnitzel, *frijoles, platanos* (fried bananas), and tortillas. We all understand that this fusion is not unusual, but innately us. We are a family of moves, of adjustments, of acceptance.

My grandchildren smile as my daughter and I jump between German, Spanish, and English before completing one sentence. These sentences make up the foundation of the mosaic that is my life.

As I said earlier, I am not in the real sense of the word a *survivor*.

And I still have no answers . . . only languages, pictures, memories, stories.

La Boda

SPEAKING GERMAN, HEARING SPANISH

Ernesto immediately took me to the home of his sister Irma and her husband Eugen Liebes. I would stay there until we were officially married. The next day, Irma, her two daughters, Margot and Chita, and I went shopping for material for the wedding dress. I admired a very beautiful and heavy fabric and, despite strong warning from Irma, naively ignored the tropical climate and purchased the white I had always dreamt of. Only one woman in the capital was known to style hair (this was 1937), and we engaged her for the wedding, which took place a week later. Eighty to one hundred people were in attendance, most of whom I had never set eyes on. Ernesto had the frame of the *chuppah* made, and I helped decorate it. There was no catering service in San Salvador, so the Liebes family and other friends cooked and baked for the lunch which followed the religious ceremony. While the guests stayed, we left for our honeymoon trip to Guatemala. We traveled by car to Guatemala City, Antigua, and Lake Atitlán. It was incredible; I felt like I was in another world. I looked at the flowers and the trees and the ruins, feeling far away from the Concertgebouw in Amsterdam. The trip was an adventure. At times, with the flat tires and endless unpaved roads, I did not think we would ever reach our destinations. But Ernesto was in charge. We reached our beautiful destinations and indeed had the most beautiful honeymoon imaginable.

Nuevas Tradiciones

SPEAKING SPANISH, REMEMBERING DUTCH, LEARNING ENGLISH

We led a beautiful and relaxed life in El Salvador. In the early thirties, Ernesto joined with partner Toto Lassally, and together they eventually created Lassally, Reich y CiA. Ernesto left the office one day a week to go to the *finca* (plantation) the firm had acquired after the war. Every weekend, I accompanied him. We would leave early in the morning, walk with the supervisor through the plantation, eat lunch, and return home before sundown.

We loved to get together with our friends and entertained often. Our daughter Ruth, who was born in 1942, was a happy child who preferred to eat in the kitchen with her *nana,* the cook, and the gardener. She loved scraping up her food with the help of tortillas instead of eating with her boring parents in the dining room.

About every three years, we would take a long trip to Europe, often spending most of our time with my sister, brother-in-law, and nephew in Amsterdam. After World War II, we routinely sent food packages to the family. One year, upon my arrival I inquired about them. A simple question turned into a conversation I will never forget.

Georg, have you been receiving the food packages?

Yes, thank you, but we have needed them less and less.

Oh? Well, did you give the food to someone who could use it?

Absolutely. I gave it to a former coworker of mine who has a family.

Yes? Do I know this man?

I do not think so.

Try me. Who is he?

Well, he is German.

Jewish?

Well, no. Not Jewish.

Not Jewish? And German? Who is this man? Do you know anything about him? Could he have been in the war?

I don't know.

Don't you care? He could be Nazi! What else do you know about him?

Wilma, all I know is that he is *hungry*.

I cry as I retell this story to my granddaughter. It moved me in so many ways. Because of this conversation, I was able to turn away from the easy way out, the act of hating. Georg made me see how humanity holds us together; how essential it is to take that second look, to give that second chance, to really listen. I thank him for it.

Y la Nueva Vida

SLOWLY FORGETTING DUTCH, PRESERVING GERMAN, LEARNING SPANISH

After returning from Guatemala, we stayed a few days in a hotel and then moved to the small *pueblito* of Chinameca in the eastern part of the country. Ernesto bought coffee from the small *finqueros* in the sur-roundings and I often accompanied him, walking or riding on mules. Ernesto also oversaw the processing of the raw beans in a rented *beneficio*. Near this *beneficio*, we rented a small house with a big yard. In the yard, there was an outhouse and farther away a *pila* in which to bathe. This was to be our bathroom—a completely open and exposed space. In my honor, some boards were erected. I used to throw my bathrobe over them, managing to cover my upper body but leaving my lower legs exposed. I was satisfied with the solution. With a *huacal*—a bowl formed from the dried fruit of a tree—I threw the water over my body. Two maids helped me with the cleaning, cooking, and laundry. The dry season had started, and constant dust became our greatest enemy. Though we swept and mopped several times a day, we could never completely get rid of it.

Our kitchen was not connected to the house. The stove was fired with wood *(leña)*, and I did not really manage to cook on it. I did pre-pare bread dough, which one of the maids baked in the oven. *Leña* was thrown inside the oven and as soon as it was consumed, the loaves were put in its place. I never learned this technique, but definitely en-joyed its delicious finished product.

The maids doubled as my teachers. I used to point at things and they told me their name in Spanish. We laughed together as I struggled with my accent and the new language. Every two to three weeks we took the complicated trip to the "capital" to see the family and buy vegetables, meat, cheese, and butter. In Chinameca we only could get chicken, eggs, tortillas, beans, and bananas. Was it a hardship? Not at all. It was an adventure and a fascinating experience.

After two months we returned to San Salvador and rented a house in a location where few Jews lived. It was convenient for Ernesto as he could reach his office downtown on foot. The neighbors were friendly.

Where do you come from?

Germany.

Oh! We love the Germans.

Well, we do not love them. They are Nazis and hate Jews and we are Jews.

Yes, and we are Catholic.

It was more important to them that we were German than that we were Jewish. At the time, this made me feel uncomfortable; German nationalism was not an easy subject to digest.

Around this time, Ernesto was working hard to get my mother out of Amsterdam. Eugen Liebes tried to get a visa from the United States while Ernesto never stopped trying to get one from El Salvador. We were eventually denied the visa by the Salvadorean Minister of Foreign Affairs, and we lost my mother a few years later. I believe this is the harshest example of anti-Semitism we experienced during our years in Salvador.

During the war, we spent a lot of our social time with the other Jews in the community. These included French, Germans, Poles, and Americans. We tended to stick to our own simply because we were all struggling to maintain our Jewish identities. After the war, we integrated more German non-Jews into our lives. We spoke German and reminisced about the places we had all tasted, witnessed, experienced.

La Comunidad Israelita

LEARNING SPANISH, IMPROVING ENGLISH, TEACHING GERMAN

I loved Salvador, but in one way or another was always reminded that I was a foreigner. Life was completely different from the one I was accustomed to. Identity was a complicated subject. Being Jewish and a member of that small community helped.

Two couples took turns hosting Friday evening services in their homes. Saturday morning it was more difficult to get a *minyan*. On holidays, a bigger house served a bigger assembly. Slowly, more refugees were admitted and as a result our community grew. Younger members had children and it became easier to get a *minyan* together. Eventually, a former teacher got permission to enter the country and he became our cantor, rabbi, and teacher.

Ernesto would wake up early every morning and study Hebrew. This ritual began before our marriage and lasted until the end of his life. I was involved in the more social aspect of things. We Jewish women became members of WIZO (Women's International Zionist Organization) and started fundraising. Later on, I even became *la presidenta* of the (WIZO) for several years. My timidity prevented me from enjoying the responsibility of public speaking and the duty of asking for more and more money. Even so, I enjoyed the work and felt we achieved a great deal. Despite my shyness, we raised a significant amount of money and, through contacts in South America, sent it directly to Israel. At our frequent board meetings, I would serve the Salvadoran *fresco (refresco)*, the typical fruit drink, along with German pastries that I baked. Our meetings would be on the porch, and we would often talk for hours about the *fincas*, the children, the husbands, Europe, vacations, and yes, WIZO. Of course I also joined several Salvadoran charities, contributing money and some work to orphanages, newborn babies, the blind, and the deaf. I managed to donate food to the homeless and knit for the Red Cross during the war.

One afternoon I noticed a boy who, while trying to walk up a hill near our home, kept falling down and getting up again. I could see his misshapen legs and the small stick of wood which served as his only support. I offered to drive him to where he was going and he agreed to let me help him. He came from the poorest slum near our house. He soon became dear to Ernesto and to my daughter; we tried to help him in various ways. Our economic contributions were small but our intentions were to instill in him moral values and to organize his education. We wanted to help him plan for his future and most of all to be honest. We made sure that he received the appropriate surgeries and health care for his polio and insisted he finish school. Eventually, he entered the university. He always had jobs to help him along. With his never-faltering persistence and courage, he managed at last to become a judge in El Salvador. We were always proud that he resisted the pervasive bribery and threats. The connections with my family continue. My daughter and I know his children and my granddaugters are their friends. Ernesto and I were always proud of his remarkable achievements and truly unique character.

One strict obligation of my daily life consisted of taking care of our home and making sure the *almuerzo* (big meal of the day) was ready for Ernesto when he came home from the office. It was not rare that a foreign visitor would be with him. He was always home from the office around noon and after the *almuerzo* we would take a short *siesta*. He would then return to work. He had mastered the Latin way of conducting business and understood the differences between the American, European, and Salvadoran perspectives. He used to tell us that most Latin businessmen enjoyed chatting the first thirty minutes of a meeting about families, politics, and soccer while Americans and Europeans walked in, shook hands, sat down, and right away got to the point. Ernesto was able to skip between the two genres effortlessly. I accepted these two different outlooks and adopted them as my own.

Our daughter Ruth often accompanied us to the *finca* and sometimes brought friends along. She loved these excursions and soon learned to ride one of the mules. She attended the American school in San Salvador from kindergarten to eighth grade, then we decided she needed a stricter and better education. We enrolled her in a boarding school in Vermont.

The separation from our only child was painful but necessary. "No hay mal que por bien no venga" (There is no bad that does not bring some good). This transition brought me to a new phase in my life. I decided to start teaching German.

A Salvadoran executive of German descent wanted his Salvadoran wife to improve her skills and suggested that I have weekly chats with her. These chats turned into a small career for me as I began to give lessons to many adults and young people. Little by little, I began to be approached by people I didn't know. My teaching brought me several very good new friends. Teaching my "old" language was a way to embrace my original identity. As I taught German mostly to Spanish-speaking people, I taught in Spanish, and it is really ironic to consider that most of my pupils spoke better Spanish than I did.

We enjoyed Ruth's visits home and marvelled at her adventurous spirit. She became known for the "viajecitos" she would organize to the different natural wonders El Salvador provided. Ruth would call all who were interested, organize the transportation, lead the climb, and get everyone back by sunset. I was always waiting for the group with *fresco*. I often went along and enjoyed the gorgeous hikes with friends and family. Even people from the American embassy called our home to find out about our wonderful "guia," and our Ruth began to include the embassy personnel on her adventures. Our country was and is beautiful; Ruth helped us to never forget it.

I am not in the real sense of the word a *survivor*.

A real survivor survived the concentration and death camps. A real survivor was hidden by righteous people. A real survivor lived under a false identity. I survived because I left Holland shortly before the war. Many survivors ask themselves: "Why was I spared?" or "Why did a higher power or destiny choose me?"

I have no answers.

As I sit at my small kitchen table in Houston, Texas, with my youngest granddaughter, I think about my own story. My granddaughter listens to my words as if they are golden, and I smile as I think of the small details that make my family so unique, so beautiful, so *especial*. Who knew I would spend my life in Latin America mixing *frijoles* with challah, bar mitzvahs with *quinceañeras*? This is the story of the journey and the destination, the memories and the *nueva vida,* the people we won and those we lost. This is my story; this is my world of survival.

In 1931, one semester before my final tests to become a librarian, the Nazis stopped my studies. I was able to get work as a librarian until leaving for Holland in the summer of 1935. I moved in with my brother Max, his wife Liza, and their small child. I enjoyed Holland and easily made new friends; Amsterdam was an exciting city, and I explored it on my *fiets,* my bicycle. My sister-in-law was expecting a baby and would have preferred to stay home, but since she had a work permit she could not afford such a luxury. I cared for their only child and did household chores while she worked, and quickly settled into my new life.

My brother Max had a friend, Heinz, who had emigrated from Germany to El Salvador years before in order to work for Goldtree Liebes, the firm of his relatives. Max and Heinz corresponded often, and we all used to gather around and listen to Max read these letters out loud; El Salvador was an exciting and far-off place. I was intrigued by the details, the description of new fruits, the stories of coffee and *fincas,* the different language and people.

In June of 1938, I met Ernst Reich, who lived in El Salvador. He got our address from Heinz and decided to drop by on the way to visit his family in Germany. He was in Europe to negotiate the emigration of two sisters, a brother-in-law, and his mother. I still do not know how Ernst (later Ernesto and finally Ernest) foresaw the coming events. His Salvadorean passport—he became a naturalized Salvadorean citizen in the early thirties—allowed him to travel freely in Germany, which at this point was extremely dangerous for a German Jew.

Ernst left Germany having made good progress on his mission and returned to Amsterdam to spend a week with me. Liza gave me free time during the day and we went to the country, the beaches, the lakes; I was the guide and he the follower. We talked for hours upon hours and finally, at the end of our week together, he asked me to wait for him. After taking care of his family, he would work on my emigration. He assumed I would be safe in Holland. In the weeks after Ernst's return to El Salvador, things in Holland grew progressively worse. We were all nervous and now knew that war in Europe was inevitable.

One day in late September of 1938, I woke up with the flu and the memory of a dream. As I ate breakfast with Max and Liza, I told them about the dream I remembered from the night before. I dreamt that Ernst had written to ask me to marry him and come immediately to El Salvador. They laughed and called it wishful thinking and claimed that my fever was the cause of such hallucinations. An hour later, a cable arrived from Ernst stating that the consulate of El Salvador in Amsterdam had been instructed to give me a visa and that I should book a passage on the *Crijnssen*. The boat was to leave three days later.

I forgot about the flu and arrived at the consulate the minute it opened. After nervously waiting for the consul to confirm the visa, I was finally granted the precious stamp on my passport. I then ran to the shipping line office, where I found lines and lines of people. I never thought so many people would wish to travel on such short notice, but the sense of impending war was undeniable. People were hysterical as they waited to get to the front of the line. At last it was my turn. When I stated my request, showing my stamped passport with the sacred visa, the clerk gave me a bewildered stare. "There is not one bed, not one cot unoccupied on the *Crijnssen*. It was completely booked months ago." My heart sank and I began to feel numb. As he uttered these devastating words, a phone rang nearby. The man who answered lifted the receiver and motioned to his coworker not to let me go. I waited.

"Miss, a lady from Paris just canceled her reservation. We have a long waiting list, but you are here, you have a valid visa, you have a valid passport. If you are willing to travel second class you may have her place."

If I was willing? I nodded my head, still feeling numb, knowing that I would be leaving everything I knew and everyone I loved on September 30.

I now had two days to settle pending business and say goodbye to friends and relatives. My mother called from Berlin and we spoke for a long time. This would be the last time I heard her voice. She received permission in 1939 to settle in Amsterdam, but all of our subsequent efforts to get her out of Holland failed. Her sister Grete attempted to bring her to Ecuador, but German officials would not grant her permission to leave Holland. She was deported from Amsterdam and gassed in Sobibor in 1943, one year after my only child was born.

I packed one suitcase. I took everything my mother had ever given me—tablecloths, linens, bedclothes, books, and my favorite poems by Hesse and Rilke.

On September 30, family and friends gathered and accompanied me to the *Crijnssen*. We looked for my cabin and Liza opened the door. She turned around and told me that we must have made a mistake: "It seems a movie star will be staying here." I looked past her shoulder and saw an enormous bouquet of flowers on the table. I read the accompanying card: "For Wilma Bloch, (the future Wilma Bloch de Reich)."

Soon, we were forced to say our last goodbyes. As I hugged Liza, she cried. I think she felt this would be the last time we would see each other.

My sister Maja and her husband Georg with their son Peter would survive by hiding in the attic of a friend's home in Amsterdam. Their other son, Walter, was deported, together with my brother and his family. We never learned of Walter's fate. Liza and her two small children were gassed in Auschwitz upon their arrival. After the war, I was told by a survivor of that camp that when Max learned of their deaths, he stopped speaking and died of typhus that same year.

I left the city with a clear head and a heavy heart. I felt safe because I was a bride-to-be, but sensed that the coming years would be a challenge. Even so, I was young and interested. The journey excited me and the prospect of living in a new place was exactly what I was looking for. I never let myself believe that I would not see my family again. I waved goodbye to Max, Liza, Georg, Maja. I smiled and blew a kiss.

When they were out of sight, I turned to the sea and took a deep breath.

Die Reise

SPEAKING GERMAN, SPEAKING DUTCH, STRUGGLING WITH ENGLISH, PICKING UP SOME SPANISH

I shared a cabin with two women: one Austrian, the other Dutch, one Jewish, the other not. We were in similar situations yet headed to different destinations. We spent a much of our time talking about where we came from and where we were going.

By chance, my cousin Margot Jung and her husband Walter took the same boat on their way to Ecuador. They came down to second class everyday to spend some hours with me. The rest of the day was spent reading, sitting, or walking on deck. I remember one meal vividly. A steward offered us fruit. People turned their heads from the orange, fleshy substance while I put out my hand for a piece. The steward smiled and looked at me saying: "Try the papaya. It is YOUR fruit from now on."

One of our ports was Maracaibo, Venezuela. I stood on the deck and looked out; I was fascinated by the vegetation, the bright colors, the new smells. While on board, I received a detailed letter from Ernst telling me about the people I was to meet when I reached Costa Rica. However, I still had a ways to go. In Colombia, the boat experienced an enormous crisis. The majority of the passengers were fleeing Jews, and many were disembarking in Colombia. When they attemped to enter the country, their visas were not considered valid. Despair reigned. I silently sighed as I watched the people forced back onto the boat; their future was uncertain.

We next docked in Panama. Here I would separate from the Jungs, who were to disembark and continue on to Quito. We learned in Panama that Colombia had finally agreed to take those with visas. Everyone breathed a collective sigh of great relief. I spent two days in Panama and was mesmerized. I remember Ernst telling me in his last letter that I should try and buy some summer dresses at the next port. I ventured off the boat and into the stores and bought three cotton summer dresses. I never saw so many colors, so many strange-looking vegetables, fruits, people. I remember walking and walking, exhilarated by the many new sensations.

Our final port and my destination was Puerto Limón, Costa Rica. Here, I received my last letter from Ernst. He told me that I would be met by a couple in San José, but first I had to get there. The mountain train was an overwhelming experience. We traveled from the beaches through the rainforests to the top of a mountain and finally reached San José. I spent a lot of my time talking with a young man from Hamburg who was half Jewish and whom I had met on the ship. Another person from our ship, a Costa Rican returning from Europe, served as our guide on the train. He explained various aspects of life to us and eased our fears about climate, food, language. He got off the train at lunchtime and brought back a lunch of tortillas, *frijoles,* and fried plantains. This would be our first true taste of our new culture.

In San José, where I stayed for two nights, I was met by a very nice couple—business acquaintances of Ernst. They gave me lunch and dinner, showed me the city, and patiently answered many of my questions. I asked if there were any trains in El Salvador. They told me that these trains were mainly for freight and livestock and that only the poorest locals rode on them. I asked him if he would tell me about coffee. He smiled and said: "No, I won't. You will hear about coffee for the rest of your life."

Once in San José, I waited for the flight to Salvador; the small propeller plane only made the trip three times a week. After a brief flight, I arrived in the small airport and saw Ernst, dressed all in white, waiting for me at the end of the runway.

By ship, train, and plane it took me twenty-eight days to get from Holland to El Salvador.

Finally.

Chapter 12

Shared Memories

Nedda G. de Anhalt

And as I speak to myself, I reflect and invent myself.
I discover who I am.
—Octavio Paz, in *Vigilias II*

WHAT DOES IT MEAN to be a Jewish woman in Latin America? It's not an easy question to answer since it means folding back into myself, contemplating the events of the past and resurrecting them in order to offer a partial history and geography of my origins. If they had to be lined up, I'd say that Cuban, Jewish, and Mexican factors all have their chromosomes carefully implanted in my spiritual universe.

MY MOTHER, BORN IN WARSAW, and my father, born in Riga but educated in Vilna, arrived in Havana, Cuba on different dates. There they met, fell in love, married, and brought me into the world. The day and time? Five in the afternoon on the fifth of February, 1934.

I spent my childhood, adolescence, and part of my young adulthood in Havana. At the University of Havana I began to study civil, diplomatic, and administrative law, studies I interrupted when I went as a transfer student to Sarah Lawrence College in New York. Classified as a junior, I'd have graduated in another year, but I interrupted my education again. I made an important choice which I still do not regret: to marry Enrique Anhalt. And since my husband was born in Mexico and lives there, this is how the second stage of my life became a Mexican one. About this topic, choice vs. destiny, I wrote a short story about Jewish love, "A Love Story Like No Other" (in *Cuentos inauditos* [Mexico: Editorial Incaro, 1994]).

What does it mean to be a Jewish woman in Latin America? The question is asked from an abstract point of view. The concept of Latin America, an apparently magnificent idea, is utopian. We are twenty-two very different countries, strangers to each other. No one could be more different from an Argentinian than a Bolivian, for example. And if you add to this gap their Jewishness, you have to find out whether it is Sephardi or Ashkenazi. But above all, I think that being a Jewish woman in Latin America, or in any other remote corner of the earth, means something similar: a belief in one God and an inherited burden of past injustices that impels one to try to construct a more ethical and more just human order.

I don't mean to imply that Judaism dedicates itself exclusively to the past, but that it does extract invaluable lessons from history in order to live in the present and see the future as a vibrant space of potential. Judaism has always been capable of extracting a song of hope from sufferings.

Our marginalized condition engenders the need to embue our acts with moral meaning. The problem is that some Jews have forgotten this and have buried our best qualities under a frivolous or vain superficiality.

But let's take this step by step.

MY CHILDHOOD IN CUBA was a time of all eyes and ears. I gazed constantly at the sea and at palm trees, stars, lizards popping in and out of great clumps of flowers. I listened to the calls of those selling fruits and other foods, pushing their merchandise on carts through the streets.

The Cuban language in contact with music was a great literary lesson. The tastes, aromas, and colors were the language of the pagan spirit of the island. I didn't withdraw from it, but rather submerged myself in it. I lived like the vegetation or the clouds, feeling myself part of an enchanted nature. I felt Cuban but at the same time Jewish. Why?

Because at an early age my ears heard about the trial of Captain Dreyfus and other terrible stories of anti-Semitism that my mother told me. I listened to how my father went to the Cuban authorities of the time to plead, to no avail, that the passengers of the ship the *San Luis* be allowed to disembark. I listened to my parents' strategies for bringing to Cuba the only survivors of Nazism who remained from my mother's family. I heard how my father's older sister, who lived in Russia—their younger sister had died in a Nazi extermination camp—couldn't get permission to leave; the Stalin regime, with its Iron Curtain, was implacable. I listened to reprimands for not finishing all the food on my plate—an unforgivable sin when hungry children existed. I heard for the first time the word *shnorer,* without understanding what it meant. This was when my brother's circumcision was being celebrated at an intimate gathering. I was nine years old and was not allowed to watch the ceremony. I was left alone on the terrace of the house. Soon two older men, strangers to me, came and kept me company; they were pleasant. Later I found out they were *shnorers.* The truth? Ever since then, I've felt a certain sympathy for those survivors of life. I learned the meaning of a *mitzvah* through my mother's story about her maternal grandmother. She made challahs and placed them in five windowed compartments on a wooden wall in front of her house. Thus any poor person could take the bread without having to thank her. I listened to my mother's fairy tale about going downtown to Old Havana during the forties to buy cloth to cover a lampshade. She went to a shop run by a "polaco" (nowadays, "polaco" means the hole in the floor into which urine and feces drain in women's prison cells, the "celdas tapiadas," so called because the prisoners remain standing in a small dark space with walls of sheet metal), which is what any Jew, whatever his origin, was called in Cuba. A priest, dressed in a black cassock, entered the shop. When he saw the owner, they embraced each other cordially. According to my mother, that image, which would have been so improbable in the Warsaw of that time, sealed her love for the island.

My father had come to Cuba when he was young. He spoke Spanish without an accent and he wrote it perfectly. He became a public defender *(procurador público)* and had his office in the commercial center of downtown Havana. Cuba for him, as for my mother, symbolized real life, everyday life. They were in love with Cuba, their adoptive homeland.

It is not irrelevant to mention that, since childhood, my Judaism had been marked by the expressive force of anti-Semitism, the Holocaust, and also by paradox. Even though my father had been a founding member of the Patronato (a synagogue and social center located on Línea e I Street, in the Havana neighborhood of El Vedado), and even though my mother did volunteer work at the Froien Farein, and we belonged to the Beth Israel congregation (the Beth Israel temple was located on the Avenue of the Presidents in El Vedado), I did not receive a formal religious education. On the contrary, I went to a Catholic school for first grade.

This was due to health problems. I used to get nauseous and vomit if I had to travel on a school bus. The San Vicente school was near my house, and I could go on foot. Its principal, an ex-nun, was a friend of my father's. They both agreed that I would be exempt from participating in catechism and religous history classes. And so I was.

EVERY SCHOOL IS A MICROCOSM of the universe. Students breath in a certain atmosphere and are influenced by it and by certain incidents that occur. Two things particularly affected me. One teacher must have discovered in me a certain facility or talent for writing. On various occasions she let me out of class so that I could sit in an empty classroom and write a composition on a patriotic topic. After recess, in the school courtyard where the Cuban flag hung, I'd recite it before teachers and students.

The second thing had to do with my religious vocation. My two best friends, in complicity with a priest, decided to convert me to Catholicism. The only requisite for baptism was that it had to be kept a strict secret. I couldn't tell my parents or anyone. I didn't like that prohibition, but out of loyalty to them, I kept silent. I still remember pacing up and down in the park near the neighborhood church of Santos Suárez where they were going to baptize me. God opened my eyes, as He did Hagar's in the desert. I didn't go. I left them waiting for me. Later, I fictionalized that episode in my life in musical form in my story "It Happened in Havana" (in *A buena hora mangos verdes* [Madrid: Ediciones Cocodrilo Verde, 1998]).

Of all the definitions of the meaning of Judaism, Elie Wiesel's is the closest to how I feel. I paraphrase, but the idea is this: to be a Jew doesn't mean just to have been born a Jew, but to choose to be one.

That morning when I paced up and down in the park in Havana was the moment when I knew, at age twelve, that I had chosen to be a Jew.

I kept it secret for a while, but as Octavio Paz says in *Primeras letras,* the value of liberty is connected to the principle of truth. To tell a lie knowingly or, as in my case, through silence or by avoiding the truth is to exercise not liberty but slavery. One day I told my parents everything.

I remember the looks they exchanged. By the following week, we had moved out of our house and our neighborhood, and I was enrolled in a secular school, considered the best in Cuba: the Ruston Academy.

Our teachers, some Cuban and some foreign university professors who lacked the papers certifying them as such (most of them were refugees from the World War II), were extraordinary. However, at the graduation ceremony (of the *bachillerato*), I was surprised by the presence of a priest and the saying of Mass.

We Jews in the class joked resignedly about how it seemed to be a state coup. We could have insisted upon having reciprocity: if we had known ahead of time about the priest and Mass, we'd have invited a Rabbi to the graduation. We shrugged our shoulders and moved from critical remarks to comprehension.

There was a certain absurd quality to this whole incident. How to explain, then, its connection with a terrible memory that I have? The memory is of the murder of a young medical student and his girlfriend on October 23, 1946, in the Forest of Havana. They were both Jews. Their names were Syma Rambasky and Jaime Bergerman. He was the only child of a friend of my mother's. There were all sorts of rumors, but the motive of the crime was never made clear, and the murderers were not caught. It was sung about for some time in "La Guantanamera," a popular melody from a radio program which broadcast the daily news. (The composer of "La Guantanamera" was the well-known Cuban musician Julián Orbón. The most widely known singer who popularized Orbón's song was Joselito Fernández. Later, Pete Seeger made the song even better known when he added lyrics by José Martí.)

LET IT REMAIN A MIRROR and a testimony of those years that, in 1940, the Republic of Cuba created one of its best constitutions, and that synagogues, Hebrew schools, and social and cultural associations flourished without rejection on the island. Every Jewish family could give their children Biblical names or whatever names they wished. Unlike in other Latin American countries, it was not obligatory to give children the names of Catholic saints. Jews walked freely around the island without having stones hurled at them as in European nations. And it is true, also, that Jews did not belong to the powerful elite or to the Cuban aristocracy.

THE RELIGIOUS HISTORY of Cuba, as well as its social, economic, and political history, took a 180-degree turn in 1959 when the Castro brothers came to power. There came times of terror and hate which still remain.

Many Catholics fled into exile. Those who remained on the island hid behind a mask of hypocrisy. Like the Jews of yesteryear who hid from the Inquisition by converting to the new faith but continuing their Judaism in private, Cuban Catholics became Communists and/or said their prayers in the privacy of their homes. "Galeshka," "Vladimir," and other Russian names began to replace those of Catholic saints. Were they to have done otherwise, parents would have ruined their children's prospects and might themselves have been labeled "counter-revolutionaries."

The Hebrew minority that was able to do so also fled into exile. My father was very worried about the future of Cuba. He came from Russia and intuitively recognized the signs of despotism: freedom of the press vanished, workers lost their freedom to strike, the effective surveillance system of the CDR (Comites de Defensa para la Revolución, or Committees for Defense of the Revolution), the ironhanded control of ration cards, work and school identification cards, the speeded up trials, executions, and more. . . . How right my father was! But he was not able to do much, because he was surprised by death.

In 1961, my mother and brother came to Mexico. On the journey, my mother wore, pinned to the lapel of her coat, a Cuban flag made of metal. She also brought the small mahogany bust of the poet and Cuban patriot José Martí and a few tablespoons that she had brought with her from Warsaw.

I don't wish to jump to conclusions, but I can affirm that my dreams and expectations had been suspended between these two poles of Catholicism and Judaism without my giving up either conscience or truth. As a Hebrew Cuban, I felt myself doubly wealthy, with riches that belonged to me but that I also had to deserve. It was true that while I was growing up in that privileged space, stimulated by a kind of vital luxury, some of the worst tragedies of the second half of the twentieth century had happened: the injustice of the *San Luis* ship, the Holocaust, the bombs on Hiroshima and Nagasaki.

Having joined my mother and brother in Mexico, I completed my studies in humanities there. I received a Master's degree in Latin America studies from the University of the Americas in Mexico City, where for six years I taught courses in Hispanic American literature. My son was born here. Here, beginning in 1984, I have published my books and engaged in cultural journalism. For eighteen years I wrote a weekly column of literary criticism for the Saturday supplement of the newspaper *Unomasuno*. In this same paper, I launched the column "Upcoming Films," where I was the first to unmask Leni Riefenstahl, the first to publicize Alfred Hitchcock's "Memory of the Camps" and Claude Lanzmann's "Shoah," among many other films.

I HAVE SPENT MORE YEARS in Mexico than on the island where I was born. In 1968 I became a Mexican citizen. I am sure that there are anti-Semites in Cuba, but I did not encounter them. In Mexico I have, and at all levels. We cannot ignore the fact that the Latin American anti-Semitic best-seller *Derrota mundial*—with antecedents in *Mémoire pour servir a l'histoire du jacobinisme* by the French Jesuit abbot Augustin Barruel (1741–1820), the first book to declare the existence of a "Jewish conspiracy," an accusation repeated later in the anonymous libel *Los protocolos de los sabios de Zion*—was written by a Mexican.

Mexicans are a people surrounded by ruins, churches, and volcanoes and inhabited by the ghosts of nationalism and antiforeign sentiment, which includes anti-Semitism. This anti-Semitism stems, in large part, from their Hispano-Catholic heritage. But it would be absurd to reduce Mexican anti-Semitism to a simple side effect of religion.

The topic is complex, because Mexico is a country capable of harboring massive contradictions. Here, Jews of Ashkenazi as well as Sephardi origin have found a home. And to be fair, I have to admit that on a professional level I have never suffered rejection because of being Jewish. More than that: without seeming too innocent about it, I feel that people have helped me precisely because of my Judaism. My politics have inspired the opposite response.

Because I fought in favor of human rights in Cuba, and because I have been in favor of reestablishing democracy on the island—or, said in a simpler way, because I have opposed Fidel Castro's forty years of tyranny—I've suffered all kinds of rejections, hostilities, and exclusions in Mexico.

An example: several years ago, a Mexican Jewish student presented her dissertation at the UNAM, the National University of Mexico. She had selected the work of three North American Jewish women writers and compared it to that of three Mexican Jewish women writers, of whom I was one. During the examination, two university professors, assuming the role of supreme arbiters of definition of Mexican nationality, told her that I could not be included in the thesis because I had not been born in Mexico.

The student answered that, following that reasoning, she would have to eliminate another of the writers as well, since she had not been born in Mexico either. Curiously, that case had not bothered them, but mine had. The student asked if my exclusion were related to "political" reasons. They denied it emphatically but insisted: either she remove me from her thesis, or it would not be approved. The three Jewish Mexican women writers were reduced to two.

What is paradoxical about this dictatorial pronouncement about nationality is that it came from two Mexican professors who, like me, had not been born in Mexico and were Mexican citizens by naturalization.

This incident must provoke a reaction of bafflement and repulsion. Something very sad underlies it: a lack of spiritual solidarity. If I have made a point of mentioning this, it is because I want to be clear about something. It is known that the UNAM is the citadel of Castroism and that Mexico has friendly relations with the official government of Cuba.

But one must write one's work honestly, independent of envies, competition, prizes, and recognition. Thus it is not surprising that when my book of aphorisms, *Crítica apasionada,* defines the *curriculum vitae* of the ideal critic, it also offers a synthesis of my identity:

That he should be born on the most beautiful island that human eyes have ever seen.

That he should live, by choice, in a country he loves because it enjoys a singular fame: that of having no double.

That he should belong to the chosen race: that which God chose to have suffer.

What more can you ask?

Thus it is not strange, for all these reasons, that being Jewish in Mexico should be a simple matter for some and difficult for others. For some Jewish women who are not "politically correct," it will always be difficult.

I am aware that I am swimming against the current, but it is my choice. And although this choice may have come with a high price, I am not sorry I made it.

Chapter 13

Judaism
An Essential Tool

Graciela Chichotky

WITH FOUR RUSSIAN GRANDPARENTS (one from Odessa and the others from who knows where), I was born in Buenos Aires in 1958. The story goes that my paternal grandfather, in urgent need to escape the European inferno, looked for a ship that would take him to the United States, where he could meet his brother. The question was unexpected: "Which city?" "Any city!" "Buenos Aires?" "Buenos Aires!" And so he came to settle in this country, where he never saw his brother again, and began a family line that now includes dozens of us. Of my other forebears, little is known.

The Judaism that was passed on to me was vague and diffuse. Of my four grandparents, I only knew the ones on my mother's side. Her father died when I was twelve years old. He loved Yiddish music and spoke Yiddish with my grandmother so that their daughters would not understand. At one point he tried to teach me a bit, the Hebrew letters and a phrase: "Ich Farbrengn zer guit" (I'm having a good time). He told us only a few things about Russia: that they used to warm their hands over heated stones, and that his last glimpse of his country before emigrating was of Cossacks' boots on the grating under which he was hiding. Once he found me looking for Jewish surnames on the obituary page of the newspaper. It pleased me to find them: I felt a surge of pride as I recognized myself in them. He explained to me that I shouldn't take pleasure in the death of a Jew, and for the first time I felt a sense of belonging, of community, learning that the misfortune of one Jew would necessarily affect me, too. On another occasion, he heard me swear by God. My grandfather told me, in a joking way: "Don't bother Him for insignificant things; He has so much to do. . . ." He never knew how that sentence of his gave me a sense of a God who was concerned about us, who was interested in our fate, a God who "had so much to do" and yet cared about me, a small girl in the Argentine Republic. I think that my Zeide José was a good Jew in his own way, a way that was secular yet inseparable from the common destiny of Jews with their roots in the People of the Book.

My grandmother passed her culinary wisdom on to us. Her gefilte fish, her *blinchikes* (blintzes), and her *eksifleish* (bittersweet meatballs) were truly memorable creations. She was never observant, and she ate pork right up to the end of her days. Nevertheless, when she gave out the recipe for her incredible *blinchikes,* she'd explain: the cheese ones are fried in butter; the meat ones in oil. She gathered the family together for Pesach, Rosh Hashana, and for the end of Yom Kippur. The only difference between the three dinners was the substitution of matzoh for bread. No ritual, no lighting of candles, no Seder made these meals different from any other family gathering. Nothing but the greetings: on Pesach my aunts and uncles would wish us "A gut yontef," while on Rosh Hashana and Yom Kipur they would wish us "A gut yur." In any case, the aromas of my Babi's apartment, and of her entire building on those days (she lived in the heart of Villa Crespo, a predominantly Jewish suburb), were unforgettable. When we went up in the elevator, we could smell roasting chicken and gefilte fish on every floor. Even now, anyone who wants to breath in the aroma of "yontef" has only to poke his nose into any building along Avenida Corrientes in downtown Buenos Aires.

My formal Jewish education was nonexistent. Somewhere in the world there exists the man responsible for this. He may be a rabbi, or he may be so assimilated that he has baptized his children. What is certain is that he is ignorant of his decisive role in the Jewish education of a family of five children. When my elder sister was old enough, they enrolled her in a "schule," a Hebrew school. And this man, then a child, taunted my sister, calling her a "rotten apple." She didn't want to go back, and that was the last of the Jewish education of the entire family. My parents, feeling that we should all be educated the same way, focused on culture: English, piano, guitar and singing lessons. The five of us became a chorus, with a repertory in four voice parts that included Christmas carols, Negro spirituals, and songs from *The Sound of Music*.

As for our identity, we knew we were Jews but nobody ever asked what that meant. On weekends, we'd go to a sports club named "Hacoaj" (Hebrew for "the force"). Nowadays, Hacoaj offers more intensive Jewish education than it did then. At that time it offered very little as a Jewish institution: a few words in Hebrew such as *kvutsa, haverim, maagal,* etc.; a booth-building competition on Succoth; and a communal Pesach Seder with lots of songs and meagre food which constituted, even so, my first introduction to Jewish ritual. A single premise was important in our education, an undebatable premise repeated over and over with the urgency of the essential: we absolutely had to marry Jews. However unlikely it seems, all five of us did just that.

There were a few things that defined my identity. At age eight, the time of First Communions, my school offered a class in catechism. The children who wanted to take it stayed on after school. I assume that they had let the parents know about this, but no one said anything to me about it. I found out about it one day when the teacher said that those who were going to stay should form a line (in those days, nobody went anywhere without lining up first and waiting). Without knowing what it was about, I got in line with my friends. The teacher pulled me out and said, "Not you." It was a strange feeling. As if there were something for "them" and not for me. I think it was the first time I felt different. A long time later I learned that some of my classmates were Jews, too, and I began to feel a sense of fellowship, an awareness that we all had something in common.

At one point we spent the summer in Córdoba, about six hundred kilometers from Buenos Aires. It was the year when we had participated in the Sukkoth competition, learning nothing about the holiday but a lot about how to build a booth with branches. Excited about this new skill, the first thing we did when we reached our rental house was to build a *sukkah*. The neighbors' daughter came over to play with us. We all chopped down vines and branches, and for several days we worked along on this project. It was clear to all of us that it wasn't a hut, it was a *sukkah*. To all of us but our newly acquired friend, who bewilderedly asked what a *sukkah* was and what made it different from an ordinary hut made out of branches? Finally, she asked the definitive question: "Why do you all insist on tying everything you do to being Jewish?" I didn't have an answer, but I could tell that in the very question there was a weightiness that was hard for me to understand.

Since nothing in life falls on barren ground, all this was building into a coherent identity, a vague idea of belonging to something shared with other people who were also scattered around the world. The idea was that there was something different about us as Jews that could be perceived by "the others" and which we necessarily had to acknowledge.

But there was something inside me, something intrinsically mine that had not been taught to me (except, perhaps, by my grandfather): the notion that there existed Someone who was protecting us. I began to pray at the age of ten. Each night before going to sleep, I prayed for the health of my whole family, including my grandparents, aunts, uncles, and cousins. I imitated my only model, the children I saw praying on television, kneeling beside their beds with their palms together. Living in a country as Catholic as Argentina, it was common to see people crossing themselves as they passed a church. So by the time I was twelve, I had invented a litany where I prayed for "all the synagogues in the world" as the bus I was riding in passed in front of the synagogue on the Calle Libertad. On our visits to the "shil" at the end of Yom Kippur (we went at five in the afternoon, all dressed up after a good meal) I learned the formula of some *brahot* (God of Abraham, God of Isaac, and God of Jacob), which I quickly included in my prayers. Gradually I constructed my own Judaism, my rituals and my personal way of communicating with God.

BUENOS AIRES HAS A VERY INTENSE Jewish life. Even now, despite the terrible crisis the community is going through, there are many youth centers that are open on Friday and Saturday evenings. Young people up to age eighteen gather for *peulot* (cultural and recreational activities) and then go out to the movies, to eat, to dance, or to one of their houses, where they gather to sing songs with someone playing a guitar. There was a *madrih* (youth leader) at one of the youth centers who invited me to join them. (How we met is another story.) I was seventeen years old. This *madrih*, who would one day be my husband, was a believer and was preparing for *mitzvot*. Besides our physical and chemical attraction, he showed me a world where Judaism had a prescribed form, where I didn't have to invent it all myself. Thus we began to search together. At first we tried joining a neo-Orthodox group of the Benei Akiva where, besides learning a lot, we could see this type of life close up. Finally we made contact with the Latin American Rabbinical Seminary, presided over then by its founder, Marshall T. Meyer z'l. (A great fighter for the cause of human rights, Marshall Meyer helped to rescue not only Jews who had been detained for political reasons and were being tortured for being Jews, but also anyone else who came to him in search of help. He was later decorated by the democratic government of Raúl Alfonsín and awarded the Order of the Liberator General San Martín, the first foreigner to receive such a distinction.) At the Seminary we continued our search, trying to find a way to live Judaism that would unite the inner world with the outer one, that would permit us to live in both realities without neglecting either of them.

The number of synagogues in Buenos Aires is incredible. It is not comparable to New York, of course, but in some neighborhoods there is one every hundred or two hundred meters. When we married, in 1979, we helped to found a new conservative community, "recycling" an old synagogue in Villa Crespo that no longer had a *minyan,* near where my grandmother still lived. The Ioná Hebrew Center became quite a phenomenon. Started by a group of friends, the community soon had a primary school (preexisting); a *madrihim* school; groups for children, youth, and adults; a bi-weeky publication; and volunteer activities. Leaders of defunct or underpopulated communities would come ask Ioná to take them on to return them to life. The center eventually had three branches (two synagogues in the city plus a country club in the suburbs). At High Holidays it would offer six parallel services for young people and adults, and throughout the year there were enormous numbers of bar and bat mitzvah ceremonies, as well as about five weddings per week. In such effervescence, we maintained our contact with Latin American reality. One of the purposes of Ioná was to carry on the struggle for a more just society, based on Judaic sources, and to reassert the prophetic messages of liberty and solidarity. I remember an interview with Eladia Blásquez that appeared in our magazine *(Kol Ioná),* in which she asked a question that never stopped resonating in my mind: "We are horrified by the death of six million, or of two million. The death of a single person does not produce such horror. How many deaths does it take for us to be appalled? Two, three, ten human beings?"

THE CHALLENGE TO JUDAISM in that era was that many young people were straying from Judaism to join the ranks of those engaged in the national struggle: the country's reality demanded urgent involvement in a social activism that young people felt was all-absorbing. They tended to feel that if they joined the Communist Party, or the Peronist Party, they should leave the Jewish community. To be a Jew was regarded as doing nothing, just singing little songs in the synagogue on Fridays and closing out the world. Those who joined the armed struggle left behind all identity that was not that of "Argentine to the death." Jewish communities were shrinking terribly. Lamentably, many of them did not survive this disastrous period. Those were very difficult years in every sense. Our communitarian task had to be to forge a common path of endeavor. The prophets of Israel came to help us. Their messages of social equality and of respect for human life were the underpinnings of an unarmed fight to preserve Jewish identity by offering young people a place where they did not feel disaffected from national reality.

In 1983, after four years of communitarian effort at the center, my husband decided to complete the rabbinical studies he had begun. He resigned from his accounting practice and from his position as general director of Ioná, and, with a one-year-old daughter and my newly acquired profession as a biologist, we left for Jerusalem. After two years in the Eternal City, we returned to Argentina, where Eduardo received his *smiha* and became a rabbi.

Our first assignment was to a small community of a thousand people in the city of La Plata, fifty-seven kilometers south of Buenos Aires. Even though the community had existed for eighty years, my husband was the city's first rabbi. Extremely secular and affiliated with the political left, the Jews of La Plata thought they needed a rabbi like they needed a hole in the head. The students at the school greeted him with signs that said "Khomeini keep out." The first Friday night religious service was attended by my husband, my daughter, now three years old, the organist, and myself. With time, they came to understand that religion is not necessarily the opiate of the people, that it is possible to seek social involvement and purposefulness through our millennarian sources as well. We went through two years of colossal challenge that culminated in a reawakened *kehila,* pledged to all the human values of Judaism. Our next assignment was to the Israelite community of Santiago de Chile, where we are still working and have been for the past eleven years. We now have four children, aged sixteen, twelve, eleven, and six.

TO SPEAK OF LATIN AMERICA as a whole is perhaps an error. Each country has its idiosyncrasies, and it is unwise to generalize. Argentina is an essentially Catholic and inquisitorial country. Most of its inhabitants share a totalitarian mentality which believes that the ideal human being is the prototypical Argentine. No one remembers that the much-vaunted Argentine character is made up of contributions by Spaniards, Italians, Jews, and other people who have molded the national culture and language. Everyone should be equal; no one can be singled out as different, because anyone who is constitutes a menace to the others. The jokes about Galicians, like those about Jews, form part of national culture. The official anti-Semitism that has made it impossible to ever find those who have profaned Jewish graves or the assassins of the AMIA makes Jewish life doubly difficult there. Chilean reality is different. Not only is there more respect for the distinctive qualities of each cultural group, but there is also a perception and appreciation of the dignity and worth of belonging to a community. This makes it easier to find a Jewish base from which to contribute to the country, since every individual is socially permitted to participate in his or her own way.

Our undertaking here in Chile continues to be to show that it is possible to lead a dual existence. That one can be both Jewish and Chilean without neglecting either of the two. As in every community in the world, assimilation is a force which corrodes our roots. It is the great challenge, this great riverflow of merger where our blood is lost. Mixed marriages, people who become estranged from their communal rites, the large number of people who identify themselves as Catholic whose last names are Lewin, Goldberg, or Cohen: all these become ever more worrying. In Chile we have a small but considerable number of people who return to the Jewish community after two or three generations of Christianity. A grandmother dies and they find in her things a pair of candelabra or a moth-eaten *siddur,* and the questions begin. Or a search for origins turns up a *marrano* Jew. But these are the miracles of our people. And miracles don't happen every day, as we know. We know that that is not the norm.

RABBI TUVIA FRYDMAN, Z'L, conjectured that Judaism survived four thousand years because it was useful and stressed that it should continue to be so if it wants to endure. What use is it to be Jewish? If Judaism as a culture is only a burden of guilts and dangers that do not include any benefits, then it makes no sense to continue it. If, on the contrary, Judaism brings me something without which I could not live, I won't give it up for anything. Let's look at a clear example. In a tropical country, woolen hats are unnecessary. If someone were to start campaigning: "Let's revitalize the use of woolen hats, keep them from extinction," people would take him for a madman. But in the Arctic, there could never even be a "Pro-woolen Hats" campaign. Woolen hats are necessary. Everyone simply uses them.

The big problem of assimilation is that people don't find their Judaism useful. They feel that they do not need that woolen hat. The mission of those of us who are engaged with the community enterprise is not to show off how attractive our hat is, but to make them understand that it is cold outside and that Judaism can give them warmth. According to Frydman, the usefulness of Judaism is triple: it functions as a frame of reference which is larger than ourselves, as a cosmic compass (to tell us where we came from and where we're going), and as a source of meaning for life. If we can manage to make this understood, we will have won the greater part of the battle.

Assimilation worries us. But there is also a paradoxical change in respect to what happened in the seventies in Argentina. The military repression has been inverted. During that period, we struggled because young people were leaving Judaism to submerge themselves in national reality: we were losing Jews. Now they are hiding from reality by submerging themselves in Judaism: we are losing world citizens. The proliferation of ultra-Orthodox groups that promise instantaneous answers to existential dilemmas endangers the mission of Jews which is, precisely, to improve the world that they are evading. Philosophers attribute this to globalization and postmodernity, which lead us to return to medieval magical thought. The second current challenge to Judaism should be a return to the point of equilibrium, a return to the center, so as not to interrupt our contribution to humanity.

There is an excellent Argentine comedian named Enrique Pinti. His political monologues are surprisingly astute. In one of his skits about Latin American identity, he says that Latin America is a continent looking for its roots, that it has to dig within itself in order to find its identity. And he continues, "And here we have Moisés Rabinovich, a *poncho* on his shoulder and a *quena,* an Andean flute, in his hand, hunting for his Latin American roots in Lake Titicaca."

Being a Jew in the Diaspora, in any diaspora, is complicated. One must recreate one's own roots, feeling that somewhere along the way they have split and divided. In Latin America we must struggle to define and explore our ancestral origins, as well as our ties to this land so rich in pain and struggle. They may be essentially compatible. A book on this topic that was particularly striking to me is Mario Vargas Llosa's *The Storyteller.* It seems incredible that without being himself Jewish, he has found in the history of our people the model of cultural colonialism that tried to decimate the native peoples of Latin America. Someone takes on the responsibility for saving us from our perfidious beliefs and thus tries to convert us into something that we are not, so that we will stop being ourselves although we will never manage to be "them."

I am convinced that our contribution to humanity must be based on our identity and our specificity. I don't believe in John Lennon's dream, where he imagined a world without nations or boundaries, where we would all be equal. Equal to whom? Would we all eat tofu or hamburgers? Would we all wear pants or tunics? My dream is of a world with boundaries, with different nations, where everyone respects everyone else and themselves. Where we all understand that just as we protect whales so that they will not become extinct, because the world needs its whales, so, too, should we be concerned that no one should stop being what he or she should be. If I see a Hindu eating beef, if I see a Catholic who does not go to Mass on Sundays, or a Muslim drinking whisky, I feel that humanity is losing the richness

conferred by diversity. It may be that we will all end up eating hamburgers and wearing blue jeans, but that is not going to make us more
human, nor will it keep us from hating each other. If we can manage to
understand that each one of us has not only the right but also the obligation to be him- or herself, each one of us could contribute the best
of him- or herself to make this a better world.

Chapter 14

A Passion to Remember

Sonia Guralnik

MY WHOLE LIFE IS IN MY STORIES. Memory infuses all I write. Word by word, I embroider the tapestry of memory. When my stories are all told, they will be a great woven coverlet of words that my descendants can pull over themselves, wrapping themselves in layers of memories that may shelter them and may help them make sense of things. In this historic moment, in a Chile that is deeply mine although in many ways I am still a foreigner here, when forgetfulness wants to chill everything, memory is essential, and I hold fast to the words that persist in remembering and preserving the past, allowing its horrors and loves to intertwine. Chile is my country, and so is a distant Russia that no longer exists. Embroidering my tapestry, I forge identity and make the future: the layers of the recollected past will comfort and fortify the hearts of those who follow me, and, knowing this, I combat forgetfulness and help others to do so, so that our history is not lost. As I recover memories and set them in words, I realize that mine is not a history of great events, but an account of a succession of small episodes, little incidents, like most of women's histories through all time.

There's a beautiful poem by Enrique Lihn that says "I'm alive because I write." I, too, feel grateful to my writing. I don't know if everything began the way I remember it, or whether, way back there, long ago, I drew things on the Russian snow and imagined where those beautiful stories of my people came from. What I remember as the beginning of my effort to capture my memories in words was one afternoon in my apartment, after I'd been summing up what I'd done in my life, which consisted of having children, cooking, scrubbing, and taking some odds and ends of courses, I decided to write a story about a war, a war because, beginning with World War I and the Russian Revolution, there have been so many in my life.

The story of the war was told to me daily by soldiers who came from the front and had no way to get back home. It was a struggle to survive in the postwar blockade, when there was no kerosene, or sugar, or medicine. We lived on sardines and other river fish and on roots. I don't remember now how that first story of mine turned out, and it doesn't matter: it gave me a glimpse of how my stories and my life would intertwine.

I would write about how, after that war, the journey to America followed. In Russia, I spoke Russian, the language in which I learned to read and write. At home, we spoke Yiddish. We were all completely bilingual. When we came to Chile, I had to learn Spanish, the language in which I now think and write. But in my dreams, the languages get mixed up together: *mestizaje* occurs. The first poem I ever recited was by Pushkin, then a whole poem by Hayyim Nahman Bialik, "The City of the Massacre," in Yiddish. My mother wanted us to keep speaking both Russian and Yiddish, but my father thought that because we spoke Spanish at school, we should speak only Yiddish at home, because of its relationship with Judaism. My mother continued to read in Russian until she died in 1951; she used to trade books with other Russian immigrants, and she was especially fond of Pushkin's poems and of Tolstoy, Turgenev, and Chekov. She would read anything in Russian, but was never comfortable in Spanish. Through my mother and her readings, I was introduced early on to the world of words.

By the time I started school in Chile, I knew how to speak some Spanish, but I didn't know how to write. We arrived February 5, 1930, and classes began just a month later, on March 15. I was in the fourth grade. I had learned a lot of words in order to play with my new friends. The first word I learned was when I was invited to play *luche,* hopscotch; my new friends drew a court on the ground and jumped through its squares, and that's how I found out that *luche* was a game, not a food or a stadium. I had no idea how to write the alphabet in Spanish. It might as well have been Chinese. And then I was baffled by the relationship of sounds to letters: I didn't understand the *s* or the *c,* the *ch,* the silent *h.* They were all puzzles to work out. Several years later, I could speak and write Spanish, but my dreams were always in Russian. Sometimes, I still dream in Yiddish or in Russian.

Then came the Spanish Civil War and I marched with other students, singing the Republican songs. My last formal education was at Girls' High School Number 3, and although I'd have liked to go on to the university, I didn't. I enrolled in a course the gas company was offering on how to cook. World War II took place, and the Holocaust. A newly created Israel fought its own wars. So many wars have followed: Vietnam, Nicaragua, Iran-Iraq, Lebanon, El Salvador, the Gulf: so much strife during my lifetime.

But we should not forget about the war we have lived through here in Chile, a war without declarations or missiles. I am, in truth, an expert on wars, but I can find no rational explanation for the nocturnal, hidden, vicious, and fratricidal war we have endured here. It was during this war and its losses that I began my own battle with words. In the midst of the unbearable, sitting alone in the afternoons, I began to write my first words and stories in a notebook, trying to absent myself from the war that surrounded me on all sides. My nephew was arrested and killed, my daughter was forced into exile, my family was divided: everything that had been built up came tumbling down without my being able to do anything. I wrote to preserve memory, because I am Jewish and I know that memory is fundamental. I wrote in search of a way to understand the truth about what was happening, a truth I could not find in the kitchen at the bottom of a casserole, or by being a worm hidden in the earth, pretending to be uninvolved in what was occurring.

Sometimes I cry about those times, and sometimes I wake up at night in terror. But I've smashed the worm that was growing in me, and I've put myself together piece by piece, constructed myself with memory and with words, words that derive from a past of meringue pies and catering and teaching cooking lessons, a past I do not renounce, but which came to seem insufficient. I would not have been capable of writing a book without the support and encouragement of Pía Barros, my teacher, without Soffia, our writing group, without my friends' sometimes merciless criticisms, without the "Keep on, Sonia"s.

The success in 1984 of my first book of stories, *El Samovar,* pleased me, but I wasn't sure it made me a real writer: I had just collected memories, told the stories I remembered from childhood and filtered them through my adult perceptions. Pía Barros tried to convince me that literature is an artifact of memory, that the act of choosing one word rather than another is to create.

When my second book, *Relatos en sepia,* was published, I joined the Society of Writers. I had always wanted to participate in cultural affairs, and this seemed to be the right route. The country needed change, and I was the country. Holding my new registration card, on which I was officially listed in print as a "writer," I walked all around my house, holding the card as if it were a sacred object. I showed it to my children, to my friends. It was proof.

But a little after that, when I introduced myself as Sonia Guralnik and someone asked me, "The writer?" I was overcome with modesty and answered, "Not yet. But I am an apprentice writer."

Every afternoon I would sit with my notebooks and, in my careful handwriting, struggle with words, with narrators, with time frames, and with structures. I invented stories based on minimal truths which gradually evolved beyond their origins and became stories I would have liked to have lived, or to have been told, or which moved me.

When I delivered my third book to the publisher, Editorial Sud-
americana, something changed in me. That morning, life seemed
clear: it was meaningful, and I had worked hard for this. My steps were
confident. With my registration card in my wallet, I strode across Santiago almost singing out loud. When I reached the office, I greeted the
secretary and said, stumblingly:

"I have an appointment with . . ."

The smiling girl asked me my name. With a firm voice, I said, "Tell
him that the writer Sonia Guralnik is here."

And even though a wave of insecurity threatened me, I paid no attention to it: I was holding a book, *Recuentos de la mujer gusano,* in my
hand, at home the central character of the next book awaited me, and
Mrs. Guitel could not be far behind her. I was eager to continue my
storytelling, and written words were accumulating in my notebooks.

"Yes," I repeated. "The writer is here."

My Family's Journey from Russia to Chile

My first book was titled *The Samovar* because it includes a story about
one of the few items we were able to bring with us from Russia. It has
been in my home all my life, first in Russia and now here in Chile. We
lived in a town named Ameldnik, which was on the Bug River and had
a population of one hundred fifty thousand. The Christian city was on
one side and the Jewish city on the other. The Bug River was a tribu-
tary of the Volga, and shipping was important. Ameldnik was near the
city my mother came from, Vinnytsya. Ameldnik was destroyed during World War II because it was part of the agricultural zone of the
former Soviet Union, and the Germans were very interested in its
wheat. They entered the city in October of 1942. We read about it in
the Chilean papers and felt very sad. I loved that city. My school was
there, and my river, the river I swam in during the summer and skated
on in winter. It all exists clearly in my memory: where the house was

located, what the storage cellar looked like, and how scared I was to go down there alone—I'd always get my little sister, Dora, to come with me when I had to go down to get a jar of jam. After World War I, when food was scarce, the yard was turned into a vegetable garden and the trees were cut down. It's the kitchen I remember best, with its big hearth—we even took baths there, in big wooden tubs.

As a child, I was a dreamer. I dreamed more than I talked. When I read, I would be the characters. When my real life was disagreeable, I preferred to be the book characters. I had to take the chickens to the *shochet* so they would die a kosher death, and I had to ride in car 36, the last car, while my friends could ride up front. I complained to my father, because I was ashamed to travel second class. My father said that even though the last car was open sided (they only let me ride up front on rainy days), there was no difference; both cars got there at the same time and so there was no reason to be ashamed. To get even, I dreamed, I imagined everything. In the book *Corazón*, I crossed the Andes, I was Anna Karenina, I suffered hunger with Knudt Hamsun, and no one noticed the chickens under my twelve-year-old arms.

We left Russia because we were Jewish and because my father was going to be sent to Siberia for disobeying the Commissar of the town, who ordered him to stay in his shop. My father left in 1928, taking my brother Haim with him, since he was the oldest. A year later, my mother, my sister, and I left Moscow by train. In Moscow, we said goodbye to Aunt Bruche, the youngest of my mother's sisters and the only one who had married for love. Uncle Ravinovich, her husband, who was the Commissar, got our passports for us, since they were no longer being issued. After a month-long stay, we left at Christmastime in 1929, amid gifts, tears, photographs, and enough keepsakes for the rest of our lives. Departures were like this, for always, and emigrants were never seen again. Aunt Bruche was the mother of two girls our ages with enormous black eyes, and we had played with them every day during our stay. Our train crossed all of Europe: Germany, Holland, Belgium, and France to Marseilles, where we embarked on the

Liberté, the steamship that would take us to America. We were traveling second class: those in first class had the top deck, we in second
class had private cabins, and those in third were divided into men's
and women's dormitories. We were lucky enough to have a cabin for
the three of us. Mamá never let go of our hands. Mamá's older brother,
Flimman, had gone to Chile in 1913, and we were sailing to Buenos
Aires in order to take the trans-Andean train to Santiago, where my
father and brother were.

In Buenos Aires, we were met by a group of seven representatives
of the Jewish Committee, who spoke to us in Yiddish. Because there
were already stories going around of girls being kidnapped for prostitution, they asked Mamá to not let us go out of the Jewish hostel
where we stayed. She kept us there, locked in, during the eight days it
took her to make all the arrangements for the next part of our journey.

The trans-Andean train from Argentina to Chile took more than
thirty hours. Mamá got off at the stations to buy fruit and bread, and
the train supplied hot water for tea. It caught our attention that groups
of men were drinking a strange tea, passing around a little cup with a
straw they all drank through; we thought those must be the Indians
we had been told about. At that time we had no idea what *maté* was.

We had left Moscow in the middle of an exceptionally cold winter.
We were all three of us wearing floor-length fur coats, with fur hats
and muffs, which my mother insisted we put on for our arrival in
order to look elegant. We got off the train in Santiago in midsummer,
and the first thing I saw were the mountains. I didn't know whether all
this was real or a story, and I was so steeped in all of the Russian and
Jewish stories my mother had told me that it seemed more likely to me
that we were in a story. I'd seen tall mountains in illustrations of Russian stories. But these in Chile seemed too steep, and I asked if they
weren't about to fall on us. There at the Mapocho station, my Uncle
José's family was waiting, all dressed for summer. I didn't know any of
them. But there was my brother Jaime with a plaid suitcase full of
Chilean candy. Papá embraced Mamá and they wept and no one paid

any attention to us. I suppose they hadn't known whether they would ever see each other again.

Papá had brought all his books, his tallit, his phylacteries, all his prayerbooks, and books by Maimonides and other ideologues who have contributed different ideas to the religion. In contrast, my mother brought all her books of Russian literature so as not to forget Russian, beginning with Pushkin, Chekov, and Tolstoy (my greatest heroine was Anna Karenina); the eiderdown comforters; the meat grinder and the knife for gefilte fish; the green felt tablecloth her sisters had given her as a wedding present, with its fluffy pompoms all around the edges (which the rats eventually ate); the samovar; the Shabbat candelabra; and the clock, all in wicker trunks, and she only allowed us to bring one *matrioshka* each.

My father was a man austere to the point of avarice, who said that we had to save for the bad times because Jews had always had to emigrate—a man full of precepts, without any sense of humor, full of nostalgia for his synagogue and his lost brothers. He'd get sad on Saturday after-noons, because it was time to pray by a river: Mamá would say enthu-siastically, "Well then, go over to the Mapocho," and he'd say, "That's a river with no fish, dirty, full of stones." He'd go anyway, but not hap-pily. My father prayed three times a day until the day of his death, when he said his afternoon prayers and died at dawn the next day, a Saturday.

My mother was a warm-hearted, understanding person. She always managed to get things Papá said "No" to. There was a wedding and I had only one pair of school shoes; she explained to Papá that in Chile, children had both school shoes and dress shoes. Papá said that you should only have one pair of shoes and when they wore out, then you could buy another. I remember she said, "It's that Sonischka is grow-ing." She wanted to tell Papá that I was beginning to need other things. Mamá was optimistic and enthusiastic, full of hopes for this new life; Papá was nostalgic, full of memories and losses that didn't allow him to appreciate the new. My mother was sociable, traded books with friends, and was a voracious reader. She obeyed the precepts, but without Papá's strictness. She wasn't interested in cooking; she used to tell my sister and me, "Don't take on domestic tasks, you'll have the rest of your lives to do those; this is the moment to learn." My mother was a devotee of education, of the professions, of knowledge. My mother was the first in town to bob her hair, a great scandal. She was an innovator.

We were very observant. Saturdays we had classes. Papá wanted us to walk to school on Saturdays, but since I couldn't manage that, Papá agreed that we could go by streetcar, even though on Shabbat travel is not permitted. I respected my father, but it seemed to me that you didn't go straight to hell if you ate a piece of pork or a shellfish. He kept fasts religiously, and even today I fast on Yom Kippur. My house has its *mezuzah* in the doorway and its Shabbat candelabra. My children have not followed all of my customs; they've made mixed marriages. Far from grieving over this, I feel integrated into the whole world, into all beliefs, and closer to my God of pardon and goodwill, the god of morality and ethics who loves all the people of the world.

Since I was born into a home of practicing Jews, my early memories are of family events where Judaism played a role. I remember when I was little, at home, on the eve of Yom Kippur, a bird was sacrificed for each of us with a prayer that says: "This animal will suffer all that you might suffer during the course of this year." Jaime had a young rooster, Dora had a little chicken, I had a chicken, and my mother had a hen. Father would say this prayer, holding each animal over the head of its recipient. Sometimes I feel as though all the sorrows of my life have occurred because my father wasn't there every year to hold the chicken over my head.

I AM JEWISH, AND what I am (Jew, immigrant, Latin American, woman) is what I write. Writing and being are fused: being a Jew, an immigrant, a woman, a writer, a Russian-born Chilean are all part of my reality, my memory, and my writing. I wouldn't describe my writing as being about topics which are particular to Jews, immigrants, women, or any narrow category. Ethics, which does interest me, is not the property only of the Jewish religion. Every religion (and every category of human being) includes both despicable people and great ones. I wouldn't say that there are any topics that are exclusively Jewish, but there is a Jewish world view, a women's world view, an immigrant's world view. The stereotype of the Jewish mother, as a character, is like the stereotype of the Italian mother, just as the miser may be found in Catholic, Protestant, and other cultures. Not even the stereotypes of characters are uniquely Jewish, although the anti-Semitic use of them is.

One's identity is indivisible. The writer, the Jew, the Latin American, and the woman are inseparable from one another; their interrelatedness makes me what I am. I learned how to be Latin American when I was marked as different by my Jewishness and blondness in a high school where everyone else looked otherwise. Being different has been what has marked my life and my writing. Difference is what has taught me respect for everything that is dissimilar to me, and love for difference has taught me the politics and utopia of dreaming of a society without exclusions. My desire for justice is for everyone, not just for Jews. Yes, I am a woman writer, a Jew, and a Latin American, but that is not a definition; it is barely a first introduction. When we came to Chile, the servant ate in the kitchen, but in Russia Antoschka ate at the table with us. The violence of discrimination always makes me take the side of those discriminated against.

Chile is so class-prejudiced, valuing only connections to the country's forty founding families, that even if those connections don't exist, people prefer to invent them rather than admitting their *mestizaje* with Indians, Jews, Arabs, or whatever it is that separates them from a concept of *criollo* aristocracy. I think that only very recently, and related to the national need for memory, texts by immigrants or ones that offer us a past are being considered important. But this is only in the last three years or so. On the other hand, Chile values education. When we arrived from Russia, we discovered that universities were free and that primary education was compulsory. On Echeverría Street, when we lived there, the *carabineros* came looking for some children because their parents had not sent them to school. They made the parents send their children to school. In this country of green vegetables and fruit all year around, education was not a privilege but a requirement. My mother greeted Dora's fellow university students with an enthusiastic "The doctors honor my house," and knowledge was on every street corner, within a hand's reach.

When I was first beginning to write seriously, I met women like myself who struggled with problems like mine and had the same difficulties with words, because we had somehow gotten the idea that language was by men and for men and that we women did not fit into it. The sadness of being a woman was transformed in the process of writing into the joy of discovery; the words "gender identity" made me part of half the world, and I learned to write by women for women, from a distant memory, where history in a big sense was narrated by men and the little stories, those that created identity and memory, were told by women.

Memory is the fundamental base of what I write; I hardly ever write anything that is pure fiction, because what I do is reconstruct a country, a childhood, recollections that are my own or that I heard, fragments of what I am and what the generations to come will be. I reconstruct and build with construction material made of words. My whole self, and all my selves, are made of words, which build themselves into books, which make me what I am and what I will be in the memory of those who read me. I cannot separate memory from my texts, any more than I can separate being a woman from writing my texts. Memory is the largest construction of our minds; without it, we don't exist, we are not here, we will not be. I came to Chile with an immense memory which I have been recovering little by little through these years. I didn't realize then how much fit into my little head, all the songs, all the prayers, all the stories, all the frozen lakes of a nostalgia I would discover with the years. I have memories of persecutions of others, of myself, mixed with political persecutions, which one of my daughters suffered. I have griefs fused with other griefs, and each recollection gives me a root, a deep connection with Europe and America. I am part of every being and present in every gaze, and when I am not here, I will be memory in others and I will not cease to exist.

Every afternoon I construct a bit of memory in my notebooks. With those notebooks, I have a passport that says "writer"; I have converted myself into a person with her own name and identity. I am still someone's daughter, someone's wife, and someone's mother, but I do not exist only in those roles. Writing has converted me into the witness of my own conscience, free to speak for myself and for others.

Chapter 15

Poetry in the Clouds
A Costa Rican Journey

Rosita Kalina de Piszk

MY PARENTS IMMIGRATED to Costa Rica, where my mother's family had been living since 1930, in 1932. My father left the rest of his family in Poland and never heard from them again after 1940. By the time my parents arrived in San José, my maternal grandfather had already established a small shop in the central market, and his unmarried children helped him with it. The family was very close, and gradually the children married, with the exception of one of my uncles who remained single and made a great fortune.

I was born on October 3, 1934, and, in the poor neighborhood where my father rented a bar, El Polo Sur, spent a happy childhood playing doctor with the neighborhood children and splashing in the open water pipes that came down from the Paso Ancho washing area. We weren't there many years, and I was very young, so my recollections are not full-fledged memories but more impressions and intuitions that I've tried to express in my poetry. Among the experiences of those early years are recollections of the radio and World War II news, the lack of news of my father's family, the prevailing sadness of the home in which I was growing up, which I later realized was due to my father's loss of his brothers, sisters, and parents in the Holocaust. They are profound memories, unhealed wounds, the pain and insomnia of which lacerated my senses as a child and adolescent. These impressions of the family are very much my own: my sister did not live through this, since by the time she was born, in 1943, we lived in a much more centrally located house, still modest but by now with a servant. My father, who had been a jeweler in Poland, rented a shop and started a business repairing watches and selling jewelry, porcelain, and silver items like the old clock I have in my dining room, which reminds me of the old jewelry shops, first Hermes and then Joyería Kalina, where my mother also worked beside my father while my sister and I chased 'round, each with her own interests and problems. Sundays were interesting: the whole family gathered on the beautiful farm owned by my rich uncle in Santa Ana. His land had a marvelous view of the mountains, a river splashing along between rocks, a house full of valuable antiques, and a bird enclosure with pheasants and a peacock who strutted like some of the teachers I knew at the Escuela Perú. My father never went out to that farm since the rich uncle, according to him, was not very Christian, as we might say, and Don Isaac Kalina refused to accept people who were different. Perhaps because of that, my rich uncle didn't leave me anything when he died, but I forgive him because I loved him too much to feel anything else for him.

My sister Ruth was born when I was eight years old. I was never close to her, since my mother's obsession that I should become the family star kept me fully occupied. It meant that I had to go to an upper-class school where I didn't fit in. It meant endless piano lessons and all the tedious practicing at home, with my uncles applauding me for playing Clementi's Sonata well, or the Chopin waltzes. And it eventually meant the National Conservatory of Music, where I learned theory and harmony. When they signed me up for ballet, and I performed dressed as a rabbit at an assembly held in the National Theater, I was so plump and nervous that I fell on my face in center stage. That was the end of ballet classes for me, and I was left on my own to turn into a tall, skinny heron, all legs and elbows. I think that all this kept me separated from my generation for a few years, since I shared very little with my Jewish friends except the obligatory Friday dinners and attendance at the humble synagogue of that era, where we learned to read Hebrew poorly and speak it even worse. I have managed to completely forget those scraps of Hebrew, and if I speak and understand Yiddish, it is because I learned it from hearing it spoken at home. When I think about who constitutes my generation of Jews in San José, the ones who are thought of as "good Jews" are businessmen, industrialists, some professionals, and me, turned into a rebel by my demanding mother and father in a home where affection came mostly from the paternal side.

THE JEWS WHO IMMIGRATED before the war were deeply rooted in Judaism, as was the post-war wave of immigrants, who brought more painful memories with them than did the first group since the majority came from the ghetto or from concentration camps. Their sense of Jewish identity was very strong, apart from the great emotional wound that they suffered. The numbers tattooed on their forearms impressed me deeply, even though I never met or knew much about anyone in my father's family, which disappeared without a trace. I have always looked for that family, with no success. Even when my husband and I visited Russia in 1983, I kept looking for the surname Kalina, with no luck. Even today, my sister Ruth keeps looking and tells me about her efforts in this regard. They are wounds that never heal and that make you abhor that ungrateful past that has so scarred your mind with its horrors, even though you were born in a democratic country like Costa Rica, which welcomed the Jews who escaped from concentration camps and began to find new lives in the country that generously took them in.

My experiences as a Jew in my parents' home were profound and deeply influenced me. Sometimes Ruth and I would slip off with my friend Ana to watch religious processions during the Catholic Holy Week. We felt something very strange when we saw the angels and the virgins and the image of Jesus crucified amidst all that pomp and circumstance. Ours was a simple synagogue in a modest neighborhood. I never accepted that the women had to pray behind a curtain and that the men had a place of honor in the religion. When I asked my parents about this, they accused me of being a rebel and an intransigent. Things are the same in the present elegant synagogue on the Paseo Colón: the women upstairs, the men downstairs in the large room. Now, a Reform synagogue exists and another that is Lubavich, but I've never been to nor am I interested in them. In reality, I seldom go to the synagogue, except on holy days like Yom Kippur and Rosh Hashanah. I am a largely nonobservant Jew and have chosen to be so.

MY CHILDHOOD WAS MARKED by poverty, and by parents who were rigid and embittered by their economic and social situation, even within the nascent Jewish community in Costa Rica. I never went to a Hebrew school because there wasn't one. There is one now: it goes from preschool all the way up through high school. In grade school, I was the first in my class in academic excellence, and I had a wonderful teacher, Miss Soledad, who helped me along for six years. I had a more difficult time with some of the other teachers and with the director of the school, whose prejudice against me often made me unhappy. Once I stole a picture of Robert Taylor, who was my masculine ideal in that preadolescent stage, from a classmate's bag, but I felt such remorse that I sneaked my idol back into her schoolbag at recess the next day.

The religion teacher, Miss Marta, let me into her classes without my parents hearing about it. I knew more about Christianity than did my Catholic classmates. Once I answered a question about the martyrdom of St. Stephen. My classmates all turned around and stared at me incredulously. By age twelve I had already read the classics—the Greeks, Verne, Tolstoy—and it hadn't made me any happier. I played the piano, I spoke English, and it didn't make me any happier. They refused to let me carry the Costa Rican flag in the school parade, even though I was the best student. I left the parade and watched it from the sidewalk.

Once I reached adolescence, although I was still painfully shy and very conscious of my family's poverty, I was finally allowed to attend a fairly democratic high school where social class was not so conspicuous as in the private school. But again in high school, they refused to let me carry the Costa Rican flag. Again, I refused to participate in the parade. All this must have influenced my poetry, since I find there a tone of rebellion in spite of being a good Jew, although not in a religious sense. That's why my first poems examine and reflect upon my childhood, my poor neighborhood, and my later ones the existence of religions, political credos, and ethnic differences. To a certain extent I feel satisfied with my past—it allowed me to see things that my Jewish compatriots didn't experience. I worked for several years at the Costa Rican Authors' Association, and that, too, helped me to free myself of fear of expressing, poetically, how I see the truth.

It has been very pleasing to be a first-generation Jewish writer in Costa Rica, since my books have been well received by journalists as well as praised in essays in various of the country's university magazines. I'm often called for television interviews or to serve on degree committees. Since what I write is pretty much existential and somewhat polemical, there has been interest in analyzing my poetry and my stories. I wrote for twenty years for the opinion page of the country's most eminent newspaper, *La Nación,* as well as for the Sunday literary supplement, *Ancora.*

As I've said, my childhood and adolescence made me extremely sensitive to social problems and religious differences. I constantly felt anti-Semitism in grade school, and sporadically in high school. The loss of family members in World War II, family relationships, Jewish and Catholic friendships—all these created a fertile world for literary creation. My relationship with Jewish topics has been meaningful, since, despite not having studied in a Hebrew school, I have always been fascinated by the Bible and the people it describes. Since childhood, I have read everything I could get my hands on, from the ancient Greeks to, later, Tibetan and Hindu texts. In other words, there is an important religious synthesis going on in my work, since being Jewish did not keep me from being interested in other paths, even though I did not become personally committed to any of them. My primary concern has been with a more universal vision of humanity—its surroundings, its religions, and its religiously motivated wars, which have always seemed to me to be an aberration—and, above all, with a wider perspective on other cultures sometimes devalued because of skin color. Others' ways of worshipping the gods, their lack of tolerance as in the Inquisition, and their slaughter of indigenous people have all helped the world become an interplay of huge superpowers with enormous economic and military power. All this has nurtured the expression of a wide range of topics, not just Jewish or Costa Rican, but wider and richer in terms of new emotions that flowed forth as I wrote poetry, essays, and stories. Since poetry is in some ways more intuitive than rational in its production, when I reread my poems, I sense in them a rebellion against a status quo that I've been rejecting ever since childhood, which I continue to feel even as I get older. I believe firmly that without conflict literature cannot exist, and that is what I see in my writing.

IN MY POSITION AS A university professor, I have always been interested in Jewish writers, especially the twentieth century North Americans like Bernard Malamud, Philip Roth, Isaac Bashevis Singer, and others. Whenever I've traveled to the United States, I have had the opportunity to buy books for my students of North American literature. And I even wrote my thesis for the *licenciatura* about Malamud: "The double pattern of suffering in *The Assistant*," some of the chapters of which have been published in scholarly journals.

As for the Jewish themes I incorporate into my work, I can affirm that the Book of Job has been a source of inspiration for several poems for, above all, the divine injustice of punishing a human being in order to test his devotion. I've reflected on Genesis and the creation of the world, where I found some contradictions, above all in respect to the creation of woman, who is left secondary to man. I have also been profoundly influenced by Nazi genocide, which I never could understand, but which I remember as an open wound in the hearts of Jews whose only crime was to have been born Jewish into a European inferno the likes of which the world has not seen for many centuries. That nightmare, which I did not live through personally but which marked me from childhood on, is present in my poems full of underlying questions: How could God permit this to happen? And if He could, what can we believe in?

In my poetry and stories I include recollections of grade school and high school, too. It is interesting that my best women friends are Catholic schoolmates from high school and college. My Jewish friends are also very dear to me, and we see each other once in a while, but the Catholics visit my home month after month, and we talk about the past and live very intensely in the present.

I think that memory plays a major role in the life and work of every writer. Everything that is written functions because of the power of one's recollection of one's own life and the lives of others. In the twentieth century, and the beginning now of the third millennium, literature is conditioned by memory and the desire to memorialize, which is what some critics have said of my collection of stories, *Esa dimensión lejana* (That distant dimension), in which writing or literary discourse goes as far as memory can reach, exploring events of childhood, adolescence, and adulthood. They say that every book contains a part of the author, whether or not the author intends this.

AS A COSTA RICAN OF Jewish origin, I lived intensely through the years of the 1948 revolution in Costa Rica, and I have always been interested in the politics of my country and of Latin America. I cannot imagine how being Jewish would make me turn away from something as essential as the land where I was born and lived my whole life, just as I cannot imagine how I could stop being Jewish or separate myself from the meaning for a Jew of the state of Israel and Israeli literature, or the importance for me of my trips to Israel, especially the Congress of Jewish Latin American Writers in Israel in 1984, when I lived and shared with my companions a marvelous country that welcomed us and received us as its own, where we met Itzhak Rabin, we had readings of poetry and stories, and we traveled around the country from north to south and from east to west, in incredible friendship and companionship. Thus I feel very comfortable being at once Latin American and Jewish. But with the passing of time one becomes more universal and stops thinking in terms of particular countries.

WRITING THESE WORDS HAS been an opportunity to think about what participating in "Jewish Latin American (rather than European) hybridity" has meant to me. My hybridity is that of a Costa Rican Jew as a child, an adolescent, and an adult wife, mother, professor, and human being. This hybridity is reflected in my home, too, where I have a Jewish candelabra, a *mezuzah*, etc. and a little terrace onto the garden, with indigenous things—typical decorated carts, bull horns, and pre-Columbian vases, which may or may not be authentic but which I like to keep to remind me of the precolonial era of this country.

I WOULD LIKE TO CONCLUDE by appending a part of a reflective essay I published in the newspaper *La Nación* on August 29, 1986, with the title "Days Later":

> I spent several days as a patient in the Hospital México in San José, the week before Mother's Day, August fifteenth. Mother's Day is one of those holidays celebrated every year, sometimes with great ceremony, sometimes with tears of sentiment, and in a few cases, with remorse or forgetfulness. This particular Mother's Day has been memorable for me.
>
> There were six of us women in the ward, and each of us hoped to be released before the fifteenth of August so we could celebrate this important date with our children and parents. When we started conversing, this ward of six beds became a microcosm in which our lives and experiences were shared. We became aware of the extent to which women, whatever their age or economic condition, manage to undergo

surgeries, difficult childbirths, and possible later complications with strength of will and courage, as long as they can be with their families.

Through the big window, we could see the tops of trees, blue sky, and the uncomplicated clouds. A song that emanated from nature and bathed the room of anxieties in peace and calm. At four in the afternoon, the room would fill with anticipation: the daily visiting hour was approaching. Would our children come, our parents, our brothers and sisters? Our arms weighted with intravenous tubing, our aching bodies, our open hands all readied themselves to reach out happily to family hands. Across the hall, the priest from the La Dolorosa Church talked to a patient who was about to have a hysterectomy. He offered her the rite of Annointment and the prayer resonated in that part of the hospital like a psalm offered to all who suffer.

In the double rooms in the rear of the floor, cries were heard. A mother of five cried out in grief, her body mutilated by cancer.

They were the last cries of a pain unsilenced by morphine or hope of rest. It was a profound and ancient wailing sound, saturated with chemotherapy, cobalt bombs, preventive surgeries, and care. Beyond the possibility of cure, her voice reverberated in desperation. An old woman came over to me, in tears. "I hate coming back to the hospital for chemotherapy." Her eyes reflected her body's weariness. Her shoulders bore the weight of her struggles and of her efforts multiplied by pain.

On the other side of the ward, the childbearers sang a multiple song of joy. The nurses ran back and forth; the new mothers bathed their babes; the pediatricians, gynecologists, and surgeons raced around in a frenetic dance to add moments to time, to illness, to death. And this constant activity is multiplied every day, at every hour. And that microcosm is a universe of cries and pains, of yells and shuddering moans of new canticles, the voices of those who see the world for the first time and whose little bodies feel the lullaby of familiar and unfamiliar tenderness and whose lips feel the pearl nectar that soothes and feeds them. And amid the silence of the hopelessly ill and the hopeful who received injections and serums and blood for their thirsty veins, I looked toward the immense window and gazed at the serene sky and the August rain beginning to fall and told myself that nothing is in vain, that it is just and necessary that all these women should enjoy Mother's Day with their families, that it is not just like any other day, and that they need as much love as they give.

On the fourteenth, a few days after I left the hospital, I returned to the ward to visit. Most of my companions had gone home. New patients had filled the beds. There was just one familiar lady there still recuperating. I greeted her affectionately. "You know," she told me, "yesterday I dreamed of your gold charm. You explained to me that it was a Hebrew letter that represented the number eighteen. And you told me that its meaning was 'life.' They've operated on me, I feel better, and I expect to see my children here in the hospital tomorrow. It doesn't matter where Mother's Day is celebrated, the important thing is to be alive enough to look out the window." I kept silent.

She continued, "My dream about your charm was very beautiful. But it wasn't you who was wearing it. I didn't recognize the person with the charm." For an instant I thought about this. I answered her: "Dear lady, I think that you were wearing the charm yourself. It's a symbol of life, and it is worn around the neck of the person who, like you, awaits her children's visit on a bed of hope, and like you, has the faith to receive Annointment before surgery, and like you, and many others, lives a double life of work and dedication to home and children."

I looked out. The same trees, the same sky, different clouds. I listened to the sounds of the wind and the cries of the woman in one of the back rooms. It seemed to me that feminine spirit was intensely present in that hospital. I held the charm in my fingers and went down the stairs slowly. I felt part of the chain of life and death as I heard a sacred canticle that burst out of the tops of the trees in homage to so many women who would celebrate their Mother's Days in operating rooms or in giving life to a new hope in the birthing room.

Chapter 16

From Toledo to the New World
A Story of Secrets

Angelina Muñiz de Huberman

I KNOW THAT MINE is not the life story you expect. It's not the usual one; it's not traditional. Rather, it's a tale about a life story. Or the tale of a life. Thus I've set myself the task of telling it in different ways in each of my books. Once again, I'll tell it here.

The key to what happened was a war. But this is not unusual. Many lives are changed by war, and destiny takes command amid chance occurrences and whims of good and bad luck. Order is overturned and the compass of history loses its magnetism and the routes of travelers become unrecognizable. Then the exile begins that is the awakening after the sleep of memory. From one country to another, until finding a nest in a treetop.

My key was a war, the Spanish Civil War, which turned into World War II. It was a long war that is still not resolved. Neither in History nor in my own history. The remains of Fascism and of Nazism have not disappeared, and the offshoots are hard to eliminate. A bad weed never dies.

I was born where I should not have been born. If there is any special place in which to be born, why Hyères? Is that any kind of place to be born? It was a safe place and a place chosen by my parents. A place that does not appear on many maps—I always have to explain where it is. Hyères is in the south of France, in Provence, in the province of Var, near Toulon, across from the islands that bear the same name. Hyères exists and thus I exist. But the question remains: why Hyères? Because an uncle of mine, a Swiss Jew, had a summer house there. And that house saved me. If I hadn't been born there, my mother would have remained in Madrid in the middle of the Civil War, and I don't know whether we would have survived. My parents, who were Spanish, decided that I should be French, and, since my uncle's house was available, that's where my life began.

But my parents did not leave Spain together. My mother, with my older brother and pregnant with me, crossed the border to France. My father, a journalist, remained in Madrid. Only when the newspaper sent him to Paris as a correspondent were they reunited. They stayed in Paris for two years, then, seeing the European war looming, thought about emigrating to America. Their country of choice was Cuba. My parents were also fleeing from a personal tragedy: the death of my brother, who had been hit by a truck in front of our house. And so our reduced family embarked at La Pallice in the year 1939 for a journey into the unknown. I was then one year old. The ship was the *Oropesa*.

The Oropesa

I've often written about the *Oropesa*, and it figured on the jacket of one of my books. This English ship obsessed me, and I think I remember some scenes from the crossing, which was engraved on my child's memory, something so powerful that it will always stay with me. My love for the sea was awakened at that moment and I still yearn to travel by ship. That's why I put my characters on shipboard.

The ship carried a miscellaneous lot of passengers. Most were Jews, but there were people of all nationalities. I remember, or I think

I remember, mistily, the stateroom, the children's dining room, the deck, the stairways. I remember a young sailor in white who was very handsome and the captain, who seemed very tall to me. These memories, plus what imagination adds and my parents' stories, have resulted in many of my written pages.

Memories of journeys by ship are shared with other people and create special ties. Hence the expression: *shifbruder*. My parents became friends with José Luis Sert and his wife Moncha; he would later become a famous architect, recognized worldwide, and a professor at Harvard.

The arrival in Havana is engraved in fire on my memory. Foreigners were not well received and were interned in Tiscornia, a concentration camp. When my father heard this, he erupted in insults to the authorities and what he said, in gentle words, was that they could not intern him because he was everyone's father. The fact was that they did not intern us.

I was sorry to leave the ship, and I was full of emotions. What I could not know at that moment was that the ship and its crew had only few days left at sea. This would be its last voyage. On the way back to England it was sunk by a Nazi submarine.

I would have another relationship to the *Oropesa,* one which I would not discover until many years later when I met Albert Huberman, whom I would marry. His parents, Polish Jews who had been living in France, had emigrated to Cuba in 1927 on the same ship.

Caimito del Guayabal

Cuba was my paradise. My parents settled in the country, in a town named Caimito del Guayabal, and dedicated themselves to rural life. For me, it meant a life of total freedom surrounded by nature, without having to go to school, and without conflict of any kind with anyone. Being an only child has advantages and disadvantages, but at that time,

I was aware only of the former. I got used to living among adults and I listened to my parents' conversations, which were always about three things: the war; stories about the family, now scattered all over the world (Spain, France, Belgium, Casablanca, New York, Argentina); and my brother's death.

The farm in Cuba ended up being an economic disaster, since my father didn't know anything about agricultural work and had invested all his money in Canadian potato seedlings, even though the other farmers had warned him that potatoes wouldn't grow in that soil. And sure enough, the potatoes had tumors on them and were unsalable. My Swiss uncle, now established in New York, came to his rescue and suggested that he open a branch outlet in Mexico of his medical products laboratory. This was why we moved to Mexico in March of 1942.

Mexico

We arrived in Mexico by plane, which meant another great adventure and marked me as a traveler at an early age. Mexico was a difficult place right from the beginning. The first incident took place the first time we left the Hotel Gillow and took our first steps toward the Zócalo. My father was robbed and a fountain pen that the last president of the Spanish Republic, Manuel Azaña, had given him at a press conference was stolen.

At the same time my father was setting up the laboratory, a school was found for me, since I was already five years old. Gordon College was near our house [in Mexico City] and satisfied my mother's desire that I learn English. Attending that school was fundamental in defining my identity, since a large number of the children were Jews. Some had been born in Mexico and others were survivors of concentration camps. Thus it was natural for me to become part of the group. One of my friends was the niece of a rabbi, and I began to become directly acquainted with Judaism.

From then on, I played with my multiple nationalities and, depending on who I was talking to, I could seem Andalusian, Madrileña, French, Cuban, or Mexican. Until one day a great confession on my mother's part showed me which path to take.

Judaism on a Balcony

On the balcony of the house at Tamaulipas 185, my mother said she needed to tell me about something important. And this something was that I was of Jewish origin. She had waited until I was older to tell me this; older for her meant age six, the age I was then. That immediately made me feel older. She told me that we had always been Jews, that we descended from Spanish Jews who had not obeyed the Edict of Expulsion in 1492 and who had led a double life in order to survive: Jew at home, Christian out in the street. She told me that our Judaism had been transmitted through the maternal line and that if I learned how to make the sign of *shaddai* (putting together my ring finger and little finger, and my middle and index fingers, with a separation between the two sets) I would be identified as a Jew. To this was added her last name which, although it sounded very Christian, was really a translation from the Hebrew: Sacristán for Shamash. The relationship with the *shaddai* was confirmed. My grandmother, whom I never knew, knew some words of hispanized Hebrew and knew something about *kashrut*, which she transmitted to my mother so that she, too, could pass it along to her children.

Hearing that story right then was for me a wish fulfilled. Now I could strengthen my ties to the children at school. My mother, who always carried a Bible around with her, began to read it to me, beginning with Genesis, as our story, not in a religious way. What I had thought of as exile from Spain because of the Civil War I now began to view as a much more ancient exile.

That my mother's confession should have taken place on a balcony

(a place separated from the house and yet in full light) gave me something to ponder. I interpreted it as related to a secrecy that was still very
present.

A few days after the confession something took place on the door-
step of my house while I was waiting for the school bus that was also a
revelation. A drunk man came stumbling by and, when he saw me,
shouted: "Blonde Jew!" *(Güera judia!)* With this, my Judaism was
confirmed for the entire world.

Writing during Childhood

Two years after this confession, my mother started telling me about
Jewish traditions so that I would remember them. By then I was eight
years old, which, according to her criteria, was an advanced age, almost as though I were an adult. What she told me was that from then
on I had to observe the world around me and remember these observa-
tions. This exhortation also occurred in a special place: facing the sea
in Chachalacas, Veracruz, and, appropriately, it is an image that I retain to this day with absolute clarity. After that, she made point of telling me stories about the family so that I wouldn't forget them and so
that one day they would be useful in my writing. Because another of
her fixed ideas was that I would be a writer.

It's curious, but my father, the writer and journalist of the family,
did not encourage me to write; from the time I was a child, he criti-
cized my writings as complex and lacking clarity. The two argued
about me, and my mother would tell me not to pay any attention to
him. This confused me, since it seemed to me his opinion was more
important, since he was a professional writer. As the years went on,
my mother's insistence on telling me family stories so that one day I
could tell them finally achieved its purpose.

A year later, when I was nine, I decided to write my first stories,
which my mother treasured and kept as proof that she was right. These

first stories came out like a game. We were spending a vacation in Cuernavaca, at the home of some Jewish friends who had invited us, along with a Spanish couple in exile who had a son my age. This boy became my great friend, even though he suffered from mental retardation. One day, we'd run out of games to play and didn't know what to do next, and it occurred to me to suggest that we write stories. That's how it all began.

The Beginning of the Jewish Writing

Since I considered that, in my case, Judaism was a labor of rescue, I thought I would dedicate my efforts to rescue. Together with the topic of Spanish exile, I united the two themes of rescue and exile symbiotically. The two were topics that I implanted in Mexican literature for the first time, in the decade of the nineteen sixties. That does not mean that there was no Jewish literature before me, but that it had remained part of its own community, and what I did was bring it into the mainstream for the general public. Of course it was not an easy task and I had to be very patient, since publishers delayed accepting my books for years since they didn't want to take risks with something new. Seymour Menton has pointed this out: "Angelina Muñiz has been thrice marginalized: as a Spaniard, as a Jew and as a woman." Since I introduced a foreign element at a moment of pronounced Mexican nationalism, I added new literary forms that went beyond traditional concepts of narrative, and the result was even stranger. José Emilio Pacheco considers my work as "the most personal of these last years, the most resistant to fashions, tendencies, currents." Thus I have struggled against the current, but it has been worth it.

The Jewish topics I prefer are part of a search for mystic and heretical elements. My writings are full of cabalists and alchemists. Sephardi literature regains its place. The Holocaust is represented in its poetic form of silence. I have taken historical characters, like Benjamin of

Tudela, and transformed them, an example of the imaginative and reno-
vational possibilities of Jewish thought as opposed to the static forms
of Western thought.

Nevertheless, this irrationality is manifested to such an extent that
in the reviews and studies of my work, the role of mysticism is often
emphasized, but without the writer ever specifying that this is a Jewish mysticism. There is a certain embarrassment about mentioning
the words Jew or Judaism. Of the recent reviews published in Mexico
of *The Merchant of Tudela*, very few mentioned that the book is about
a historic Jewish figure. They spoke at length of the literary qualities
of the book, without ever discussing the obvious. Of course, to be silent is to consent, as the saying goes.

The Statutes of Memory

This desire to relive the clandestine life (perhaps as a reflection of my
family's history) is an effort of historical memory. Memory as an art
which keeps life moving along on its course. Memory as a form of ap-
prenticeship: from the biblical genealogies my mother made me learn,
to what I considered more amusing: the names of countries and their
capitals, mountain ranges, rivers and lakes. Or language games like "A
ship has come from Havana laden with . . ." and then you had to imagine
cargo beginning with each letter of the alphabet, the first person starting with *a* and each successive player repeating the whole list and add-
ing an item to the end. Or "I spy, I spy." "What do you see?"
"Something." "What letter does it begin with?" "It begins with an *a*."
"What letter does it end with?" "It ends with an *a*." And you had to
find that item in the room or place you were in.

And later on, the learning of songs, poems, and sayings was important. All of this on cold or rainy days, or when ill, when it wasn't possible to go out. And if it took place in front of the fireplace (always a
favorite place for me), then even better.

In the case of an exiled child like me, another part of memory was the storytelling about members of the family. There are things that come out of all the corners in the world, that are never abandoned. Photographs in the first place. People's faces, so that they'll never be forgotten. Tracing similarities and likenesses. The past generations. Grandparents posing for the photographer in their best clothes. A photo is something crucial. Parents. The surprise of seeing your parents when they were children. The rest of the family: aunts and uncles, cousins, nieces and nephews. Learning the names and stories about each one. Who died in infancy or very young. The mother or father's second marriage. The step-father or step-mother. The half brothers and sisters. The children born outside the marriage. The adulteries. The incests. The adventurer brother who disappeared and was never heard from again, or the one who returned, like the prodigal son, sick with tuberculosis or malaria. Waiting for the end of the war to know which ones survived or how they died and where. Some photographs brought by travelers and given to the family, as a final keepsake, after having been told of the final words. The photos that keep piling up in boxes and then fill albums. The special album for my brother, from his birth until a few days before his death.

Other factors of memory have been recollections in sequence that can be unwound like skeins of neutral color. And, then, to one's great dismay, the discovery of gaps that cannot be filled in, great holes in memory. After time has passed, when those who remembered have died and there is no one left to ask, all one can do is imagine, invent, make every effort and not find the solution. Then, what I've called pseudomemories are born. The need to finish the stories is peremptory, and the literary ending surges up, not the true one or the desired one. The ending that rounds off, seduces, or horrifies.

The sense of justice is something united to memory. Those small stories that we don't want to have get lost because if they were lost it would mean a double death for the memory's holder are told over and over again. They should, above all, restore the sense of justice. What parents tell most often are their memories of childhood, what has caused the most pain, and what has been most frightening. Although, of course, there are also images of beauty and reassurance. I remember that my parents' stories of their sufferings as children, the unjust punishments, the illnesses and premature deaths, made me weak as if they were taking place at the very moment of being told. It was then that the word took on life and substituted for reality. That gift of the word that, by means of its evocation, turns the past into the present. The word as the only possibility of bringing the dead back to life.

The Magical Word

The discovery of the magical power of the word is the consolation of all grief, of all injury. In the labyrinth of memory, the word takes on the rhythm and the multiple meanings that are necessary to reach the abyss of conscience. The word recovers its Orphic depths—profoundly rooted in the labyrinth of memory—it extracts the ancient magical meaning, evoking and creating a new reality.

The canticle of the word washes away accumulations of impurities and offers its sacrifice before the initiated. The word is the only road of access to the reclusive world of the spirit, ever more desecrated and humiliated. Orpheus's lost path becomes ever more difficult to find, if it has not already been totally covered over by the spreading weeds of the spurious and the traffickers. For those who still continue to search for the talisman of sound, the law of magic is the star that guides.

To recognize that identity of the word was to recognize, from infancy on, my own identity. To know who I was, thanks to the word that named the world around me. If I asked my parents for a dictionary and an encyclopedia as birthday presents, it was because I sought not erudition, but rather the key to untangle the mysteries of words. From that moment on, I was a field sown with stars fallen from the sky.

Heritages

The obsession with words marked my attitude toward religion and the idea of God. My parents were freethinkers and never instructed me in any religion at all. My mother's origins led me to consider Judaism as my source of identity. As for my father, he came from an aristocratic family which had lost its wealth and for which religion was never a major issue. My studies of religion came later on and were my own decision. The following are some linguistic-religious anecdotes from my childhood:

The church was a forbidden place for me, one I associated with darkness and dimness. In reality, I was afraid to go by one, and always thought the church people would notice that I was not Catholic. Added to this was my belief that our not going to church was due to it being English, *cosa de ingleses,* since I mispronounced the word for church, *iglesia,* as *inglesia.* The day I was going to have my tonsils removed, when I was seven, I realized that I could die during the operation and asked if the word God, *Dios,* was written with an *s* or a *z* at the end, *Dios* or *Dioz.* Life and death were united by the idea of God, and it was important to know how to spell it. And I thought the name of God was hidden in the arrangement of the letters, almost a Cabalistic interpretation.

Another religio-linguistic episode that I recall happened when I told a Catholic girl that I did not attend church. She was scandalized and asked me whether I was an atheist, to which I answered calmly that I was not from Athens, but from Hyères.

As an adolescent, I enjoyed indulging in little subterfuges used by *converso* Jews in Spain, which my mother showed me. When, at the end of the school year, the girls were all preparing to go to Mass (even though it was a public school), I mysteriously fell ill that day.

Objects of Religious Significance

I should confess that my parents were somewhat unusual. They did not bring with them any religious objects or family souvenirs. My father always traveled with the articles he had published in *El Heraldo* of Madrid, the newspaper where he had been editor-in-chief when the Civil War broke out, articles which my mother had glued neatly into notebooks with black covers with the dates written by them. He also carried around copies of the books he had published and a few unpublished manuscripts. All his life, he kept his press pass and his journalist's insignia with the Republican flag on it. And I've already mentioned the pen which President Azaña had given him, which did not remain long in his possession. My mother, on the other hand, always had with her the Bible that I later inherited. But the extraordinary thing was another possession that my parents lugged from country to country: a trunk. A trunk is not unusual. But the contents were. It was a small trunk, in which they kept all the clothing, toys, books, notebooks, drawings, pencils, erasers, pen tips, picture cards, and skates that had belonged to my dead brother.

Exile as Accumulation

I've spoken extensively about exile throughout my works—openly or codedly—by means of the topics I've chosen or their symbols. Exile has not been an exclusion but rather an accumulation of my various heritages. The European world, the nostalgia for abandoned places, the repose ultimately found, although not mental quietude. That awareness of not belonging to the place where one happens to be. The feeling that the effort to belong is not worth it, so one may as well affirm the difference. Instead of assimilation, opt for tolerance of others' and one's own individuality. Insist on the rights of the minority, respect for otherness. Establish pride in one's own pursuits in the face of the fear of losing it. Acquire the certitude that others will not speak for one and that the moment to speak out has come. That the only property is the fragmented world of words which are recovered in order to create a new order of things.

For a while, I waited for others to speak who were more qualified than I. Surrounded by silence, I took up the word. Because of the emptiness of exile, especially Spanish and Jewish, I began to write about that. It was a kind of revelation: if not, I would not have had the energy to forge ahead in the face of indifference, envy, and other obstacles. In Mexico there is a great conspiracy of silence in reaction to the unknown or different. It is a cautious society. There is great fear of what does not follow established patterns that everyone accepts. If anyone stands out for originality (remember the case of Alfonso Reyes), it is best to ignore him or criticize him. Octavio Paz found the perfect word for it: *el ninguneo*, the nobody.

Leaving aside the impotent *ninguneo*, I preferred to keep writing according to my dictates and not in the reigning fashion. I find satisfaction in not having been sidetracked from my ethics or my aesthetics and in the presence of those people who appreciate my efforts and for whom my literature is necessary. I don't cheat myself or them. The minority has a right to exist, and a right to be different. This is the accumulation that exile authorizes. This is its wealth. Something that does not have to conform, or have conformity built into it. Something powerful which, in the eyes of others, is terrible.

I think that, if I had not assumed my identity as a Jew and as an exile, I would not have written as I have.

Chapter 17

Uruguay
A Story in Episodes

Teresa Porzecanski

MY FATHER CAME FROM A family of Ashkenazi Jews steeped in the cultural tradition of Eastern Europe, and my mother from a family of Sephardi Jews who belonged to the Islamic cultural tradition. My father's family journey began in the early nineteen twenties when my grandfather, Cusiel Porzecanski, born in Latvia, married to Ida Lina Halpern, who came from Lithuania, began to worry about the future of their children in a country affected by the strong influence of the German culture of that era. They were living then in Liepaja, a Latvian port, and they had a prosperous store with a bakery. But anti-Semitism was increasing, the future looked uncertain, and the great wave of European emigration was getting underway, stimulated by the image of a splendid America. The family's eldest son, Bernardo, had been accepted to and was attending a secondary school—the "gymnasium" in those days—but it would be difficult for the others to gain admission. There were many exclusionary clauses for Jewish applicants. On the other hand, immigration to the United States was becoming increasingly restricted and, in 1924, it was closed completely. It was no longer possible to obtain visas for the place in which my grandfather's two brothers had established themselves.

Nevertheless, Bernardo was in contact with one of his mother's uncles, León Halpern, who had left Lithuania and settled in Montevideo two years earlier. Uncle León urged him to come settle there, too. Bernardo traveled to Uruguay in 1924, was reunited with his uncle, and found work in a glass factory. He began to send my grandfather promising letters about his future in Uruguay. And so, in 1926, my grandfather Cusiel, my grandmother Ida Lina, my aunts Berta and Frida, my uncles Aron and Nachman, and their brother who would be my father, Abram, who was then fourteen years old, all embarked on the steamship *Wurtemburg* and crossed the Atlantic, heading for the port of Montevideo. My grandparents' eldest daughter, Ana, who was already married and had two children, did not wish to travel with them and stayed on in Liepaja, Latvia. (A few years later, Ana came to Montevideo for a visit. Realizing that the war was imminent, my grandmother invited her to stay and to bring her family over, but she refused. Ana returned to Latvia and she and her family were never heard from again. Presumably they were killed by the Nazis and buried in a common grave in the woods on the outskirts of Liepaja.)

The crossing was peaceful, one might even say joyous: I'm looking at the photographs of all of them smiling broadly on the ship's deck, the five brothers and sisters posing, arranged in a line from tallest to shortest. My father often used to tell the story of their departure and of the voyage itself. It was probably his favorite story, the one he told over and over again to my brother and me. He used to describe how his big brother Bernardo had had a lucky prescience about getting out of Latvia and about how he finally managed to talk the rest of the family into joining him. He used to recall how they had sold the store on Albertstrasse, which was also where they lived. Over and over again, he told how difficult it was for them to find someone who would buy that business, and how otherwise they would not have been able to get enough money together for the journey. He'd smile when he recalled how "by pure chance" a purchaser had appeared out of the blue and, even in this time of economic difficulties, had paid a high enough price so that the family could leave for America. This "pure chance" my father interpreted as a message from destiny, as a miracle which had saved them from being slaughtered later on like his sister Ana and her husband and children.

My father landed in Montevideo when he was fourteen years old. He knew how to speak Latvian, German, Russian, Yiddish (which they spoke at home), and Polish (which he had learned from a servant who took care of him when he was little), but he did not know a word of Spanish.

THE STORY OF MY MOTHER'S side of the family has as its protagonist my grandfather Isaac Salami (who later changed his last name to Cohen), who at age eleven had left the city where he was born (Damascus, Syria), embarked as a stowaway on a French ship that stopped in Dakar, and then crossed the Atlantic to Buenos Aires. My grandfather Isaac's family was very poor. His father was a tinsmith and had never gone to school. Isaac was the only one of their three children who managed to finish the five years of primary school, and he knew how to read and write in Arabic. My grandfather Isaac was eleven years old when Sultan Hamid decided to recruit boys for the army, which was preparing for war. The sultan's representatives went from house to house gathering up, forcibly "drafting," boys suitable for the war. My grandfather, with his parents' consent, decided to escape this fatal destiny and travel to America. He arrived in Buenos Aires on a morning in 1907 and got in touch with other Syrian immigrants. He went to live in slum housing and found work as a street vendor of tools and notions. Since he did not speak Spanish and had no one to teach him, at night he would repeat dictionary words out loud.

My grandfather Isaac often told me the story of his arrival in America. For him, too, this was a central event in his life. His memories of his country were precise and detailed. My grandfather felt special pride in having made his way all by himself in an unknown country. He only stayed in Buenos Aires for two or three years. There he met my grandmother Teresa, who came from Beirut, Lebanon, and, in 1910, they both moved to Montevideo, where they married and began their family. As time went by, my grandfather prospered economically and sent for his two brothers, who came to Uruguay and lived here for the rest of their lives.

My own childhood memories are of events that occurred years after my father had come to these shores, since he began his own family in 1942, sixteen years after immigrating. In the nineteen fifties we were a typical secular middle-class Jewish family, living in a rented apartment in the center of the city, and naturally we didn't have a car or too many luxuries. My father was a dentist and had his office in a room of the apartment where we lived. He had graduated after long years of sustained effort, studying at night and working at various jobs during the day. His first job had been delivering newspapers, helping my grandfather with the newsstand he had set up. Then my father worked as an apprentice at a fur store, sewing hides and furs. At the same time he worked for many years teaching Spanish to immigrants from Germany who continued to arrive. He finished secondary school in a night school, passed the exams in Spanish, studied drawing at the school of arts and trades, and eventually registered as a student at the school of dentistry.

Once my mother's father, Isaac, married my grandmother (who had also come from Buenos Aires around 1910 and was a seamstress), they set up housekeeping in a rented room. They managed to buy a sewing machine that could be paid off in installments, and my grandmother cut and sewed slips and petticoats which my grandfather then sold in the Old City, the colonial center of Montevideo. Over the years, my grandfather established a marvelously successful wholesale business in cloth and imported articles. Then he bought a respectable house in Rodó Park and a car.

My grandparents Cusiel and Ida Lina were a mismatched couple. She was robust, quite tall, and blonde and had very pale skin. He was small, quite slender, much shorter than she, and had darker skin and hair. She was quiet and pensive; he was jovial, voluble, and sociable. I remember my grandmother's visits to my house every Thursday. She had been a bread baker, and she'd make us sweet rolls full of poppy seeds and raisins. And she brought us chocolates. She'd have me sit on her lap while she told me stories; she spoke heavily accented Spanish with lots of Yiddish words thrown in. Especially her words of affection, which were all in Yiddish.

My grandmother was a calm woman who moved slowly. She had had a practical life, dedicated to caring for her seven children and keeping her house. In contrast, my grandfather was a remarkable conversationalist. He could tell stories better than anyone, and was acclaimed for this in his circle of friends. I remember exactly the glass of soda water and red wine that my grandfather used to drink every Saturday morning in the Café Sorocabana. I was five years old when he took me to his café gathering for the first time. In the midst of all these old Jews dressed in dark overcoats, their heads covered with big gray hats, I—a small girl—listened to my grandfather laugh and tell stories I did not understand. His laugh fascinated me—it was so loud and rotund.

My father had brought his stamp collection with him, taking great care of it. He had lots of Latvian stamps which showed when Latvia had been ruled by the Germans, when it had been under the Russians, and the few years when it had been an independent republic. My father used to show those stamps to my brother and me when we were children. And he explained the value they had for him: they reminded him of Latvia's history. He encouraged us to collect stamps, too. And so we had an album with stamps from Uruguay and other countries, but especially lots of stamps from Latvia, Lithuania, and Eastern Europe.

I always remember the large pendulum clock that my grandparents brought from Europe on the ship. That clock hung on the wall at home throughout my childhood. Its chimes, which I thought had a sad sound, lulled my dreams. The clock was set in a rough wooden case, neither highly adorned nor well polished, which had a little door with a glass panel through which you could see the face. Every time my father had to wind the clock, he'd climb up on a chair, fit a huge key over a shaft, and very slowly give it three turns to the right. I've often used the image of this clock in my writing, particularly in my novels. When the family house was closed down, my father flew the clock, carefully wrapped, to the city of Beer Sheva, Israel, where my brother lives. My brother took care of cleaning the clock and getting it running again, and since then it has been on one of the walls of his house.

From my maternal grandmother's house in Beirut, I still have an engraved bronze jug that was used to hold water for washing one's hands in the morning. My grandmother passed it on to me, cautioning me: "This was from my house, over there in my country." And I have kept it, with the same respect.

The Judaism my parents introduced me to was completely secular; there was the idea that to become too ritualistic and ceremonial about Judaism revealed "backwardness" and "ignorance." My father was liberal in his ideas, completely autonomous in regard to religion and religious matters, although during the Jewish holidays he liked to get together with the family to eat together, converse, and share the evening.

My mother's side of the family, Sephardi Jews from Syria, was not very religious either. It was more a matter of a Jewish identity defined by genealogical connections, family ties, and a network of friendly relationships. The only one who was a little more observant was my grandfather Isaac, who liked to be called to read in the temple. He and a group of other immigrants from his country founded various Jewish institutions in Uruguay, B'nai B'rith among them. But my grandfather's militancy within Judaism had more to do with the institutional organization of the new Jewish community in Uruguay than with the observance of religious rites.

Thus my parents' influence consisted of transmitting to me a Jewish identity not tied to ceremonial formalism, but connected to a system of moral values and a way of seeing the world. I think we always had the sense of having come from someplace else, of having known other worlds, of having crossed over not only oceans but also ways of being and living. Whenever he'd see me emulating what the other girls in primary school were doing, my father would invariably remind me, "But you are a Jew; we are Jewish." And I'd ask something like, "But what does that have to do with it?" And he'd answer, "Because we think differently."

When my mother talked about another Jew, she'd say, "He's one of ours." And thus a tenuous boundary was constructed between our Jewish identity and a society that was gradually becoming more open and that, during the first decades of the twentieth century, had absorbed and incorporated the particularities of many different groups of immigrants.

My brother and I attended a free public primary school: our classmates were not for the most part Jewish, nor did they know what it meant to be Jewish. We spoke Spanish at home, since the languages my father knew (German, Yiddish, Polish, Latvian) were not the ones my mother knew (Arabic). One day my father appeared with a Yiddish teacher for us, a heavy-set man who made us learn the letters and write them and who read us poems by Hayyim Nahman Bialik. The teacher came to our house once a week and made us learn poems by heart. My brother made fun of our Yiddish teacher. He thought he was fat and boring. I was always the one who did what I was asked and paid attention. Every week my father would ask what we had learned. I think my father brought in the Yiddish teacher because he wanted us to feel a part of Eastern European Judaism. In some way, he wanted us to have contact with that world he had left when he emigrated. But for us, Yiddish was a distant language only spoken by grandparents and other old people. My grandmother Ida Lina spoke it with her children. It was spoken by the grandparents of the other Jewish children. But it seemed to us really odd to have to speak it ourselves and to learn to write something so opposite to what we'd been taught in school: those "backwards" letters seemed really strange to us. But still, in my depths, I knew very well that those letters were something that the other children at school were never going to learn, something that was connected to my own story and that of my ancestors, because of being Jewish. I accepted it. My brother rebelled against it, he wouldn't sit still, and he teased the teacher. Sometimes the teacher brought along his own small son, who was four or five, because he didn't have anyone to leave him with. Then my brother would tease the boy and make fun of him. But I felt sorry for the son and for the teacher, too, and I thought that if I didn't study Yiddish, the teacher wouldn't have anyone to teach. This feeling of pity washed over me every time I'd hear two old Jews talking on the streetcar: people would look at them strangely, as though they were speaking an exotic, somewhat mysterious, language. Where did those old men come from? What language were they speaking that no one else could understand? I didn't understand much either, but I knew that they were Jews, that they were connected to my own story, that they were like grandfathers of mine who wandered through the world and had come here from afar.

From the age of eleven on, I read lots of books of all kinds, good and bad, and I loved Spanish language classes. By then I was already writing what I then believed was poetry. I must have been twelve or thirteen when I was given a notebook with blank pages, bound in leather with gold letters on its cover: "My Diary." I think it was one of my aunts who gave it to me. So then I began to write every day. First I wrote "chronicles" of daily events, but later the diary included thoughts and commentaries about topics that preoccupied me in early adolescence: the world of adults and my permanent opposition to what they thought or did, awareness of the passage of time, ideals of social justice, good and evil, awareness of death, loneliness, silent rebellion against many of the norms of the social world. In addition, at fourteen I began a prolific correspondence with friends in other countries. Some were children of my father's friends, others were strangers with whom I'd exchange postcards, photographs, or stamps. Many of these letters contain comments or complaints about situations I had to put up with as an adolescent, and they were helpful to me as needed spaces of introspection where I could construct a personality.

At age sixteen, these commentaries gave way to stories that included characters and situations and in which dialogues and descriptions were included. They were my first short stories, some of which were eventually published in 1967 in my collection, titled *El Acertijo y otros cuentos* (Montevideo: Editorial Arca). At first glance, it might seem that my Judaism is not visible in my writing. However, if Jewish identity is a way of understanding the world that has been constructed and reconstructed during the course of thousands of years, it is undeniable that my writing is impregnated with it, and that my own relationship to literature is connected to an underlayer which is universal but is also Jewish, a complex web of sufferings, losses, iconoclasms, searches for moral ideals, preoccupations with justice, comprehensions of the meaning of abandonment and despair: all these universal topics to which Jewish history has made special contributions.

EVERY AFTERNOON WE BOUGHT the newspaper *El Plata,* which on Wednesdays included a literary page edited by a literary figure of that time—Eugen Relgis. One day in 1954 when I was twelve years old, I put five of my poems into an envelope and sent them to Eugen Relgis, asking him for an opinion. Two weeks went by and one afternoon, unexpectedly, I got a telephone call. It was Mr. Relgis. He asked me how old I was and then he said: "Your poems show great sensitivity and care in the selection of words. Keep writing and send me your poems again in a few years and we'll publish them." Later on, when I was about sixteen and had written half a dozen short stories, I took a course in art history with a wonderful professor who spoke to us about architecture and art in prehistoric cultures. I became good friends with this professor, and one day I got up the nerve to show him three stories that I had written without any idea what I would do with them. My professor—Florio Parpagnoli was his name—read them carefully and wrote me a letter in which he commented favorably on them, saying that I had all the right instincts, and encouraged me to continue writing. That letter was very important to me: at age sixteen I did not really know what to do with my writing, nor did my parents really know about my "secret" activity. Parpagnoli's letter positioned me before a new world: the world of writing. What was I going to do with this? What place was writing going to have in my life?

Each of my novels contains something distinctive associated with Judaism. In *Invención de los soles* (Invention of the suns), for example, I write in a tangential way about the story of a deathcamp survivor, with references to a distant Europe, to countries of which there only remain photographs or obsolete objects. But also present in that novel is the Ashkenazi family genealogy, as a fleeting touch, a sense of inadequacy and rebellion on the part of the protagonist. In *Mesías en Montevideo* (Messiahs in Montevideo), one of the protagonists is Jewish and communicates with the father of his father's father through a vision. *Perfumes de Cartago* (Perfumes of Carthage) narrates the story of a family of Sephardi immigrants who reach Montevideo in the decade of the nineteen thirties. *La piel del alma* (The soul's skin) relates a tragic story connected with the Inquisition's condemnation of a young Sephardi Jew in the Toledo of 1487. (All books, Montevideo: Editorial Arca.)

A strange cosmopolitan sensation impregnated my experiences in childhood and adolescence. I, unlike my classmates in primary school, had relatives scattered all over the world: in North America, in Europe, even in South Africa. And some of those relatives had been killed or had had to escape. And their children had appeared in other places and were cousins of mine. My forebears had overcome many risks, much poverty and sacrifice, and I inherited a feeling of having walked in other places, of having lived those other lives. I was Uruguayan—Latin American and from Montevideo—but my life history began in other times, in remote places that I would have to go see someday. I listened attentively to a world of references to times before my birth: there were no boundaries either in time or in space.

My childhood in the Uruguay of the fifties was hardly a moment on the time scale of world history and its panorama of other countries, other customs, other landscapes and colors. That feeling of being heir to many worlds, often contradictory, of being the product of so many intertwined circumstances, has been crucial in my personal history, in the choice of my vocation, and in the way in which I have constructed my own subjectivity.

If all my writing is a journey, memory is the essence of travel. Memory is a mobile entity. It transforms itself, it rewrites itself unbidden, it resists my control. Memory shoots out as if hurled by an autonomous mechanical spring. It can be triggered by an aroma floating through the dawn air which carries me back to the garden of my childhood. An empty perfume bottle, a simple perfume bottle can make me skip back forty years in search of a color or a familiar face that has been deeply hidden in the folds of forgetfulness. I have been able to touch my memories as if I were touching this table on which I write. But it is through writing that the fundamental process of memory is set in motion, the process that establishes a certain distance between ourselves and the experiences we have lived, that allows us to contemplate our recollections. Writing, for me, is always an experience of being in transit, always a nomadic experience that uproots me and turns me into a traveler crisscrossing through memory in ever different ways.

Chapter 18

Of Spices and Spells
From Morrocco to Buenos Aires

Mercedes Roffé

MY GRANDPARENTS ON BOTH my mother's and father's sides left Morocco during the first decade of the twentieth century. Various branches of the family left Morocco around then to come to different parts of America. Some went to Argentina, others to Venezuela, others established themselves in Sao Paulo, Brazil. Our family myth tells it as a kind of emigration for the sake of love, where some left their homelands in order to follow more adventurous others who were already in America. No one spoke of wars or of protectorates, of internal or external politics. But it is obvious that the great swells of Moroccan Jewish immigration to Argentina—and very likely to the rest of Latin America—coincide with key moments in Moroccan history: in the first decade of the century, when Spain, France, and Germany were disputing the protectorate, and then during the mid–nineteen fifties, after independence. By 1912, when Morocco was divided up as a protectorate by France and Spain, my parents and uncles had all been born in Argentina, in the province of Santa Fe.

Since my parents were cousins, first cousins, it is very difficult to separate the routes of the two branches of the family. In truth, they all seem to have arrived almost simultaneously, or during the same era. My father's mother seems to have gone directly to Rosario, where my grandfather met her. Her name was Mercedes Abetán, and she had come to America as the adopted daughter of Isaac Oziel and his wife. No one in the family inherited this woman's beautiful gray eyes. When she died of cancer at the age of thirty-four, my father was only six. He, his father, and his three brothers then went and settled in Buenos Aires with my mother's family. Thus they all grew up more or less together, or just a few blocks apart, in the San Telmo neighborhood, where some years later my brother and I and, only a few streets away, my cousin Reina would be born.

By the time I was born, three of my grandparents had already died. My maternal grandmother died when I was three. So I never had access to their stories or their memories, except in a very indirect way. One of my parents' aunts lived with us; she had been born in Ceuta, Spain, but had come to Argentina at a young age. So she could remember the towns of Vera and Margarita, where they had lived when they first came to America. Of "Europe," as she called it, she could only remember the Calle de la Muralla, which is the first thing you see when you disembark in Ceuta from the Mediterranean. When I had the opportunity to visit Morocco in the seventies, the Calle de la Muralla was lined with little ground-floor shops where everything from jellabas to transistor radios was sold. The only personal memory my great-aunt had of those years in Ceuta was of her older sister's wedding. Her sister married the man who, years later, as a widower with six children, would go on to marry the youngest of the sisters—the grandmother who died in Buenos Aires when I was three. And it is not odd that my great-aunt would remember that wedding all her life: the celebration in Ceuta had gone on for six days, with singing and dancing through the streets "from the groom's house all the way to the bride's house," as she'd tell the story in her old fashioned, somewhat nasal Spanish.

In any case, there was not much opportunity at home to talk about first experiences. She was so young when she arrived that she was almost the same age as her older nephews, who had been born and brought up in Argentina, in those provincial towns, until they were old enough to study and travel. Then they all moved to Buenos Aires.

Many of the family treasures I remember from childhood were brought from Morocco. I recall household objects, brooches and jewels, and the gold bracelets soldered with lead made by the prisoners of the Ceuta jail, of which every woman had one or two. These bracelets found their way into a poem in *Cámara baja,* a bare mention next to a reference to the myth of the "valiant Moor," a more-than-familiar myth. Other objects? A few iridescent crystal goblets with honey-colored bases and gold rims. My mother still has them. For me those goblets are the synecdoche of our journey, symbols of survival. There were also three engraved bronze Moroccan trays at home; one of them worn almost bare, with all the engraving worn down. My parents made a table out of another of them, a kind of bar with little wheels: the tray formed the tabletop. Very handsome. And a mortar, which at home was referred to by its Arabic name, *almirez.* The *mano de almirez,* the pestle that was used to grind, was also made of bronze, not very large, with two ringlike handles on the sides. Most important of all, the relatives had brought words, old-time words, words that were pieces of words in other languages—Arabic, Greek, Hebrew, Spanish from centuries back—words or expressions of a different order that required special pronunciation or intonation or gesture, a kind of secret language, a language of intimacy.

It wasn't until I was an adolescent, however, that I made a journey that allowed me to glimpse what it would have been like to settle in those Argentine country towns. One summer, on a car trip from Buenos Aires to the province of Corrientes on the bank of the Paraná River with my aunt and uncle, we drove through all the towns where the family had lived. My only recollection of one is of the endless fields of the pampa, rain, and a barbed wire fence.

"This is Margarita," they told me. "This is where your father grew up."

It must have been a hard life, I thought, for that gray-eyed girl who dressed her children in velvet clothing and lace shirts and let their curls grow halfway down their backs whether they were boys or girls.

A few kilometers later, the car stopped by a shack with a wooden roof and a wet dirt floor. The rain continued to pour down. Someone had died, and we had to go in and express our sympathy. The owner of the house commented that even though he had lived there for more than sixty years and despite the fact that a car with loudspeakers had been announcing his mother's death all over the town, the neighbors had been reluctant to come and pay their respects.

"Because we're Jews," he said abashedly. The memory remained fixed, for me, in a word my grandparents didn't know: "Macondo," I thought, with that physical sensation that is sometimes produced when you glimpse a point where time and space merge.

During my childhood, half of the adults who surrounded us in Buenos Aires were foreigners from different places. Of the children living on the block where I spent my first ten years, one was the nephew of an Italian couple and others had typical Spanish nicknames. The first friend I made in school was a Japanese girl. Her parents had just come. My brother and I became friends with her and her sister and a brother who was a little older, who still had very vivid memories of his country and used to talk to my father about Japan. And in high school—a public school in the center of the city—many of my schoolmates were daughters of Jewish European parents.

I think everyone talked about their experiences once in a while. Especially the adults. At that time, my father was very eager to hear about the historical and political experiences of others, and he really enjoyed talking about these matters. But I don't know that it was a question of "an immigrant's sense of identity." I think that at that time, in the country, there were various factors that favored or strongly promoted integration, and it was not well thought of to insist upon differences, so people didn't talk about their different backgrounds or countries of origin. I sense that it was something more complex and subtle than what is sometimes reduced to or ridiculed as "repression" or "prejudices." I think that what was expected was that the condition of being an immigrant—of having just arrived and still feeling like the Other, the alien—would be temporary and would not prolong itself enough to become an identity in itself. A perception of immigrants as a permanent category of citizen would have been perceived both as the failure of an entire national project and also as a personal, individual failure to adapt.

I don't deny that other people may have had more difficult or more complex experiences than I did. It may well be that in other sectors of Argentine society, anti-Semitism would have been more noticeable and problematic. Some feel that anti-Semitism was a component in the sale of Argentinean passports to escaping Nazis, or the Tacuara episodes of the nineteen fifties as well as in other more recent acts of violence that are still being investigated. Even so, I think that certain criminal acts and various forms of state terrorism have not, for the most part, been a major part of most people's Jewish experience in Argentina. I myself have had only the experience of being a young Jewish woman of middle class living in Buenos Aires with friends of many different backgrounds and sharing with these friends the good times and the bad: liberties when they existed and, when they didn't, repression and panic.

I don't know that one can speak, in the case of Argentina, of "immigration literature," either, unless to refer to a certain kind of urban folklore, local *costumbrista* writings, music hall skits in which the immigrant is not the writer but the subject, and a caricatured one at that. What is being caricatured, above all, is the melting pot phenomenon so common at the beginning of the century, when poor immigrants from various countries lived together in the same building and, later, in the same neighborhood or on the same block with older middle-class Argentineans, all narrated, in these humorous sketches, from a supposedly "local" (Argentinean?) point of view. As for a literature written by immigrants, I don't think the concept exists. Being asked to participate in an anthology of Jewish writers is a relatively new event for me: so far, in every instance, the invitation has come from someone living in the United States.

I've never thought of myself as a Jewish writer. Maybe because I never write about topics or conflicts or traditions or language that I associate with my religion. Of course there are elements in my poems that could be traced to Biblical or Sephardi traditions, but I think that they are much less evident than are elements of other cultures: Greek and Latin, the golden age of Spain, French decadence of the end of the nineteenth century, or even what I would call a feminist genealogy, which would include Djuna Barnes or Violette Leduc.

It's difficult to discern a clear division between the fact of being Sephardi and the act of writing within the traditions of the Spanish language. If I play in a text with Saint Teresa, is it with the Carmelite mystic, with the doctor of the Church, or with the Jewish intellectual? And the discourse of love that is central to an important part of my work—who is to say whether it stems directly from the Song of Songs, from *jarchas,* from Diego León, from St. John of the Cross, from Fray Luis, from the story of the six-day wedding in Ceuta, from Borges's shy reticence, from Pizarnik's always-absent "you," from Silva's affair with his sister Elvira, or from the relationship of the hungry Violette with Simone de Beauvoir?

Something I am grateful to Argentina for is that it has never made me use or desire any explicit identity marker or any adjective at all after the noun *writer* besides my place and date of birth. Which does not mean that I deny any of the aspects, like being Jewish, that make up my life. I think that being Sephardi and, at the same time, being immersed in Spanish literary tradition ever since I began grade school makes it very difficult to separate and catalog traditions or influences. Even when a typically Jewish element appears in my poetry, is it because I am Jewish that it is there? Then how do you explain the four Mayan definitions that I wrote during these past two years? Does my Jewish origin explain my translations of Jerome Rothenberg's *Khurbn,* about the Holocaust? Then what genealogy explains my translations of Anne Waldman's poems about Milarepa, or of Native American poems about creation or the coyote or shamanistic experiences?

An occasion on which a Sephardi experience or an allusion to the Sephardi world entered a text of mine explicitly was in *El tapiz* (The tapestry). *El tapiz* is a book I wrote between 1977 and, I think, 1982. What poured out first were some fragments in prose, highly elaborated, in a register of language I could hardly recognize as mine, as contemporary. The composition of the fragments moved along: every night, a nun slipped out of her convent in order to embroider a tapestry of flowers with threads unraveled from her own habit. The scenes proliferated and faded, or not—we'll never know. After a certain time the profile of "The Author" appeared, the biography of the one who—unlike me—could have written those texts. The author was described as Ferdinand Oziel—the same surname as the man who had adopted that gray-eyed child who never found out that she would be my grandmother. I think the name Ferdinand came from an edition of Saussure's *General Linguistics* which we were working on at that time at the Losada publishing house. Ferdinand Oziel, author of *El tapiz,* had been a painter born in Orán in 1876, son of a Jewish father—a shipping merchant—and a French mother—a noblewoman from Limoges disinherited because of her dishonorable marriage. The model for the mother could be traced back to one of my mother's aunts, a very beautiful older woman with skin that was very pale and fragile as paper, snow-white hair, and very bright blue eyes.

At a certain point, I would have been tempted to say that all is memory, that there is nothing besides memory. I even insinuated this in a poem:

No hay nada	There is nothing
Nada	Nothing
más allá de esa mullida	beyond that scattered
hostil	hostile

capciosa	captious
vía láctea:	milky way:
la memoria	memory
No hay nada	There is nothing
más allá	beyond
de la novela florida	the flowery novel
que ella juega	that she arranges
arma	sets up
destroza	destroys
entre centelleos	amid sparks
hechizos	spells
despojos	shards
—machos y hembras.	—males and females.

Fiction is still, like some dreams, a combination of different scraps of memory. But recently I've had recurring experiences as I write that make me qualify such an all-encompassing statement. Experiences which are not new, but which I thought would be limited to moments like the composition of *El tapiz*. With the possible exception of the postscript, where Oziel's biography is recounted, as well as the honors and hardships that critics offered him during his brief career as a painter, the main body of the book, *El tapiz*, was composed of a succession of what I always privately called "visions." Another time, as in dreams, the visions included bits of both my own daily life and the political life of the country—it was written during the era of the dictatorship. Thus the erotic body alternates with the body broken into bits by torture and, in the text, fully articulated sentences are mixed with fragments and stammers that are barely salvaged from the splintering of multiple censorships. I expected that this experience of visionary writing would end when I finished writing that book, when I was still relatively young. *El tapiz* was followed by two books that perhaps could be associated with memory, above all if memory is taken to mean both memory of what has been lived as well as read. *Cámara baja* is primarily a book constructed as a patchwork, with scraps of read texts strung together again by the thread of personal life experience. Of course the operation is not such a simple one, given that one lives as one reads, or lives what was read, or interprets and feels what is lived through one's readings. In that sense I say that memory is memory of what has been doubly read.

The experience of vision, on the other hand, emerges from a different mode, and has other echoes and other repercussions. The book I'm writing now, to my surprise, stems primarily from that other source, from that other depository of marvels that is perceived by vision. Of course the visions I am referring to have no mystic or religious significance. Rather, the word "vision" refers to the way in which a visual or auditory image inserts itself into our awareness, whatever its content may be. In that case, the role of memory is crucial, but secondary: it's like the switch that makes a photo begin to move like a film, to extend itself, to acquire development and duration. Elements can be added to the composition, before or after the written word. But the initial stimulus is something else. This stimulus is not much discussed. In general, this whole topic is not often considered. Nor is it often discussed within Jewish tradition. Maybe because there is a long anti-iconic Jewish tradition which is, in a certain sense, antivisionary. Which does not mean that there is not also an equally long tradition of Jewish visionaries, both male and female. A recent telephone conversation with my mother about some questions that I had about Jewish tradition and dreams made us both think about this topic, this type of experience that is so common but so rarely analyzed. I think that memory, vision, and reading form an indivisible sheaf. Even more, as that medieval song says, a sheaf that we should not even dream of dismantling.

Asked what it means to be a Jewish Latin American woman writer, I can only say that I am more comfortable defining myself as a Latin American poet, or as an Argentinean poet or writer. As such, I don't feel forced to hide any aspect of my identity as a Jew, nor do I feel obliged or coerced to behave or write as a Jew. Both these things are an enormous privilege: to neither hide nor represent, nor be ashamed, nor feel obliged to fill ethnic pigeonholes in order to pacify one's conscience and promote the well-being of others—whether the others are Jews or Negroes or indigenous people or Eastern Europeans or North or South Americans.

In Argentina it has never occurred to me to think about Viñas or Gelman or Aida Bortnik or Pizarnik as Jewish writers. The first thing I read about Pizarnik when I was an adolescent was—ironically—her obituary, which mentioned the La Tablada cemetery. The notice touched some chord in me, for an instant, a chord that was both intimate and familiar, and yet, at the same time, I was aware of a distance, a difference: it was about a Jewish cemetery, but it was another community's cemetery: our dead were buried in the Avellaneda cemetery.

As a writer, I think in a language, in a tradition, in a succession of recollections, visions, and readings which I share or don't share, which unite me or don't unite me, with other writers. The Song of Songs, the *jarchas,* and Ibn Gabirol abide comfortably in me alongside *The Metamorphosis,* Catullus, Sei Shonagon, *The Wings of the Dove, Amadis,* Garcilaso, St. John, Sor Juana, the French decadents, Darío, Virginia Woolf, Tsvetaeva, Carrington, Barnes, Leduc, Borges, Orozco, Pizarnik. That is the pantheon, and that is the only Promised Land.

Chapter 19

Saint Anthony's Intervention and Other Accounts of Growing up Jewish in Mexico

Diana Anhalt

It was a fine funeral. The deceased, a rich man with many children, had lived most of his adult life in Mexico, given generously to Israel, and was buried on a Sunday, so the event was well attended. Karina, his niece once-removed and my former student, was among the mourners. She greeted me warmly.

"How are you?" I asked.

She sighed. "I'm so desperate I'm lighting candles to San Antonio."

Never having heard the expression before I asked for details.

"Look," she said, "San Antonio, Saint Anthony in English, is the saint of lost objects: lost glasses, lost keys, lost dogs, you know. He finds things. But his specialty is finding husbands. My Catholic friends told me to collect coins from thirteen married men and visit San Antonio's Church on June 13, his feast day. Once there, I had to place the coins on his altar, light a candle, pray, and do the same thing when I got home. It's supposed to work better if you tie San Antonio's image upside down, probably in the belief that discomfort speeds delivery."

We laughed.

"But I couldn't, I couldn't bring a saint into my mother's house so I just keep lighting candles—and praying."

People were milling around the grave, their voices hushed. The service was about to begin. We veered away from the crowd. "But Karina, you're Jewish," I said.

"Yes, I told my friends but they assured me San Antonio will be flattered by the attention, from a Jew no less, so this is a sure thing!" She gave me a good-bye hug. "Now just promise you won't tell my mother."

A few months later Karina's mother called. "Karina left for the States a few days ago or she would have called you personally. She's getting married in May to a very nice rabbinical student from New York. Remember my uncle's funeral in July? Well, she met him there."

THIS STORY GOES TO PROVE three things: Saint Anthony is no anti-Semite, even if he is a saint; miracles in Mexico are as plentiful as potholes; and to be Jewish in this country is to believe in them.

Here is another miracle I believe in. A Jewish child, one of many, was rounded up and sent to Auschwitz during the war. She had only her mother's photograph to remind her of home. Fearing the Gestapo might take it away she folded it in four, back side out, and placed it in her mouth under her tongue. The child left home, literally, with her "mother in her mouth." The photo survived the war. She survived the concentration camp.

Like her, I also left home involuntarily, but under far more propitious circumstances, bearing my language in my mouth and the taste of snow and my grandmother's borscht on my palate. Unlike the Polish child, I was not forced to leave home because I was Jewish.

I was forced to leave because my parents were Reds. They fled the Bronx and the ghosts of their radical pasts during the so-called McCarthy era. At the time, from the late forties and throughout the fifties, membership in suspect organizations, your signature on a controversial petition, or your refusal to swear you had never belonged to the Communist Party could result in the loss of a job, a subpoena, or both.

I was eight years old when we became part of that long line of political dissidents, fortune seekers, draft dodgers, and tax evaders who,

for centuries, have entered Mexico seeking sanctuary. In the beginning I didn't think much about growing up Jewish in Latin America.
I was too busy indulging my other minority identities. I was a
"gringa" and a "Commie's daughter." I had no time to be a Jew and,
though I never denied it, I chose not to be, at least not at the beginning. At the beginning I preferred to be a "gringa," until I discovered
I really wasn't. I had nothing in common with the children who attended the American School with me.

In my America I had never met anybody like them and probably
never would have had I remained there. They came from places I'd
never heard of like Waco and Duluth, wore crinolines and Mary Jane
shoes and believed in God; their mothers cut the crusts off their sandwiches and belonged to the Junior League; their fathers worked at the
American Embassy or with a U.S. corporation and voted Republican.
They rarely learned Spanish because they would be leaving in a year
or two anyway, and some actually used the word "Spic" to refer to
anyone who wasn't American.

There were exceptions of course, and I found them, but for a while
I recited Grace in the homes of my Christian friends, crossing my
fingers and lowering my voice when I reached the end: "For health
and strength and daily bread thank Jesus Christ, our Lord." I learned
all the words to "Silent Night, Holy Night" and "Oh Little Town of
Bethlehem" and went caroling with the Girl Scouts. We even had a
Christmas tree, once, although my parents made me place it upstairs
in the playroom, not in the living room where everyone would see.

Being a "gringa" was not easy but being a "Commie's daughter"
proved impossible. For one thing, outside a small circle of intimates,
no one knew the details of my parents' political pasts. As a matter of
fact, neither did I. (They swore me to secrecy nonetheless.) They
weren't "Famous Communists," like some of my friends' parents, and
their names never appeared in the newspapers. As eager as I was to cul-
tivate the role of underdog and rebel, I had nothing to go on. Being
Jewish, however, helped account for my oddities: my New York

accent, my scuffed orthopedic shoes, my preference for reading over television, my sardine sandwiches. In fact, there were times when, in my mind, being Jewish and being Red were pretty much the same thing.

However, we were not just Jews, we were English-speaking American Jews residing abroad. In the sanctified tradition of our American forefathers world-wide who turned everything they touched into a replica of Boise, Idaho, a small group of Americans, including my parents, started the American Jewish Club. We held Passover Seders, met on the High Holidays, and organized a series of edifying lectures on cultural themes. Within months we had attracted the attention of the FBI. Apparently, some of our speakers and, no doubt, some of our members, were suspected of being Communists. To make matters worse, our president shared an office with Alfred Stern who, along with his wife Martha Dodd, was wanted in the United States for conspiracy to commit espionage. We decided to disband.

Soon after, the former members met to establish the American Jewish Synagogue in Mexico City. For my parents, it was, undoubtedly, safer to be Jews than Communists and, by then, they had reason to believe they had been identified as the latter. (The embassy refused to renew their U.S. passports in 1953 after my father was seen leaving suspected spy Alfred Stern's office.) Thus, although my father was one of the temple's founding members, he never received much credit, perhaps because he was a radical and didn't believe in God.

The congregation rented a house, purchased some prayer books, and hired a Reform rabbi. Mexican Jewry was not ready for us. In Mexico during the fifties, being an American was bad enough, but to be American and Reform! That was unheard of. Some of our members joked, although it might have been true, that when an Orthodox Jew passed in front of our temple, he spat three times and crossed the street. After our young rabbi left we hired a Conservative, out of respect.

While the vast majority of Americans were confined to "Little Americas" of their own making, we Jews had a decided advantage, an entry into Mexican life our gentile American friends did not share.

Under the illusion that, as fellow Jews, we must share some things in common, the Mexican Jewish community occasionally included us in their activities and allowed us to join their sports club and raise money for Israel.

We might be Americans, recently arrived, but we were after all Jewish and by definition "paisanos," compatriots. Well, more or less. Some Jews, it seems, fully qualified for "paisano-hood," while others just scraped by. It all depended on who was passing the judgment.

For Central and East European or Ashkenazi Jews the only full-fledged "paisanos" were other Ashkenazim. The same held true for the Sephardim, Jews originating in Spain and Portugal or migrating from the Middle East. Since we were descended from Polish Jews, we were generally accepted by our fellow Europeans, but not by the Sephardi community. The opposite, of course, was also true. (That these two populations, and several others, were able to overcome their differences long enough to establish a sports club is, in fact, a miracle in itself.)

Though my upbringing was hardly religious I had always felt comfortable with people who were like the people I knew in New York, most of whom were first or second generation Jews born in the United States. According to family legend, when my sister Judy was three years old she wandered down Jones Beach, pausing at each beach umbrella to ask, "Are you ticklish or Jewish?" so a sense of Jewish identity pervaded my childhood world. In spite of this, the terms "Ashkenazi" and "Sephardi" were not part of my vocabulary.

Regardless of the differences separating them, the Jewish community in Mexico wrapped their Judaism—the religious traditions, values, shared histories, and languages—like a shawl around their shoulders to keep out the cold and the outside world. Centuries of persecution and migration, and now their convergence in a foreign country, bound them—occasionally the entire community but, more frequently, sizable segments of it—together.

The Europeans, for example, shared not only a culture but a language, Yiddish, and for my monolingual parents this was a straw worth grasping. In their desperation to communicate, they dredged up tattered bits and pieces from their past, interspersing English words whenever the Yiddish evaded them. (Years later, once their Spanish improved, they did the same thing, substituting a Spanish word for a Yiddish one.)

Shortly after his arrival, my father was introduced to a man named Jaime, pronounced "Himay," a common name which means James. To his ears, accustomed to the names of childhood companions, it sounded like "Hymie." He had never met a non-Jewish Hymie. Assuming the obvious, he gave up on his Spanish altogether and inquired, "Farshteist Yiddish?" (Do you understand Yiddish?) At the dinner table that evening my father regaled us with a detailed description of his encounter with Jaime. "The man must have thought I was nuts. Either that, or that my Spanish was the worst Spanish he'd ever heard."

"Or that you swallowed your gum," I interjected. (My five-year-old sister and I thought that was hilarious.)

Despite our differences, we Jews were drawn together under that metaphorical communal shawl because every single one of us belonged to a decided minority in Mexico and was an immigrant, a fairly recent one at that. In the United States, on the other hand, the large waves of Jewish migration, marking the beginning of the century, had been reduced to a trickle after the American government imposed quotas in 1917.

Thus, when I arrived in 1950, few Mexican Jews had been here for more than two generations. True, Jews had originally arrived with the first conquistadors. But during the 1640s the Holy Inquisition efficiently eradicated any traces of Judaism in Mexico. (In 1875 twenty-five Jewish families resided in the country.)

Because the experience of immigration was more recent and its effects more immediate, being Jewish in Mexico meant living within a stone's throw of the ghetto and just steps away from the Holocaust. I met people with concentration-camp numbers etched into their forearms, learned what the phrase "siege mentality" meant, and discovered that Jews continued to arrive in Mexico from Aleppo, Turkey, Iran, Argentina, and elsewhere.

Judaism travels well. It was instrumental in helping people adapt to one side of their lives in Mexico, the Jewish side. But, in some ways, few places could have been more inhospitable and, at the beginning, adaptation was difficult. Certainly that would account, at least in part, for Jews' cleaving together. Although a few would eventually migrate to the United States or the provinces, the majority would remain in Mexico City. Those who didn't customarily sent their unmarried daughters to live in the city with relatives or to board with respectable "paisanos" so they could meet and, God willing, marry a Jewish man.

Years after I arrived, my husband's uncle Morris, known more for his charm than for his accuracy, told me a story, possibly apocryphal but "true," in the same way a fictionalized account often is. He claimed that, according to the Mexican census bureau, five hundred thousand Jews lived in Mexico in the early 1940s. (Even today, we probably number no more than fifty thousand, a decided minority in a country of approximately ninety million.) He knew the figures to be grossly inflated: "Well," he told me, "it turned out that every Protestant, Confucian, Moslem, Seventh Day Adventist, Christian Scientist, Mormon, Non-Believer, in short, anyone who had identified themselves as anything other than Catholic had been lumped into the same category, 'Judío' [Jewish]."

When I arrived in Mexico I knew virtually nothing about Catholics except that they were Christians. Christians believed in Christ. We didn't. I had known some Catholics at public school in the Bronx, but to me they were just kids, American kids. Some were my friends; others weren't. That was the extent of my experience with Catholicism.

In Mexico, however, Catholicism, like the chorus in an opera, is always there, if not on stage, then in the wings. Images of the Virgin of Guadalupe and Jesus Christ find their way onto matchboxes and tee-shirts; crosses and shrines sprout alongside highways to mark the sites of fatal accidents or miraculous apparitions. No town is without its church, no church without its saint, no Catholic without a saint's day, no saint without a feast day and, among the less educated, few of the devout without some prejudice: the Jews killed Christ, they are greedy, control world finance, and sprout horns.

Certainly, Mexico had no monopoly on anti-Semitism, but it was out in the open here: newspaper articles regularly identified subjects by religion as in, "The Jew Pedro Birman murdered his wife . . ."; *The Protocols of Zion* and other savagely anti-Semitic tracts were sold over the counter by otherwise reputable bookstores. (My father complained to the manager of Sears Roebuck because they openly displayed them in their book department.) It was not unusual to see swastika flags sold alongside Mexican flags on street corners.

My husband's father purchased one, a miniature Mexican flag, and fastened it to the radio antenna of his car on national holidays. He was a Mexican citizen, his naturalization papers bore the signature of President Portes Gil, and he embraced his new citizenship with pride. But if someone had asked him his nationality and he had replied, "I am a Mexican," their most likely response would have been, "No, I mean your real nationality."

Foreigners were not encouraged to assimilate. The newly arrived were known to cling to their heritage like the ship-wrecked to life rafts. (I've known third-generation Spaniards born in Mexico who have never "lost" their Castilian accents.) On the other hand, in one generation my parents had become, or at least considered themselves, fully Americanized.

Becoming a Mexican was more difficult. While Jews often chose not to assimilate, any attempts they made to do so were, more often than not, frustrated. Their recent migrations, the cultural and religious disparities, the tight-knit groups within the Jewish community itself, and the still-vivid memories of the Holocaust helped explain their isolation. It also explained why conversion to Catholicism or intermarriage between Jew and Gentile—and even between Sephardi and Ashkenazi Jews—was, and to a lesser extent still is, relatively rare.

Occasionally the obituary of someone long forgotten, topped by a cross, will appear in the paper. The old-timers who remember will see it and mutter, "Ya se murió el renegado" (The renegade has died).

There is another, less obvious, reason for our alienation from mainstream Mexican life, all the more worrying because it is impossible to fully comprehend. I think of it as an undercurrent flowing out of Mexico's most remote past, rising out of its mystical, surreal, occasionally violent nature.

I felt it when I saw a *curandero*, a witch doctor, roll an egg slowly up a child's body to "cleanse" it of evil. It invaded me on the Day of the Dead when relatives commune with their deceased and set out offerings of flowers, food, and drink. The unease was there at the burning of the Judas during Holy Week, when celebrants exploded the immense papier mâché Judas figures—bearded Satans with aquiline noses, a rat with an uncanny resemblance to a former president, a rock star, a policeman—each explosion representing the eradication of evil and the triumph of light over darkness.

It is related to an integral side of Mexican life, the irrational side, the side which believes in miracles. Miracles make me uncomfortable because of my background, I suppose, but often leave me with no choice other than to believe in them. Some are easier to believe in than others, of course, because they really happened, like the "Cristo de Oro," the Christ of Gold miracle.

Samuel Rosencrantz—not his real name—owned a dozen small apartments clustered around a central courtyard in downtown Mexico City. A developer made him an astronomical offer for the land providing he could induce his tenants to leave. At first, a few accepted cash settlements without protest, but upon visiting his property one morning he found several tenants digging up the patio.

"What's going on?" he asked.

The tailor, who seemed to be in charge, replied, "We are looking for a 'Cristo de Oro,' which, legend has it, was buried here during the Revolution."

This was a most unwelcome development and slowed down nego-
tiations considerably. Each tenant demanded a better price. The most
reluctant to settle, and the last, was the tailor. When, many months
later, Samuel shook his hand over their final agreement, he asked,
"Just out of curiosity, did you ever find the 'Cristo de Oro'?"

"Of course we did," the tailor replied. "It was you, Don Samuel."

I shared many things in common with my fellow Jews but I knew
that to be Jewish, really Jewish, in Mexico was to be many of the things
I wasn't, and there were times when I asked myself, "If these people
who are so different from me are Jewish, how can I be the same thing?"

Shortly after I met Mauricio, the man who became my husband, he
introduced me to the ancient Mrs. Ripstein. She and her husband had
arrived in Mexico in the nineteenth century, and he had fought in the
Mexican Revolution. If anyone had a claim to Jewish aristocracy, she
did. As soon as she had a chance she drew Mauricio to one side and
asked, "Is this girl you're seeing Jewish?"

"Of course she is."

Mrs. Ripstein looked him the eye and said, "Well, you're wrong."

In an attempt to humor her, Mauricio asked, "Well, how do you
know that?"

"Because I've never seen her before in my life."

I had failed the "Ripstein Test." That was not the only test I failed.
My mother-in-law had arrived in the port of Veracruz in 1925. She
made the crossing by ship from Antwerp and could still recite from
memory the names of her fellow passengers, her "shifshvesters" and
"shifbruders," knew their families, their spouses, and their offspring.
Over the years so many dozens of *shifshvesters* and *shifbruders* had
been introduced to me that I sometimes doubted there was a ship large
enough to hold them all. But I realized, at some level, that to be a bona-
fide Jew in my mother-in-law's eyes was to have crossed the Atlantic
with her in 1925 or to be a blood relative of someone who had.

Like my mother-in-law, my grandmother on my mother's side was
born in Poland, but had migrated to New York City in 1910. For Jew-

ish immigrants in those days, New York must have been much like the Mexico City I reached in 1950: old-country traditions, values, and religious observances prevailed, and nothing was more important than keeping the family together at all costs.

After my family returned to the United States in 1981, I often felt orphaned in the company of those Mexican families—both Jewish and gentile—the size of small battalions, who muster together at the slightest pretense, invade each other's homes, work together, travel together, and, in short, fulfill each other's every need. My grandmother would have felt right at home in such an environment. Had she and my mother-in-law lived in the same city, I think they would have called each other "shifshvesters." They were soul mates in a way my mother-in-law and my American-born mother never could be.

Perhaps their only grounds for discord would have been politics. My grandmother was a Socialist and voted for Eugene Debs, and, years later, for Franklin D. Roosevelt. My mother-in-law, on the other hand, was like the majority of Mexican Jews, politically conservative, anti-Communist, and pro-American. If she voted at all in the Mexican elections she would have backed the PRI, the government party, because there was no viable opposition in Mexico at the time.

Not until I married my husband fifteen years after I'd arrived in Mexico City would I realize just how much of an outsider I had been up until that point. My mother-in-law knew, of course, from the moment she met me, that I was not "one of us." Any doubts she might have had in that area were quickly dissipated by a series of nuptial "accidents": my parents overlooked a time-honored tradition when they neglected to give Mauricio a "wedding watch" following our engagement; ours was the first Jewish wedding in the history of the Churubusco Country Club; the women in charge of the flower arrangements had never attended a Jewish wedding and fashioned an arched *chuppah* out of Easter lilies; and when dinner was served, my mother-in-law sat down to her first, and probably last, non-kosher wedding banquet. But I think that her relief at her son's having married a Jew, an Ashkenazi Jew at that, more than compensated for the fact that I had flunked the Ripstein Test.

I HAVE HEARD THAT ONCE you cross into Mexico at Nuevo Laredo there are few opportunities to turn back. All you have to do is bear south on the main highway and follow the "no hay retorno" (there is no return) signs, cautionary reminders dotting the highway all the way to Mexico City. When my parents snatched me away from my certain destiny as an American child growing up Jewish in New York and crossed the border into Mexico, they delivered me over to another, quite different, fate. I became an American Mexican Jewish woman who acquired, during fifty years in Mexico, a new language, culture, value system, and a set of hyphens.

Taking on all those extra options has given me a decided advantage, unlike the terminally ill woman in the Mark Twain story: A woman visits her doctor, who tells her that her situation is critical but she might, by miracle, survive if she stops drinking, smoking, and cussing. "I can't stop drinking, smoking, and cussing," she replies, "because I don't do any of those things." So she died, of course. According to Twain, "She was like a sinking ship with nothing to throw overboard."

My Jewish and Latin American identities have given me plenty of excess baggage, so if the going gets tough, I can work miracles of my own and travel down other roads. Roads with "retornos."

Chapter 20

With All That I Am

Ana María Shua

Woman, Argentine, Jew, and writer
in that order or any other

BACK TO CHILDHOOD, let's go there, where the broth of life is bubbling, getting its flavors, that's where it starts, where it's defined, where it takes shape. And now that we're there, since we're children, off we go to school. To the Argentine public school, equalizing, secular, where all the children look like white doves in their school smocks, all alike, indistinguishable, white and pleated, with belts and hair bows for the girls, plain for the boys. Totally white, pure white: it's forbidden at school parties to wear a coat over your pinafore. We wear special collars that go around our necks, to hide our bulging flesh, a starched collar that covers any color that could possibly show through from underneath. Lined up on the steps, white gloves, white anklets, we with our short skirts, they with short pants, all of us with our knees freezing in the patriotic wind of the 9th of July, in midwinter.

Up to third grade, there are a few boys in our class, but only because there is a shortage of boys' schools. After that, we are all girls; there are not even any male teachers: once a year the photographer visits the school, once a year a policeman comes to instruct us in public safety. These are real occasions: a man in the school, what a stir, what a shock, the teachers smoothing their skirts, retouching their makeup, the directress offering them coffee. Not even our fathers get to come to school, except for an occasional school party, with their cameras in hand: if one of the students has a problem, it's the mother who gets sent for. All the same, all white, even those children with skin darker than the others, who get called out to the directress's office, pulled out of class in front of us all, made to stand out in the effort to see that they fit right in, in order to give them the white pinafores the school board is donating to them because their parents can't afford to buy them.

The school is quite a way from my house but it is the only one my mother could talk into admitting me to first grade before I turned five, compelled by a mandate of intellectual urgency: a need to save time, save that year of life, of school, a need to hurry on, the child already knows how to read and write, why wait. Later I'll find out that every Jewish mother of her generation felt compelled to do this; later I'll meet many adults my age whose mothers have pushed them into skipping a grade, starting school early, jumping a grade to enter secondary school a year sooner, it's important to hurry, demand more, work harder, skip ahead, who knows why. At that point, I don't know anything much, I'm five years old and my seatmate knows much more than I do, is a lot older, she's almost six months older than I am, although she is being pushed ahead, too. It's then that, for the first time, I hear the strange, unexpected question. Rosalba, my seatmate, asks me if I'm Jewish. I give the answer my father has taught me to give—clear, definitive, total: that's not a subject to talk about at school, I answer her, with calm certainty. Well done says my father when I tell him, well done, that shouldn't be discussed at school, the school is secular, every child is equal at school, there's no religion or color or origin or poor or rich or anything. My father is the president of the school board, and that assures me the best of all possible equalnesses. We're all equal but not everyone is as equal as I am: those children with darker skin, with mended pinafores and notebooks full of inkspots and spelling errors whose books are paid for by the school board, the ones my mother would never call *cabecitas negras,* darkies, nor would my father ever permit that expression to be used in his house, but better you shouldn't spend time with them says Mamá, because they're ordinary people, they're poor students, they're a minority in that middle-class prosperous neighborhood school, in any case many of them won't stay around long, you can't expect them to finish up with the others, some are much older than you are because they've repeated several grades, in high school there's a better atmosphere, you'll see.

But, then, am I Jewish? If Rosalba invites me to her house, so we aren't at school and we can talk about anything, what do I tell her? That I'm not anything, because to be Jewish is a religion and at home we don't practice any religion, we're all atheists and my *papá* is a little more atheistic than the rest of us? Rosalba is Jewish and her parents aren't atheists but neither are they religious—how complicated life is getting to be. One thing I'm pretty sure of, my *papá's* parents are Jewish, because they practice the Jewish religion, but Mamá's parents must not be, because they are atheists, too, like us, and they don't practice any religion. Religion seems to be something that's easily forgotten, not like knowing how to ride a bike, so you have to practice it a lot, but we don't ever practice it. My *papá* explains that religion is the opiate of the people.

In my paternal grandparents' house, the ones who are for sure Jewish, the Jewish holy days are celebrated, for example Pesach, which is when the Jews fled from Egypt. My grandfather Musa is an Arab, he came from Beirut, but my grandmother Ana is Argentinean, the daughter of Moroccans who weren't born in Morocco but on the Rock of Gibraltar, which means that they were Spanish, but of English nationality—life keeps getting more and more complicated. I'm *morocha,* dark skinned, like my *papá* and like them. A Jewish holy day is when we get together with all of *papá's* brothers and sisters and their children. I have eight aunts and uncles because two died, one of peritonitis and the other I don't know what of. On the table, they set the hairless head of a dead animal with blue eyes that stare right at me. On the table there are lots of things, some to eat and others for decoration. Then they bring my grandfather a little book with mother of pearl covers with funny squiggles that must be written in Arabic, which is what he speaks. My grandfather Musa puts on a blue poncho with a fringe and a funny little cap that he fastens to his hair with a bobby pin so it won't fall off. Why doesn't he just wear a bigger one so it will stay on better? And he starts to sing, in Arabic, things that no one understands, rocking himself back and forth. We all stand up out of respect for Grandfather, and my uncles take their handkerchiefs out of their pockets not to blow their noses but to put them on their heads, my *papá*, too, and they repeat some of the things Grandfather is singing, even though you can tell they don't understand anything at all and they say the words very differently than he does. Of course, since my grandmother is Argentinean they never learned Arabic. Then we eat chicken with really delicious rice, dark with Turkish pepper, with cinnamon, almonds, and pine nuts.

Mamá's parents are very different, they serve different foods, like gefilte fish, they must not be Jews because they don't believe in any religion and they never go to the temple or anything. I went to the temple just once, Papá took me there on the Day of Pardon to hear how they played the *shofar* and to see how all the religious Jews went running out afterward, headed home to eat because they're dying of hunger because of fasting. My maternal grandparents are Zeide and Bobe. They are blond, with light eyes like my *mamá* and my aunt Musia. The only way they resemble my other grandparents is that at the same season of the year they put those big square flat crackers that don't have much taste out on their table; that they call "matze" and the other grandparents call "masá." My Zeide grandfather, the one I don't know if he's Jewish or not, taught me how to say things in his language that he speaks with my Bobe and with Mamá, too, when they don't want Papá to understand, a language that must be Polish because they came from Poland. He says things like, "In the *yeide*'s house is . . ." and I add, to fill in the blank, "ame-haiele!" That seems to make everyone happy, except my *papá*, who gets into a bad mood. At the same time when I was starting first grade, my Zeide grandfather, the one I don't know if he's Jewish or not, made me a life member of the Sociedad Hebraica Argentina club so I could learn how to swim.

And then, no way around it, one grows up and begins sorting things out, some puzzling things get cleared up, others seem snarlier than ever. I found out a long time ago that my *zeide* and my *bobe* were not speaking Polish, but rather Yiddish, and I found out that Grandfather Musa's little book with pearl covers didn't have Arab songs in it, but rather Hebrew prayers, and I found out that I have a grandfather Meishe and a grandfather Musa and they are both named Moses. I saw the film *The Ten Commandments,* probably the sum total of all the Jewish education I received throughout my childhood, and I understood that if the two of them are named Moses it's because they were both given the same name as Charleton Heston. I learned about the pogroms and the Holocaust because at home people were always talking about those subjects and everything else, and one could fill in between the lines with more Hollywood images. Papá had had to put up with going (against his will) to some *kabbalat shabbat* at the Hebraica, late one Friday afternoon, and what a horror for my poor father: that's how they reel you in, he says, by dangling the hook of making friends and then trapping you into religion, and you could see that it seems to him the worst of all possible worlds—the strange world of my Shua grandparents, who dug a hole out in their garden to bury the knife and fork my mother used to put the ham between bread slices.

On the other hand, how difficult to understand my *papá,* who is so afraid of the *kabbalat shabbat* but who doesn't seem to mind having us participate, my sister and me, in the catechizing meetings of the evangelists in Rivadavia Park across from our house. There, sitting on roots of the *ombú* tree, we sing "There's forgiveness for the blood of Jesus, /

there's forgiveness for his death on the cross, / there's forgiveness, there's forgiveness, there's forgiveness for everyone, / for the death of Jesus Christ." For everyone, reiterates the preacher, and, although he shows us a drawing that includes children and grownups and old people, black, white, and Chinese, he repeats again, forgiveness for Jews, too. Papá, I ask afterward at home, is it true what the girls in the plaza say, that Jews killed Jesus? No, my father, who really knows about everything, explains to me: it wasn't the Jews, it was the Romans. Oh what a relief, to not be responsible for something like that, the Romans must feel really bad. I decide on the spot that if I ever meet a Roman I am never going to say you were the ones who killed Jesus.

By that time I'm pretty clear about who Jesus is, I realize that he was a very important person, I read a lot at that time, I read the whole day long, and all, absolutely all, the books I read, the educational children's magazines, the little books I check out of the school library agree about the importance of believing in God, in Jesus, in the Christian faith. Nobody tells me about any other options. And it's perfectly clear that anyone who has the chance to become a Christian and doesn't take advantage of it will go straight to hell. I never heard anything about a Jewish hell, Jews must just go straight to the Christian hell. But I've learned that my recent faith is not something I can talk to my parents about, what a blow to them, who are always so proud of not being anything. I'm fascinated by the lives of the women saints, especially the ones who get tortured a lot, especially the ones who are tortured because they refuse to give up their virtue, that part's not very clear, where they have this virtue, but I can imagine where, because sometimes I touch myself there even though Mamá says it could make me sick.

In a children's magazine I learn the Our Father and I begin to recite it every night just in case, there doesn't seem to be any special punishment for giving up Judaism, on the contrary. I even baptize myself, solemnly, in the bathroom sink, I've read that that can be done under extreme circumstances, when there is no possibility of reaching a priest and having a complete ceremony, and what possibility would I have. It's not that I'm absolutely sure, maybe God exists (I imagine Him as necessarily Catholic) and maybe He doesn't, I'm waiting for a sign, but meanwhile what does it cost me to take some steps to save myself from hell just in case? Meanwhile, I'm a writer, the most famous poet in my whole school. I write moving poems for the patriotic holiday, about the flag, the special issue decorated pen, the national coat of arms, the twenty-fifth of May, the ninth of July, about San Martín and Sarmiento and all the national heroes. I'm Argentine, very Argentine, proudly Argentine, in school they explain to me that I am also Latin American but I can tell that both my teacher and my parents have their doubts about this, we're very different from the other countries of Latin America, they explain to me, we're Europeans here, you don't see any Indians or Negroes here. In our national poem, the *Martín Fierro,* there are lots of Indians but it doesn't talk about what happened to them; they seem to have disappeared for some reason. On the twenty-fifth of May holiday, we dress up as blacks from the colonial era, but only two months later, on the ninth of July holiday, there isn't a black left because the colonial era came to an end. Little by little I figure out that the first call for liberty was the twenty-fifth of May, 1810, and that we became entirely free on the ninth of July, 1816, but it never occurs to me to wonder what happened in those six years to all the people dressed up as black Mammies who sold *empanadas* and *mazamorra* to the mothers who came to school for the celebration of May twenty-fifth. The girl who works in our house (it's bad to say the servant) has dark skin, thick lips, and very frizzy hair but you'd better not say maybe her grandfather was black because she gets really offended. Lots of people are nicknamed "Negro" or "Negra," for example my little sister, whom my Zeide grandfather teases and of whom he says they found her in a trash can in Bolivia, that's why she's so dark skinned, so *morocha;* it seems to me that Negrita doesn't much like this joke. "Shitty Jew" is a terrible insult, and it's not just anyone who dares to say that to a Jew, on the other hand, "fucking negro" is a very common insult, and even those who are *morochos* say it to each other.

We Argentines are very European, say the adults, and all of a sudden for some reason no one understands well they decide it's time to run off to buy rice, sugar, and noodles, standing in line at the store through those days when all you can hear on the radio are military marches and my parents say another revolution or yet another military coup. At school they teach me that an Argentine president serves for a term of six years, but in my lifetime none has lasted even two, six years is too long, says my father, maybe if he only had to get through four he'd make it, but no one could get through six, the military step in and remove them, but they can't make it on their own either, and then there are elections again. I want to be up on things and I read the newspapers but I keep forgetting the name of the president because it changes so often, it seems like in Europe and the United States this doesn't happen. Perón's name I do remember well because I heard it so many times, but that's from right before I started school so I don't have pictures and photos of him in my reading book like my cousin Quique does, who's three years older than I am and in all his school books he tore out or scribbled over the faces of Evita and Perón or he drew mustaches on them and his parents let him, that's really weird because generally parents don't let you draw in your school books, and they certainly don't let you tear pages out. I never used to talk about Perón because when he was president, Mamá always used to tell me not to repeat the things I heard at home because it was dangerous, and now my father, when he says bad things about Perón, always calls him You Know Who I Mean. It seems as though it's prohibited by law to say the name Perón, and that really pleases my father, when he says Whatsisname he says it as though he's laughing, but sometimes he isn't really laughing because you can see that it bothers him.

In any case, always, the government is to blame for everything that happens in Argentina, and that's why we're not like the United States or France. I never hear anyone saying that in Venezuela or Perú or in Brazil these things don't happen. Those are countries we don't talk about; they hardly exist. Uruguay does exist because we hear it on the radio and it's very close, just across the river. When all you can hear on Argentine radios are military marches, then everyone tries to pick up Uruguayan stations to find out what is going on. I studied Chile, Bolivia, Paraguay, and Brazil in school because those countries border on ours, but no Argentine would compare himself to them. They don't even come out complete on the map, only Uruguay, the rest just show the strip along the Argentine border, though once in a while people remember Paraguay because that's where they had the *Tirano Prófugo,* the Old Renegade, who's the same sort of thing as You Know Who I Mean.

All of a sudden I'm twelve years old and I'm in high school and I know about a lot of things now. The boy I like gives me his little medal of the Virgin for me to take care of while he's playing soccer but he forgets to ask for it back and I get home so in love that the little medal burns my skin but my parents see it and don't like it one bit, and we talk and we talk, and I find out, I discover with horror, that this matters to them, that for them, for my parents, who have always been fraternalistic, universalist, egalitarians, esperantophiles, and atheistic, and I wouldn't have thought they would care, it's not that they are opposed, mind you, never that, but it does matter to them that their daughter is choosing to like a Catholic boy rather than one of her own community. I weep in despair, feeling as though I've awakened from a long misconception, with my eyes open now I look around me and for the first time I realize that the clubs we are members of are Hebraica and Hacoaj, I think about who my parents' friends are and for the first time I realize that they are almost all Jews and that perhaps, only perhaps, this is not by pure coincidence.

Around then I take my first trip to the United States, with my parents and my sister. We go visit part of our extended family that lives there. My mother's father emigrated to Argentina but his six brothers settled in the United States and had their children and grandchildren. Our Yankee aunts and uncles and cousins are surprised that we can live comfortably in a Nazi country like Argentina. We try to persuade them in every possible way that Argentina is not a Nazi country,

although there may be some anti-Semitic groups, although some of
the anti-Semitic enclaves may be as important as the armed forces. We
try to persuade them that our Jewish community, one of the biggest in
the world, lives comfortably integrated into Argentine life, we try to
persuade them that we don't live, as they do in the United States, in
neighborhoods or suburbs where everyone is Jewish, because in Argentina people are more mixed together, we try to persuade them that
both my parents and my sister and I have always gone to public
schools and universities without suffering from the slightest discrimination, but they look at us compassionately and do not believe us.
They have read that our country is Nazi, they read it in books, in
newspapers and in magazines, and they are convinced that we are just
so used to persecution and mistreatment that we don't even notice
them any longer.

In 1967, I published my first book of poems. I'm sixteen years old
by now. Summing up the situation, I am very clear that:

1. I'm Latin American. At this point I'm a leftist intellectual and in
my last poems I begin to consider the notion of compromise. I'm a
supporter of the idea of the New Man and, without being a militant ex-
tremist of any party, I sympathize with the Marxist revolution. I am
clearly and energetically opposed to Yankee imperialism.

2. I'm Jewish. This concept clashes with the previous one in a
pretty dramatic way. The Six Day War provokes a huge amount of
discussion and dissent among the leftist Jews: isn't Israel an enclave of
imperialism sustained by the Western powers? Nevertheless, I come
out in favor of Israel. I'm a Jew, I defend the existence of the state of Israel and I feel that the holy war includes me. What confusion.

3. I'm not very sure about being a writer. Despite this first book,
which I wrote at age fifteen and which at sixteen I feel no longer represents me because it seems infantile, I still have too much respect for
that word Writer, which looms large. For the moment, it goes on
being a distant dream.

4. I'm definitely not a woman. That is, it never occurred to me that the fact of being female could influence my life, let alone what I write. I'm a person equal to all others. Equal. I can do anything I want if I try hard enough. That's what my parents taught me: to be Equal.

Later on, I decide to work as journalist. It's 1970, and when I make the rounds of the newspapers looking for work I feel that everyone is staring at me. At that moment, I don't notice anything strange about it: I'm young and pretty, men look at me. Many years later, replaying that scene from memory, I will realize that in those newsrooms there were a lot of men and a lot of typewriters, but not a woman in sight. My contacts send me to women's magazines. But I finally find work as a creative writer in an advertising agency, where they take me on after a rigorous selection process in which both men and women participate as equals. I go on, for the moment, without thinking of myself as a woman.

I very definitely find out that I'm a woman when I publish my first novel, *Soy paciente,* the story of a man told in first person. On the book jacket, a famous writer expresses amazement that a woman can have such a sense of humor, be pretty, and write well, all at the same time. I begin to hear other absurdly astonished voices: here's a woman who can tell a man's story! I can't understand why that should seem striking, it's happened thousands of times in world literature, it's simply the norm in writing for the theater, as well as in Argentine literature, where we have a strong tradition of women who write. I begin to hear the expression "women's literature" and "literature written by women." At first, I greet this with enthusiasm, curious to see what distinctive qualities there might be in the body of literature written by women. Little by little, I realize that I have fallen into a trap. Our personal differences are ignored, our being part of one or another literary movement is dismissed, the excuse of gender is used to lump us together in terms of our biology, we're excluded when the great general themes of literature are being discussed. Do women writers want to think? Well then, let them think about women's literature, that will keep them busy so they won't

bother us. So there are no women in anthologies of Argentine literature, or of Latin American literature? asks a publisher. Don't worry,
girls, we'll put together an all-women's anthology to compensate. I
begin to discover what I call the "women's little corral," that separate
place where women who write are all put together to protect them from
the vicissitudes of life, and meanwhile you avoid having to mix them
with the men writers, who are never called "men who write." Thus Literature with a capital L moves along one track and, on a parallel but
lesser track, is followed by Women's Literature or Literature Written
by Women. Only the Very Great can jump the barrier between tracks.

Little by little I begin to discover the importance of internal politics
in national and Latin American literature. I realize that in addition to
the obvious parameters, that is, literary quality and sales, which sometimes coincide and sometimes don't, there are other media and chan-
nels of publicity that have to do with relationships, friendships,
personal acquaintances, and certain interplays of personality between
writers and critics. On this score, we women are weaker. In general,
still, in publishing houses and the media of communication, the posi-
tions of power are in the hands of men. And men have networks of male
friends which exclude women, often without any deliberate intention.
Women excel easily when it's a matter of sales, but they have greater
difficulty in obtaining recognition by the inner circles that confer pres-
tige. Men tend to organize themselves in solidarity groups that offer
mutual praise. Women write in isolation, as free shooters. I begin to understand that the good intentions behind affording protection to Latin
American women writers may make sense in some circumstances.

I keep writing; I continue to publish. *Los amores de Laurita* is a best
seller. Laurita is an alter ego of her author and she's Jewish. She's Jewish without thinking much about it, in a natural way, just one more way
of being Argentine. I'm invited to the first Meeting of Latin American
Jewish Writers. "What kind of Jewish writer are you," asks my *bobe*,
"when you're writing in Spanish?" It is the beginning of a path that will
lead me to research and study various aspects of the Jewish question,

which will turn into more books. All of a sudden I've become an expert in certain current topics of Jewish tradition, and I begin to give lectures that turn out to be profoundly worrisome to me, because, together with a certain amount of very specific information about some topics, I have the most absurd doubts, stemming from my total lack of Jewish formation in childhood. My bits of knowledge are islands in a sea of ignorance. I can speak with a certain familiarity of the many versions of stories told about King Solomon's relationship with the devil Asmodeus, but I am never sure how many Seders Pesach has; I have a very vague notion of Queen Esther's doings, and, except for weddings and an occasional *bar mitzvah*, I have never attended a religious service in a synagogue.

And so, here I am, Latin American, a woman, a Jew, a writer—in that order or any other—writing with all I am, with all I have been, with my gender, with my Argentineness, with my Judaism, with my history, my memories, my readings, my personality, staking it all, playing for keeps, putting all of myself into every line.

Chapter 21

A Tale of Courage and Fortitude

Ivonne Strauss de Milz
as told to Marjorie Agosín

MY NAME IS IVONNE Strauss de Milz. I've lived in the Dominican Republic all my life, in the small settlement of Sosua and in the city of Santo Domingo, but I have felt most deeply connected to the community in Sosua. Sosua is where my paternal grandparents settled when they arrived in 1947 after seven years as refugees in Shanghai, where they went when they had to leave Austria. My father was eight years old when they reached Sosua. He was only one when they fled from Vienna because my grandfather would otherwise have been interned in a labor camp. My mother and her parents also came from Austria, but a little later, in 1950, when she was twelve years old. Thus my parents spent part of their childhood and all of their adolescence in Sosua and have remained very attached to the community all their lives, although they moved to Santo Domingo when they were adults. They have very happy memories of growing up in Sosua, and although all their children were born in Santo Domingo, they have continued to go back and forth and really live in both places. We all feel profoundly Dominican, and we are all very grateful to be part of this beautiful country's history and to be able to contribute to it. But now I'd like to tell you some things about Sosua and what it has meant to me to be part of this community, which is unique in Latin American and even in world history.

In the late nineteen thirties, when there was great concern about Nazi terrorism in Europe, a meeting was held in Evian, France, to discuss the problem of safety for Jewish populations. At this meeting, the only country to offer asylum to Jews was the Dominican Republic. An agreement was signed between the Dominican Republic and the DORSA (Dominican Republic Settlement Association) to enable Jews from many different European countries to come here. These refugees were guaranteed an opportunity to live their lives free of persecution and discrimination. The Dominican Republic already had a precedent for this: years before, the Luperon government had offered visas to Jews persecuted by pogroms in Czarist Russia.

The first group of refugees from Europe arrived in May 1940 from Germany via Luxembourg, and then various other groups came, including the 1947 group from Shanghai which included my grandparents and my father. Altogether, perhaps seven hundred people came. Most of those who were able to reach Sosua, a small agricultural village set aside for Jewish refugees, came from neutral places like Switzerland, Luxembourg, and, after the war was over, Shanghai. Other Jews who became aware of the possibility of coming to the Dominican Republic were not able to save themselves, since it was already too late to reach the countries that would offer them transit asylum.

I think that the Dominican Republic is unique in its history and is distinguished by its profound belief in democracy and tolerance of religious diversity. The evidence of this is that in those years when no one was letting Jews into American countries, this small Caribbean island opened its door to Jews. I also want to tell you that Sosua's history is really unique in this region. Groups of Jews had come to the other Caribbean islands, especially Curaçao, a community founded by Portuguese and Dutch Jews. But the case of Sosua is different because here the government *invited* a persecuted group to come to its shores, and no other country has done this.

I'll tell you how this community was formed. I'm basing this story on conversations I've had with my father, who has clear memories of arriving in Sosua when he was eight years old. He lives here now, as do some of the other founders of the community. There are about fifteen original families left. I mentioned that several ships arrived. The first one brought German Jews, and, two years later, another immigrant group arrived that consisted mainly of Jews of Austrian descent. In 1942, the synagogue was built; it is very small and beautiful and contains the few religious objects that we have. I don't know the origin of the Torah that is there today, but the stained glass windows were made by a Dominican artist. They are greenish blue in color. They have the Caribbean Sea as a backdrop, and they depict the beauty of the place that took them in. The immigrants who came to Sosua were not a particularly religious group. Some were more observant than others, but the main evidence of their communal faith is that one of the first buildings they constructed was a synagogue that served as a community center for all these Jews of diverse origins whose lives were saved by having come here. I think this is the most important legacy of Judaism and a proof of Jews' tenacity, as well as their capacity to continue practicing their faith despite the most adverse circumstances.

Look, do you see this lovely little town, so full of life and of people from other international communities who came to Sosua? At the time my parents arrived, there was absolutely nothing here. Everything had to be built from scratch. The Sosua community was at first a group of Jewish pioneers who worked tilling the land. Many of those who came had been practicing other professions, such as medicine. But when they arrived here they realized that it was urgently necessary to plant these fields, and they all became involved in agriculture until the community was established.

The first buildings they constructed were a school, a small hospital, a pharmacy, and the synagogue. Most people lived in barracks, the same ones you can still see out there, that were part of the synagogue. Rural life was very difficult for the settlers, and agricultural work in these fields that had never been tilled was very hard. At first, the DORSA expected Sosua to be an agricultural community with communal barracks and kitchens. They thought Sosua would be an enterprise similar to a communal kibbutz where all aspects of life would be shared and all the work would be done collectively. This expectation was short lived. It was not a success as an agricultural endeavor. Very few people had any experience in working in the fields. People with different personalities, and especially those who had lived through very traumatic experiences, found it difficult to adapt to communal agricultural work, although later on some people decided to work the fields in a more individual way. What the new settlers decided to do to enable the community to prosper was to combine individual independence and cooperative effort, and they developed a successful meat and dairy canning industry named Sosua Products which continues to this day.

My grandparents and parents worked for this food products company, and my husband works for it now. As you'll see, Sosua's history is continuous and it contributes a great deal to the island's economy. Documents show that in 1947 there were approximately eight hundred Jewish families in Sosua. My grandfather loved this land and never wanted to leave it, so he never again traveled outside this country, and that is true of many of the settlers who found peace and freedom in this refuge. That's why I don't speculate too much about Trujillo's motives in granting the visas. I am just grateful that they were granted. The other details of it aren't as important as some people think. You have to realize that the history of the community of Sosua is a story of great triumph and great courage. And it is also the victory of hope, since those who came here were saved.

Sosua's isolation has created a community which is predominantly Jewish but which includes a component of those who were already living in this area. In the early days, there were more men than women here, which meant that there were many mixed marriages that were accepted with tolerance and respect. The first mixed marriage was that of

Luis and Ana Julia Hess. Professor Hess, a very distinguished German professor of languages, still lives here. He tells of how in 1939, in desperation, he tried to find political asylum from the imminent German persecution. All the consulates closed their doors to him. Purely by chance, he walked past the embassy of the Dominican Republic and was given a visa without any problems. He was already in Santo Domingo when the first group of refugees arrived by ship from Luxembourg, and he helped to translate the agreement between the DORSA and the Dominican government. For many years, Don Luis Hess was the director of the Sosua school. As time went on, many Jews chose to move to more prosperous communities or to the United States, and more Dominicans came to live with us. This was a positive development because it produced a level of evolving communal spirit and increasing tolerance both here and in the rest of the country. There are only about fifteen Jewish or partly Jewish families living in Sosua now.

The peaceful coexistence of Jews and Dominicans can be seen in many aspects of Dominican history. The first and most obvious example is Christopher Columbus's arrival in Santo Domingo on an expedition financed by the *converso* Jews of the Spanish empire. Thus, right from its beginnings, this was an island marked by freedom of religious practice. We are not an orthodox Jewish community in a religious sense. We've kept observing traditions and holidays, but we do not have a permanent rabbi in Sosua and we often have to share one with Santo Domingo. The community of Sosua is quite different from any other in the history of Jewish immigration to Latin America, not only because of the Dominican government's legal support, but also because of its integration into the country's economy and culture.

My father was always a free thinker and inspired our desire to be open, progressive, and tolerant people. There is no Reform congregation in the Dominican Republic, but if there were one, that would be our way of life. My family, like many of the settlers, says that even though the early years here were hard and the creation of this community took continuous effort, they value the memory of the struggles they lived through, and they are proud to have created a prospering colony which is becoming better and better known throughout the country.

As for my personal life, I spent part of my childhood in Sosua surrounded by extraordinary people who instilled in me a spirit of solidarity and communal sharing. Although I was born in Santo Domingo, I spent every weekend in Sosua, where I have always felt part of the community. Later, like so many in my generation, I moved to the capital to take more advanced courses. I studied to be veterinarian, but did not practice my profession for long. I married, started a family, and settled down permanently in Sosua. My husband was born in Sosua but moved with his parents to Florida. He decided as an adult to return to the Dominican Republic.

Lately I've been involved in various community activities. Among these activities is the creation of a school where English is taught on a level comparable to what is seen in international schools. But my primary commitment is to the ongoing existence of the Santo Domingo community, its future survival, and the preservation of its history. My husband, another friend, and I are involved in several projects to strengthen the community's observance of religious holidays and services. We are putting a lot of effort into accomplishing this. We want future generations to keep alive the spirit of Judaism and preserve the historical documentation of Sosua.

My husband and I are also collaborating, together with others, on a museum. It was founded in 1990 when Sosua celebrated its fiftieth anniversary. It is in a hexagonal building with blue-painted walls that remind us of the Caribbean and Mediterranean Seas. We want to preserve a visual memory of how Sosua has been, and so we have asked everyone in the community to donate their photographs and family documents to the museum so that we can preserve a collective memory of the place. The response to all this has been marvelous, extraordinary. We have photographs of the first people who arrived by ship, of the first babies born in Sosua, of children at school, and of people working in the fields. We put together an exhibit of Sosua's history.

And we are working on a new exhibit now, one which will be an even larger display of photographs and documents.

Many of the community's children have recorded interviews with original settlers who are still living. Among them is Ella Tyaskan, who came in one of the last groups of emigrants from France in 1954. She is a marvelous person, and her life story is one of amazing risks, courage, and luck. Her two brothers came to Sosua on that first ship from Luxembourg in 1940, and, when the war ended, her mother emigrated from Vienna and persuaded Ella and her husband that Sosua was a marvelous place and a spiritual refuge for persecuted people, that Hispaniola was a beautiful island where one could live happily with very few material things. She came to Sosua and is still an important member of our community.

The Sosua community is very different today from what it was in the past. As I mentioned earlier, many families have moved away, many young people have gone to the university and not returned to live in Sosua, and many of the older people have died. I had to move to Santo Domingo with my children to further their education, but we go back to Sosua every weekend and we still feel profoundly connected to the community there. In the eighties, an international airport opened in Sosua, and, since then, Sosua has become a tourist destination. A large number of visitors from all over have come, and quite a number have decided to move to Sosua. From being a picturesque small town of European immigrants and cattle ranchers a long way from the city, it has become an international resort, bustling with hotels, restaurants, and shops, where people from all over the world gather.

Despite these changes and the gradual diminution of the original Jewish community, Sosua is proud to be the place where lives were saved and where immigrants were welcomed and allowed to begin their lives again with all the freedoms and rights that every human being should enjoy. The few of us Jews who remain in Sosua should make an effort to keep our synagogue open and to preserve the history of this remarkable town.

As you can see, this is my history and my community. I keep the keys of the synagogue and love it above all things. I am filled with happiness by the possibility of being able to continue the legacy of my parents, grandparents, and so many others who were not able to preserve their own histories. I feel very happy in Sosua. I take care of the old people and of the new generations. I am a bridge to the future and a link to the past. Historic and social faith motivate me to work constantly in this community and to keep the symbol of Sosua alive for the world to see.

Chapter 22

Too Many Names

Nora Strejilevich

MY FAMILY'S EMIGRATION ROUTE can be summed up in a few words which I remember vaguely: "Your grandmother brought Aunt Bety and me from Warsaw when we were small; your grandfather had come earlier, and, once he had set up his hat factory, he sent for us." This brief story and a sepia-colored photo of a handsome young man staring out at me with dreamy eyes framed by his mushroom-shaped hat—my grandfather—are all I salvaged from the shipwreck of maternal memories.

My father's memories were not much more extensive. His family had come from Besarabia: parents, uncles, cousins I never met. Grandfather Isidoro had settled in the agrarian community of Entre Ríos at the beginning of the century, but he tired of peasant life without tools and with too many plagues, and when he could he moved from Gauleguaychú to the capital. He launched commercial ventures which took him to the far north and far south of the country, and his fortunes rose and fell. In one of the temporary peaks of prosperity, my father and his three brothers studied at the German school in Buenos Aires, where they received a good liberal arts education. Of course, after the war, German wasn't much use to them, since they didn't wish to ever again utter a word in the language of Goethe.

One of my aunts, Felisa, finally indulged my passion for genealogy. When my grandmother Kaila died, she hung a picture of my maternal great-grandparents on the wall. I was impressed by the face of that unknown woman who watched me with the expression and eyes of my mother and of whom I know only that I will know nothing beyond that dense gaze in black and white. It is the mark of my diasporic heritage: a series of intimate and anonymous images that gaze at even my dreams, without pronouncing a word. Images that deny me all access to anecdotes and mark me with an overwhelming desire to bring them to life.

Another aunt, Bety, told me between one maté and another that she and my mother were born in a town called Visigrod, and I even held in my hands some birth certificates written in letters as legalistic as they were indecipherable. In the twenties, there was in Argentina a Jewish white slavery organization which dealt especially in women from Poland, who were sold when they reached our shores to feed a prostitution racket called the Svi Migdal. Sometimes, tired of the silence the adults condemned me to, I suggested to Mama that surely she had been brought by the Migdal and that was why she didn't want to tell me anything. This heavy-handed joke was met only with anger. It killed off conversation, which had never been very lively.

I know even less about my father's family. I found my grandmother Shlesinger's surname on the walls of the Prague synagogue, where there is a list of those taken to concentration camps. Perhaps they are not our relatives, who, according to my father, came from Romania, but just in case, I made a note of them. A list of those possibly born in 1913, like Papa. I was aware of their divergent destinies: that of an America often silent and fearful of alluding to the catastrophe and that of these victims who died without their clan on the other side of the ocean keeping their memory alive.

The formula of forgetting, I insist, was that which many immigrants used to cope with their condition of being pariahs. To escape the weight of history, to not look backwards. Tragedy, which would be reincarnated in the distant lands of the new continent in the decade

of the seventies, made evident how much memory there is in each forgetting. And those people of severed roots would not find in their dic-
tionaries any way to understand how history had crossed the ocean to
condemn them yet again. I once met a woman who had survived Auschwitz with her husband. They sought refuge in Argentina in order to
begin a new life, protected from the winds of horror. Twenty years
later, their only son was disappeared by the military junta. Dark mists
on both continents, concave mirrors, are always ready to give us the
deformed image of what we believed humanity should be or was.
Father and mother were speechless, without words to explain the un-
tellable, and one of them has already died trying to pronounce his anguish. That's why some of us are charged to conserve the remnants of
the shipwreck, take care of them. Write them.

It's said that all Argentines arrived by ship. My legacy from those
ships is a wooden box full of opaque photographs, among which was
a woman who resembles my future. I treasure that strange feeling of
being linked in sisterhood to a distant and silent passerby for whom I
developed fondness and whom I end up resembling. At the Hebrew
University in Jerusalem, an oral history researcher spoke to me of a
Strejilevich he had interviewed in Minsk. So I added Minsk to my list
of possible horizons. Visigrod, someplace in Bessarabia. Minsk?
Prague? Perhaps. Someday I'll follow the route of this imaginary map,
attracted by the mysterious magnet of indecipherable relationships.

Nobody ever understood this desire of mine to reconstruct our past,
nor why I was so resistant to accepting our limited family tree. I'm not
sure I understand either. Maybe my reaction to not having a middle
name is related to this fixed idea. A middle name, according to Jewish
tradition if I'm not mistaken, should be that of a grandmother who has
died. But I was only given one name, not for any lack of dead people in
the family, but because, according to my mother, it's sufficient to have
one name and to be named for a living person. They saved me from
Fanny, which, if placed between Nora and Strejilevich, would not
rhyme melodically. My brother was saved from Isidoro, which is not

too lamentable, in my opinion. In our country, Isidoro is the famous caricature of a greedy *porteño,* a caricature that is inevitably linked to anyone with that name. That is, on one hand they did us a favor, but at the same time we were orphaned of a middle name, a link of interconnection between generations, and it symbolizes other orphanings. Perhaps my reaction, which so amused adults, had to do with this. From age four on, whenever I was asked my name, I'd answer, "Nora Norita." Thus I solved, with everyone's approval, the lack of a middle name so that I could belong to a family group with all the credentials.

Our transnational horizons made me feel that Argentina was a perilous territory for me, that I could have been born somewhere else. This idea lent me wings, and so I nourished it. Everything could have been, or could be, or will be something quite different. Thus my mother's "that's the way it is" lost its authority on the spot. I wasn't from here or from there, but quite the opposite, and my natural state had to be that of movement. My brother liked to travel from adolescence on, and the path he opened benefited me when I wanted to launch forth on adventures: "You let him go," I reminded them, and, since they had always said they believed in the equality of the sexes, sooner or later they had to open the door for me. That's how I got to Chile, Peru, Uruguay, and Brazil. A third-world version of the Wandering Jew, but by choice. I wandered through nearby and not so nearby countries with the conviction that I was a citizen of the world. I was eager for new aromas; I wanted to discover what was beyond our limited daily life. At that time, I didn't dream of being a writer— my model was more like Madame Curie—but the narrative diet I was kept on for years finally stimulated a thirst for storytelling.

Influence of My Parents

My father, who was my guide for years in existential and philosophical matters, was secular. He read Buber and, although he supported the existence of the state of Israel, didn't consider himself a Zionist. Chito was a Jew of the Diaspora, and he knew that there was an abyss between his world view and that of an Israeli, an abyss marked by the distance opened by exile and closed by belonging to a state.

He was a humanist, a socialist. The idea of a country for all Jews, while he accepted it as an inevitable reaction to the Holocaust, seemed problematic to him. It implied a renunciation of the internationalism that had nourished and sustained the humanistic thought of the wandering people. "A state has to defend its boundaries against others, it has to attack and fight, it has to be unjust," he explained to me. "Israelis cannot, by definition, think like I do." He struggled to sustain dialogue, rather than have one army confront another. He knew that that would be impractical in a Middle East with its own history and native population, even if our tribe shared with that population many of the same roots. Jews sought refuge in Palestine because there was no other choice in a Europe that washed its hands of them, its complicity evident. In Argentina, many progressive Jews during those years understood the reasons why Israel had been created, but chose to support social change in their own countries instead. They resisted the false option of singular loyalty that sounded like a question a not-too-bright neighbor might ask: "Whom do you love more, your mother or your father?" Mutatis mutandis: "Which do you love more, Israel or Argentina?" Faced with that question, the only answer is: I want a world where questions like that are not asked.

The only holidays we celebrated at home were our birthdays and the secular New Year. We never lit candles or commemorated important dates on the Jewish calendar. We were not an exception; many secular families did not observe any traditions at all in the Buenos Aires I knew; Judaism was practiced, rather, on the level of culture, readings, thought. My parents participated in events organized by the Hebraica in which local writers and artists, particularly Ashkenazis, participated. They also used the club's library, which had the best collection of Jewish literature in the country. At home, we had a huge collection of translations of Yiddish literature and magazines published by Jewish groups in Buenos Aires.

My mother, Sarita, was a voracious reader and, although she had not finished high school, had read an impressive amount. She had remarkable recall of titles, plots, and characters; it was as though she had lived with them. She used to recommend books to me, but I rarely followed her suggestions. One of the books she often talked to me about was the Old Testament. She explained how our whole culture stemmed from it, but above all she told me about those marvelous stories crammed with images, with fantastic tales like that of Moses when he was about to receive the Ten Commandments. I still haven't followed her suggestion, the only advice of hers that had to do with our tradition. My parents had gotten married in a synagogue just to please my grandparents. My grandmother Kaila changed dishes and fasted on the Day of Pardon, but only one of her daughters, the youngest, went with her to temple. Oddly, traditions filtered down uninvited: from my mother I inherited a book that had come down to her from her family, a Bible with a bas relief of the Tablets of the Law on its silver cover. It's so beautiful, I carry it around with me. Sometimes I think that the elegant decoration of the Book is how our ancestors keep us connected to the tribe.

The Role of Memory, My Infancy

The memories I am piecing together now and many others are the subject of my writing. Playing with those misty scraps of the past has always attracted me, as though my task were that of restoring ruins or vessels whose fragments are scattered all over the planet. Memory is a province of the imagination. We rescue what matters to us, we splice in threads of our feelings, our fantasies, and we knit it all together into what we call our history. Infinite versions of a life can be told; every moment of the present produces new and different images of the infinite cavern of footprints called the past. I have a very poor memory, so all I write is interwoven with threads of fantasy. Fiction creeps in subtly without my realizing. And the forms that emerge distill their truths, as happens in all fiction.

During my childhood we lived in Olivos, a suburb in greater Buenos Aires. At that time, in the fifties, we seemed to be the only Jews there. There were differences between some of my family's customs and those of our neighbors. Although we didn't celebrate Christmas at home, Father Christmas made an appearance to all the neighborhood children, and the festivities were collective. I didn't go to church on Sundays, but I felt liberated by that: I didn't have to go to confession, or study for First Communion, or do penance for having gone out with a boy—a whole series of things that I didn't envy my friends. I've wondered how my parents managed to protect me from ever feeling discriminated against, isolated, or diminished in the face of the Apostolic Roman Catholic majority that surrounded us. I don't know how they did it, but my brother and I were both happy about my family's rejection of all religious practice. I can remember telling my friends with total conviction that angels didn't exist, that they were all a fairy tale. My identity, on the other hand, bestowed upon me marvels that my "goy" friends didn't enjoy. I was a life member of Hebraica, the club which organized championship Ping-Pong tournaments and swimming competitions. In addition, it offered vacation programs—we children got to go camping with our instructors, freed from family pressures for a month. That was pure paradise, and no one else in our neighborhood got to do this, only my brother and I. From age eight on, we went to the seaside or the mountains with our *haverim* and *madrihim,* Hebraica companions and instructors, and later with Hashomer Hatsair, a leftist Zionist group. During these four weeks of adventures, we'd hike along singing "caminemos compañeros sin cesar, / si los pies no nos pueden aguantar, / caminemos con los codos hasta que caigamos todos, / caminemos compañeros sin cesar"; we'd take turns standing night guard duty in threes, watching over our sleeping companions; we did round dances; we learned personal defense; and we'd end the day sitting around the campfire opening our hearts and finding words for our feelings. It never occurred to me to think that personal defense with sticks was a way to train us in case the Tacuara came to beat us. The Tacuara were nationalists from whose ranks came *montoneros* like Firmenich and who dedicated themselves to beating up Jews with chains as they came out of school, facts of local life that did not affect me until much later.

In my other life, in my neighborhood, I worked out an intuitive *marranismo*. I learned how to use masks in order to escape notice. I had no scruples about genuflecting and crossing myself when I'd enter the church to go play on the slide and hammock that were at the back of the chapel. If that was what it took in order to play with my friends, it was easy enough to do. The moral: belonging to two worlds was possible without any apparent conflict. The conflict didn't appear until much later on, when a college friend pointed out that my last name was "moishe." Fortunately, by then I had learned that one could not really belong on both sides, but that was the first time I felt someone look askance at me, look down on me because of my evidently inferior status as a Jew.

But let me go back to primary school. My brother and I attended a school where the director tried to eliminate all trace of the repressiveness so often typical of the traditional system. No racist comments were allowed at the Instituto Didáctico Educativo. My mother was the one who insisted on our attending this privileged school where we could speak familiarly to the director, where we were not scolded for behaving badly, and where we did not have to leave the classroom when it was time for religion class. At state schools, Jewish students had to stand up and leave the room when it was time for that required course. Sarita wanted to spare us these bitter moments by sending us to a private, liberal neighborhood school which had its own rules. I can remember the mother of one of my classmates, a German who lived across the street, saying to my mother, "You're Jews, but you're good people." These comments would only be made away from the school, since Pepe, the director, would not tolerate any mention of categories that implied approval or disapproval of anyone. But the comments were made nevertheless, and they must have weighed heavily on the adults.

Later on, when we moved to downtown Buenos Aires, I began going every Friday to the Hebraica, the club that had long been familiar but which was now only a few blocks away. Suddenly my world of Catholics, where like it or not we were the "others," was exchanged for one inhabited by "our people." Only in school were we the "others." In high school, the first thing I saw on the blackboard, in a public girls' school, was a cross. Since it was not a Catholic school, it seemed only logical to me that if religious symbols were exhibited, all of them should be included: the Muslim crescent, the Star of David, and an altar for the ancestors of my friend Higa, of Japanese origin. I persuaded a few first-year classmates, and we went to ask the director to take down the cross or put up other symbols, too. We almost got expelled: it was my first defeat in the area of social militancy. At that time I was still going on camping trips, but now with friends from the Buenos Aires, the best high school in the city. I had not enrolled there because I had listened to my elders: "Better you should become a teacher rather than spend six years studying for a degree that will be of no use to you." A high-school degree didn't prepare you for a job, but the normal school did. It seemed to make sense but they let my brother study for a high-school degree.

Skipping to another scene in this kaleidoscope of memories . . .

I am twenty-four years old and studying medicine. It's the middle of 1977, the second year of Jorge Rafael Videla's dictatorship. The police are a daily spectacle, and we cross paths with them whenever we enter or leave the university. The walls are whitewashed, cleaner than they've ever been, political activities prohibited, although certainly there are secret gatherings. I had withdrawn from the activism which was typical at universities in the early seventies. From 1976 on, the dictatorship ruled with an iron hand, and I knew that opposing the armed forces with marches and *estribillos* was as inefficacious as it was dangerous. It never crossed my mind to take up arms, although it made sense to choose armed confrontation when there was no other option in the face of violence imposed from above, as it was called in that world of those who had cause to be dissidents. I concentrated on my medical courses, an entry into research into a phenomenon that intrigued me: memory. *Desensillar hasta que amaine.*

During those first two years of the dictatorship, people began to disappear. People I knew. One of my brother's ex-girlfriends, another Nora, was taken from her work at a health center. Another friend was pulled out of a bus and shoved into a car in view of everyone. Some streets were closed at night, and, right around the corner from my house, my boyfriend and I were accosted by policemen who pointed their machine guns at us because we were kissing outside the police station. This systematic suction of inhabitants into a mysterious nothing was dumbfounding; we had lived through many dictatorships, there had been deaths and tortures, but there had never before been so many disappearances. Suddenly a black hole would open in the space just occupied by a friend or neighbor or a relative, and there would be a murky pause, during which people would be very careful for as long as seemed prudent. "Being careful" could mean moving, going on a trip, leaving one's usual haunts. "As long as seemed prudent" would be interpreted vaguely and according to very subjective criteria. I substitute taught for a friend who was having to be careful. I took over his philosophy classes and don't even remember how we managed this sudden switch, but this sort of thing was going on all the time. In a bizarre chess game, pieces were constantly being removed or substituted for each other in an atmosphere charged with fear. These empty spaces and sudden switches gave me goose pimples— we must all have felt that way, but no one said so. I began to plan a retreat. I remember it all as very hushed, as though the anguish of living in a place besieged by terror could only be expressed in voices so low as to be almost inaudible.

In June 1977, I went over to the *sohnut*, the Jewish Agency, and signed up for one of those excursions for young people who want to visit Israel. By the following month, they had accepted me to go for a year with a group of professionals. We'd spend some months in an *ulpan* learning Hebrew, and the rest of the time we'd work at something related to our professions. I wondered what job they'd find for someone who had studied philosophy, was in medical school, and did not speak Hebrew, but they accepted me and that was enough.

By this time my brother was no longer living at home, and I tried to convince him to take some time away from the dangerous circles in which he lived. Gerardo would post me on the balcony whenever he came home so I could see whether he was being followed, so I knew it was urgent that he should leave. He accepted the suggestion and went to the *sohnut*, but when he mentioned that his girlfriend, whom he planned to bring along, was a *goy*, they told him to get married. They only accepted Jews or mixed couples who were married. It was evident that for the *sohnut* bureaucrats there was no particular hurry: getting married before a trip is perfectly normal anywhere in the world. That the military was right on our heels was a detail no one seemed to take into account, even though they knew perfectly well what our situation was. Many young Jews were active in leftist movements, and we all knew what that meant at that moment. Our lives were at stake. But they acted as though they wanted to ignore that urgency, as though there were time, as though the history of persecutions had not shown them what you have to do to save yourself from the massacre. "What's happening," someone told me, "is that you live in terror, sleep with terror, eat terror, and get used to terror. And all of a sudden the phone rings and you're told Hey, they just picked up so-and-so, and you answer Oh shit, then you hang up and you go on as though nothing had happened."

My brother and his girlfriend never got out of the country. They were taken away July 15, 1977, and are still disappeared. A friend called us at home a few days later to ask why Gerardo hadn't kept an appointment, and Mother told him he had been taken away. The one who called probably said how terrible, hung up, and kept on going, feeling panic, but as though nothing were happening.

My family also seemed to be anesthetized, even after my first two cousins were disappeared. I wasn't even told about it, because no one wanted to give me such bad news. Gerardo mentioned it to me, to explain where he'd been. According to him, he'd put in the "as long as seemed prudent" time after Hugo and Abel, our cousins, had been taken away: three months. If they hadn't come looking for him by now, then surely he must be safe, since besides being their relative he belonged, like them, to the Peronista Youth. My brother's reasoning frightened me: it was a sign that we were all going mad trying to deny the undeniable. I went to see my uncle Pedro, the father of the disappeared cousins. He told me in great detail how they had chased Hugo, the older one, over roofs, firing at him. How they had forced Pedro, a doctor, with his eyes blindfolded, to feel his own son to see if he was still alive: no, he was dead. How my younger cousin had intervened to try to get them to leave the body, and how they had taken the two of them away. As a result, my uncle had lost his sanity and now spent his days putting adhesive tape on the walls to keep the enemies from spying on him. All of a sudden, the situation had become menacing: Hugo dead, Abel disappeared, Gerardo talking about hiding "as long as seemed prudent," and my parents hiding everything. Faced with all this, my desire to escape became more urgent. This was a save-yourself-if-you-can situation. But getting away was not so easy.

The Comando Conjunto squad came to our apartment after I'd packed my suitcase and said goodbye to everyone except for Gerardo, who had not come by to see us for a week. When they knocked at the door, the walls seemed to cry out. It was my mother, who yelled in a desperate tone, "I'll open the door but don't come charging in." I immediately realized who was going to enter, and I ran toward the back door. I was operating on that survival instinct that sharpens when it is already too late. My father yelled "Stop, stop!" while they ran into the apartment with big guns, ordering "On the floor, face down!" They aimed a gun at the nape of my neck and kept me that way for an hour or two. Too long, in any case, for me to stand having a gun in my neck and a boot on my back. They immediately treated me like a whore. My race for the back of the apartment proved my guilt. They searched the house, ransacking and tossing everything, and blindfolded me with a rag, and I hardly had breath to cry out to my parents "They're taking me, they're taking me!" when they shoved me toward the elevator. They were interrogating Sarita and Chito in the bedroom where they couldn't see what was happening with me.

They dragged me down to the ground floor, and on the sidewalk I kicked to put off being forced into that car—which would be the end of me—and to give me time for someone to hear my name as I shouted it out. I knew you had to shout your name when this happened so that people would know who was being taken away. When they managed, with their six arms and a lot of effort, to shove me on the floor of the back seat, they started hitting me, kicking me and repeating "Shitty Jew, we're going to make soap with you." Other variants were "Take this for crying out in Jewish," "Even if you haven't done anything, you'll pay for being *moishe*." When I had shouted out my last name, which doesn't sound like López or García, they thought it was a foreign language, spoken by one of those enemies of the state that had to be finished off as members of the international conspiracy. Reason enough to decree my condemnation. There was no way out: I was on my way to a collective grave.

They took me to a basement somewhere in the city center. A basement that only seven years later, in 1984, could be named and defined when I returned to Buenos Aires to give my evidence to the National Commission which prepared the Nunca Más report. The Athletic Club, I was told by other survivors, better informed than I. The interrogation began with so-called softening up, where they ask you for names and more names while they increase the electric shocks until you end up shouting in someone else's voice. After the softening up, they left me in a cubicle so that I could decide to collaborate, and, after this ploy, the second session centered on the Jewish theme. Since I was traveling to Israel, it was logical to think that I was going to be trained in guerrilla tactics at some kibbutz. All they needed was to find out at which one, and with which instructors. One of them kept sticking in words in Hebrew, like *haverim* or *madrih*, the only words I understood. I was astonished when they brought in a specialist in the topic, and when they noticed my surprise, they explained, "First we're going to get rid of the Montoneros, and then of the Jews."

Evidently these people knew what they were doing and were well organized; the only thing that seemed a little bizarre was that they wanted information about the Irgun. The then Prime Minister of Israel, Menachem Begin, had belonged to the Irgun: it was a right-wing nationalist group which devoted itself in Palestine to attacking the English, who had finally given up their protectorate in 1947, making possible the creation of the state of Israel the following year. I realized that these questions came from *Oh Jerusalem,* the book they had stolen from my luggage. They must have been choosing items from that book as take-off points to find out about my connections with subversive groups of other times and persuasions. They were all alike. If this method had not been applied together with the electric cattle prod, I could have laughed it off. Next, they asked about who was responsible for my trip, and, since I couldn't remember them, they described them and told me about the offices, and where the stairways were, and the corridors of that building to which I'd paid so little attention. They knew the *sohnut* building inside and out.

My liberation came about this way: someone knocked on the door of my cell, checked my identity by name and number, as usual, and, still blindfolded, I was led out to be taken somewhere, I didn't know where. I felt for the first time that I wanted to die rather than be subjected again to that torture many underwent for months and years. They led me up blindfolded to the ground floor and called me by my name. They dragged me to an office where they made me sit—not on the floor this time, but on a chair. A male voice described my family briefly, giving me to understand that they had us under surveillance. "This was an error; you were not here, you didn't see or hear anything, and keep your mouth shut because it would be regrettable if anything happened to your family." I suspected that my brother was in there; I had heard his voice crying out, and surely I wasn't wrong about that. But that "surely" left open a margin of doubt. It was never possible to be sure about anything. Once I was "outside," I found out that they had taken him away the same day they took me, at dawn. Seven years later, tying the threads together, I found out that we had all been together there at the Club: my brother, his girlfriend Graciela Barrocca, another friend, and I.

When I returned to Argentina in 1983, my teeth chattered every time I saw a uniform. I arrived a few months after President Alfonsín had assumed office, after the defeat of the dictatorship in the Falklands War. I arrived just before my mother died, defeated by the certainty of Gerardo's death. In 1988, my father committed suicide. And thus ends the saga of this family group that tried to turn its back on its past but managed, paradoxically, to repeat the tragedy: that script of grief and desolation which it had made such efforts to avoid. Sartre used to say that to be a Jew is to be seen as such. Those words described us well, since in our case the rich cultural heritage of the tribe could be summed up in a few vestiges: poor skeletons of the rich life of communities that were wiped out during the war or even before, the remains of shipwreck after the first Flood had reached us. And now I was left with an even more concise version of history, since a second Flood had stripped us of even the box of black-and-white photos that had made it across so many countries. To whom can we recur when people, objects, world, universe have been stolen? To no one. Only perhaps to the word, the memory, the recollection of that which in the moment of disaster we do not know how to name. That was why I decided to write—because I didn't know what to say.

Being a Writer in Your Country

I have not been a writer in my country. I began to write in exile, where language became my country. In Israel I began to sketch out poems, and I say "sketch out" because some of them were drawings in words. I'd send them home on the back of allusive postcards. I remember one with the image of a shovel lifting a bit of earth that was suspended in the air. The poem was called "Memory." My poetry of that era is about time, about the memories that entrap and from which I'd so often longed to escape, about distance, about feeling, the senses, or, rather, about the senseless. I'd send them with long letters to my parents, like a shared diary where I'd let them see the landscapes that surrounded me as I tred the paths of an untiring traveler. I'd paint word scenarios for them for lack of a paintbrush. My father used to draw, and, in some periods, I imitated him. But drawing turned out to be more arduous for me than storytelling. When I sat down to write, the words would come flowing out, and sometimes I'd laugh at the jokes that seemed to appear on their own. I used to remark that I'm laughing because it's the first time I'm telling myself this joke. The agility of words that surprised me by bursting out when I didn't choose them seduced me so, that the letters turned into manuscripts. But my dedication to it was sporadic. Between moves, interrogations about what direction to take in these journeys without return, in this distance in which I floated, thinking about going back, I kept noting down impressions, memories, and poems. When I ended up in Canada in 1980, sure that it would not be possible to go back soon, I began a doctorate in Latin American literature. I enrolled in a course titled Autobiography, where the professor invited us to write either an essay or the story of our lives. I chose the latter, and kept writing, and sent my first book to a prize competition. I received my first literary prize from the University of Alberta for the testimony *Una visión de mi misma.* It was followed by *Sobre-vivencias* and the novel *Una sola muerte numerosa,* and I am still writing. In all my stories, I take refuge, I remember and I forget, I laugh and weep, I lose myself, find myself, and console myself.

Objects Brought by Ancestors to the New World

I already mentioned the photographs and the thirst for stories produced by those uncut curls and mushroom hats, the distinctive clothing and infinite gazes. They were like actors playing the role of formal and serious people, but I knew that they were my aunts and uncles and grandparents, that they were just acting, and that they would start playing with me once they were liberated from those rigid and pompous poses to which they seemed condemned. In the "little room," which turned into a museum of useless household objects, marvelous things that surely belonged to those static and two-dimensional characters had been stored. There was a trunk, brought from Europe at the beginning of the century, which contained treasures like embroidered sheets and table cloths, hats my grandfather might have made in Argentina but which I was certain had belonged to my distant relatives, things like purses and shoes that I used when I played dress-up. I'd wrap those sheets around myself and become a queen, a ghost, a character from the *Thousand and One Nights,* or an immigrant of the turn of the century (when I was tempering my fantasy with a trace of realism). Sometimes I'd add the props of a pair of antique-looking candelabra. I never asked whether they came from Europe, so that they wouldn't tell me they didn't.

I didn't realize how fond I was of these objects until I had to relinquish that trunk, those linens, and my entire house, when there was no one else left in my immediate family and I was left with sculptures, pictures, books, linens, porcelain, rugs, tableware, china, clothing, more books. I'd have liked a magic carpet in order to carry it all away, but none appeared. I couldn't fit all those beloved treasures into my migrant's household, that tent I pitched and pretended was home in Vancouver and then in Edmonton, in Calgary, in Ashland. . . . And as I had to divest myself of those unique objects that my grandparents had brought from their native or not so native lands, I kept only the items that Jewish *mucos* of the Diaspora had always kept to protect themselves in adversity: the jewels. They had traveled with a handful of necklaces and rings, with a few precious stones and gold watches, because that handful was all they could carry along and might save their lives in the next Flood. And so I, who had also learned to survive in a world without certainties, held onto this minimal treasure, not as beloved as the other objects, but more practical when one rides the storms. From their eternal distance, my ancestors watch over this unfamiliar descendant who continued to journey, as did they, in pure trial and error, along this difficult road that unravels behind our steps and dissolves.

Jewish Latin American European Hybridity

I imagine hybridity as a house inhabited by many voices. In my case, the Jew clamors for gefilte fish as my grandmother did, the Argentine wants to drink *maté* and make sure you don't let the water come to a boil, the Canadian wants everyone to be quiet for a moment, and the granddaughter of Europeans wonders what the madwomen are doing, making such a huge fuss over trivia. Why don't they learn to drink tea with a sugar cube in their mouths once and for all and stop fooling around? The voices never stop, and the worst is that often they have nothing in common. But this is what it is about—understanding that we are many in one, pulled many ways by different compulsions, opposing desires, disparate histories. Without even mentioning readings: the Jewish Nora would like to revel in Yiddish literature; Nora the woman feels the urgent need to catch up on all the women writers she hasn't yet read; the Argentine Nora needs to page through all the newspapers and the most recent books written about the national reality; the

Europeanized Nora doesn't have enough time to think over Derrida, and Kristeva, and why not go back over Foucault, this is why she studied philosophy after all, to be able to understand contemporary thought. And of course, there is work, too, and taking notes on a few scenes that have sprung to mind, but it all remains half done because today I listened to a racist and it made me so angry that I started to write about anti-Semitism in Argentina, and tomorrow a meteorite will go by that will lead me to research on the curvature of the circle.

To get all this coordinated is an adventure in itself, but it would be useless to suppress any one of these voices: repression only serves to increase the volume of the conflicts. In exile I realized that in Argentina I was Jewish; but in Israel I was *dromamericai,* South American; in Canada I was Latin American; and in the United States I am Hispanic. Each place catalogs me differently, but the common denominator is foreignness. I've given up believing in any kind of monochromatic classification; I am always much more than these definitions that serve, very precariously, the filling out of forms. At the same time, out of pure defiance, I identify with all the categories, especially with the segregated ones. Which in my case are: woman, Jew, Latin American—three labels that don't seem favorable for climbing the social ladder. I identify fully with these, my great attributes, and I feel ever more part of a *mestiza* community which proclaims sincerity, citizenship, mixtures of cultures, languages, and colors. The unidimensional is nearly extinct, although many still yearn to preserve an illusory purity of blood, of mind, and of sex.

Contributor Biographies

EDNA AIZENBERG

Edna Aizenberg is professor and chair of Hispanic Studies at Marymount Manhattan College. She describes herself as *mestiza,* with Israeli, Argentinean, Venezuelan, and American strands in her wandering biography and diasporic family tree. Edna is the author of award-winning books and articles in her specialty, Latin American Jewish culture and literature. Her work on the renowned Argentinean writer Jorge Luis Borges has received international recognition. Her still-developing resume also includes the following items: correspondent for the *London Jewish Chronicle,* the *Jewish Telegraphic Agency,* and *Haaretz;* teacher of Jewish studies and English in Caracas; editor of Spanish-language B'nai B'rith journals; lecturer throughout South America and the Caribbean; wife; mother of two sons; developer of courses on Hispanic women writers that for the first time included Jewish women; and activist for Jewish rights in Argentina and Latin America.

RUTH BEHAR

Ruth Behar holds a Ph.D. from Princeton University and is considered to be one of the country's most distinguished anthropologists.

She has held a MacArthur Fellowship as well as a Guggenheim Fellowship, and she is the author of several books, among them *Translated Woman* and *The Vulnerable Observer*.

FORTUNA CALVO-ROTH

In the mid-fifties, women were not welcome in Peruvian newsrooms. And so, Calvo-Roth left her family in Lima to become a journalist. Her first stop was Mexico City, where, after a few days, she was offered a two-month contract in New York with the Mission of Israel to the United Nations. Once there, she found work as a correspondent for the Brazilian newsmagazine *Visaõ*. Later, she transferred to *Visión*, the Spanish-language sister publication distributed throughout Latin America. After stints with the assignment desk and the business section, she became, successively, managing editor, editor-in-chief, and editorial director. She did start-up work for *Vision/Europe*, a business magazine published in French, English, German, and Italian.

She left *Visión* in 1969 to spend more time with her husband and two small children and to return to the classroom, fifteen years after graduating from the University of Missouri School of Journalism. She studied theater with Stella Adler; film, television, and radio at New York University's School of the Arts; and completed the doctoral program in politics, also at NYU.

From 1975 until 1992 she taught politics, first at Hofstra University and later at NYU. She was also a partner in two media ventures—Channel 2 in Lima, Perú, and *Vista* magazine, the national newspaper supplement based in Florida. At present, she heads Coral Communications Group, LLC, producers of Nueva Onda audiobooks in Spanish, where her son Stephen is a partner.

VERÓNICA DE DARER

Verónica de Darer has a doctoral degree in multilingual multicultural education from the University of Florida. She teaches courses on second-language teaching and acquisition at the Harvard School of Education. Her research has focused on the second-language classroom and social and pedagogical process.

JOAN E. FRIEDMAN

Joan Friedman was born in Shanghai, China, and grew up in Venezuela. She has taught at Harvard and at the University of Wisconsin at Madison and has been for the past sixteen years a faculty member in the Department of Modern Languages and Literatures at Swarthmore College.

The focus of her research is Venezuelan Jewish Literature. Friedman's work appears in *Latin American Jewish Writers: A Critical Dictionary; Passion Memory and Identity: Twentieth-Century Latin American Jewish Women Writers; The House of Memory;* and *King David's Harp: Autobiographical Essays by Jewish Latin American Writers.*

Her translation of the novel *Cláper* by the Venezuelan/Polish writer Alicia Freilich Segal was published in 1989 by the University of New Mexico Press as part of its series on Jewish Latin America.

For the Bienale de Literatura commemorating the Venezuelan poet Elias David Curiel, Friedman wrote the introduction to *Collective Memory,* a catalogue of the works of sculptor and painter Lihie Talmor for the Coro Museum of Art. It was published in both English and Spanish.

Friedman's translation of *El viaje . . .* (The journey), a special edition art and poetry book, is to be published shortly by the Sefardi Museum of Caracas.

Friedman is editor of the *Latin American Jewish Studies Newsletter.*

ETHEL KOSMINSKY

Ethel Kosminsky divides her time between New York and São Paulo, where she is a professor of sociology at the Universidade Estadual Paulista (UNESP), Marília campus and a researcher at the Centro de

Estudos Rurais e Urbanos (CERU). Born in 1946 in Natal, in the state of Rio Grande do Norte, she grew up in Salvador, Bahia, where she lived until the age of nineteen, when she went to attend college in São Paulo.

Kosminsky spends time in both São Paulo, with her husband and two younger daughters, and in the United States, where her two older children live. According to her, her family has moved from place to place without ever feeling, as Marjorie Agosín says, "we are from anywhere."

ESTER LEVIS LEVINE

Levine was born in La Habana, Cuba, May 24, 1949, and left Cuba in March 1961. After living in Miami for six months, the family settled in Providence, Rhode Island. Levine received a B.A. in Hispanic Studies and an M.A. in Hispanic Studies and Education from Brown University. She has been teaching Spanish language and literature at the College of the Holy Cross, Worcester, Massachusetts, since 1979. She became assistant dean of students at the college in 1997. She and husband, Steven, have two grown daughters, Rachel, 26, and Sarah, 23.

NATANIA REMBA NURKO

Natania Remba Nurko was born in Mexico in the late fifties and emigrated to the United States in 1984. She and her whole family have always been dedicated to the arts. She was educated at the University of California at Los Angeles and Harvard, where she obtained a B.A. in psychology. She has spent much of the last ten years compiling an oral history of her family and promoting Mexican art. She currently directs a program for adolescents at the Dana Faber Research Institute.

CECILIA ROSENBLUM

Rosenblum is a testing specialist for the Educational Testing Service in Princeton, New Jersey. She writes, edits, and translates materials for a variety of ETS tests and services, primarily dealing with foreign languages and English as a second or foreign language. A native of Bogotá, Colombia, and graduate of the Lycée Français, she is fluent in English, Spanish, French, Hebrew, and Yiddish. As part of ETS's Global Institute, she has trained teachers from various regions of Latin America. She has served on the ETS advisory panel *Diálogo*, which focuses on issues of test fairness of particular relevance to Hispanic Americans. For fifteen years she has been a member of El Grupo Latinoamericano de Mujeres de Princeton, which sponsors college scholarships to Hispanic American women.

Her travels to some thirty countries have inspired a life-long interest in photography; her striking photographs of people and settings from five continents reflect the same perceptiveness and curiosity seen in her writing. In the rest of her spare time, she enjoys playing tennis and preparing her native Colombian cuisine for husband Irwin, daughters Ariela, Milena, and Katya, and the newest man in her life—four-year-old grandson Dimitri.

ESTER R. SHAPIRO

Shapiro is an associate professor of psychology at the University of Massachusetts in Boston, where she also helped design a Latino studies program, and a research associate at the Mauricio Gaston Institute for Latino Public Policy and Community Development. As practicum coordinator for the clinical psychology doctoral program at UMass Boston, she has helped found a clinical training program dedicated to delivering urban services from cultural, developmental, interdisciplinary and health promotion perspectives. At the Institute, she has worked on developing culturally sensitive community health promotion initiatives designed to improve child, maternal, and family health outcomes. She is the coordinating editor of and a contributor to *Nuestros Cuerpos, Nuestras Vidas* (Seven Stories Press, 2000), the Spanish language and culture version of *Our Bodies, Ourselves*. Shapiro is also the author of *Grief as a Family Process: A Developmental Approach to Clinical Practice* (1994), and co-editor with Murray Meisels of *Tradition and Innovation in Psychoanalytic Education* (1990).

Shapiro was born in Cuba to Eastern European Jewish parents and, after immigrating in the early sixties, grew up in Miami, Florida. Her Latina Jewish background has informed much of her sensitivity to immigrant and minority communities, and she has written personal and family narratives on it and related subjects.

WILMA BLOCH REICH, WITH JESSICA P. ALPERT

Wilma Bloch Reich was born in Posen, Germany, in 1913. In 1920, she and her family moved to Berlin, where she studied library science at a junior college. One semester before obtaining her degree, she was asked to leave school due to the Nazi codes. In 1935, she immigrated to Amsterdam, where she eventually met Ernest Reich, a German Jew living in San Salvador, El Salvador. In 1938, they married in El Salvador, and they remained married for fifty-three years until his death in 1991.

Reich's granddaughter Jessica Alpert was born in Texas. An activist, poet, and writer, she is currently a student at Barnard College in New York. "Mosaics" is her first published project.

NEDDA G. DE ANHALT

Nedda G. de Anhalt was born in Havana, Cuba, in 1934 and became a Mexican citizen in 1968. She studied civil law at the University of Havana and literature at Sarah Lawrence College in New York. She has an M.A. in Latin American Studies from the University of the Americas, where she has taught Hispanic American literature. She has published fiction, interviews, essays, literary reviews, and translations (from French, English, and Portuguese) in many Mexican and foreign newspapers, literary supplements, and magazines. She has taken part in many different writers' meetings and conferences, and has served on juries for many literary prizes. De Anhalt is a member of the Grupo de las Cien (One hundred intellectuals in favor of ecology in Mexico), of AMMPE (Association of Mexican Women Journalists and Writers) and of the PEN Club International. Currently she is the secretary of the Mexico City chapter of PEN and is working on a book on the Albert Dreyfus affair.

GRACIELA CHICHOTKY

Chichotky spent most of her life in Buenos Aires, Argentina, however, she now lives in Santiago, Chile, where she is an educator and short story writer. She teaches Hebrew and gives lessons on Jewish history in the Jewish community of Santiago.

SONIA GURALNIK

Sonia Guralnik is a distinguished author of several collections of stories, *Retratos en sepia* (1980) and *Historias de una mujer gusano* (1980), and a memoir that narrates her arrival to Chile from Russia. She is also a chef. Ms. Guralnik currently resides in Santiago de Chile with her daughters.

ROSITA KALINA DE PISZK

De Piszk is considered to be a leading Costa Rican poet, short story writer, and editor. Her works include the poetry collections *Cruce de Niebla* (1981) and *Detrás de las palabras* (1983) and a book of short stories, *Una dimensión ligera*. She serves on the boards of several cultural institutions in Costa Rica.

ANGELINA MUÑIZ DE HUBERMAN

Muñiz de Huberman is a poet, novelist, professor, and historian of Sephardic history. She currently resides in Mexico City, were she teaches at UNAM and continues to produce distinguished collections of poetry and prose. Among her narrative works are *Serpientes, Escaleras la morada del aire,* and *Las raíces y las Hojas.*

TERESA PORZECANSKI

Porzecanski is an anthropologist, poet, and short story writer who lives and teaches in Montevideo. She has written several important works documenting the Jewish communities of Uruguay, including *Perfumes de cártago* and *La piel del alma ciudad impune.* She teaches at La Universidad del Uruguay.

MERCEDES ROFFÉ

Roffé is considered to be one of the most distinguished Argentinean poets. She presently lives in New York City, where she works as an independent translator. Ms. Roffé also writes for many Latin American journals. Among her most important poetry books are *Camara baja* and *Definiciones Mayas,* both published in the eighties.

DIANA ANHALT

Diana Anhalt lives in Mexico City. As a young child she emigrated from New York City to Mexico during the McCarthy years. She has just published a story of this historical time under the title *A Gathering of Fugitives.* Her essays and poems have been anthologized and published in the United States and Latin America.

ANA MARÍA SHUA

Shua is considered to be Argentina's most important woman writer. She has written extensively in many fields from poetry to narrative, journalism to film. She is a multitalented author. Among her most distinguished works are *Los amores de Laurita, Soy paciente,* and *El libro de los recuerdos,* all narratives.

IVONNE STRAUSS DE MILZ

De Milz is a veterinarian by training, but works as a leader and organizer of the Jewish communities of Sosua, Dominican Republic, where she lives with her family. Additionally, she is assisting in the creation of the Jewish Museum of Sosua.

NORA STREJILEVICH

Strejilevich is an Argentinean writer and poet and a professor of Latin American literature at San Diego State University. She is also the director of El archivo de la memoria, a project devoted to sustaining the memories of the disappeared.